Home Bound

Home Bound

AN UPROOTED
DAUGHTER'S
REFLECTIONS
ON BELONGING

Vanessa A. Bee

ASTRA HOUSE Λ NEW YORK

For information about permission to reproduce selections from this book, please
contact permissions@astrahouse.com.

Astra House
A Division of Astra Publishing House
astrahouse.com
Printed in the United States of America

Library of Congress Cataloging-in-Publication Data
Names: Bee, Vanessa A., 1988– author.
Title: Home bound : an uprooted daughter's reflections on belonging /
    by Vanessa A. Bee.
Description: First edition. | New York : Astra House, 2022. | Includes bibliographical
    references. | Summary: "A multifaceted global memoir reflecting on Bee's adoption
    from Cameroon, her childhood experiences with public housing and homelessness
    in rural France, Lyon, and London, her immigration as a teen to Nevada, and
    eventually rethinking her devotion to evangelical Christianity at Harvard Law.
    Home Bound touches on constructions of home, and the issues of identity that can
    complicate it, including class, race, education, faith, and nationality"—Provided
    by publisher.
Identifiers: LCCN 2022006629 (print) | LCCN 2022006630 (ebook) |
    ISBN 9781662601330 (hardcover) | ISBN 9781662601347 (epub)
Subjects: LCSH: Bee, Vanessa A., 1988– | Adoptees—Biography. | Adoptees—Family
    relationships. | Essayists—21st century—Biography.
Classification: LCC HV874.82.B43 B44 2022 (print) | LCC HV874.82.B43 (ebook) |
    DDC 362.734092—dc23/eng/20220209
LC record available at https://lccn.loc.gov/2022006629
LC ebook record available at https://lccn.loc.gov/2022006630

First edition
10 9 8 7 6 5 4 3 2 1

Design by Richard Oriolo
The text is set in Adobe Garamond Pro.
The titles are set in Adobe Garamond Pro.

for my mothers

CONTENTS

Home Bound

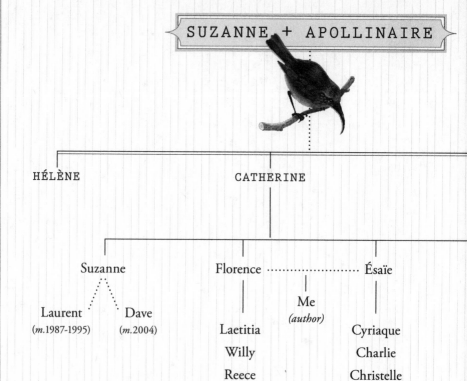

SUZANNE + APOLLINAIRE

HÉLÈNE   CATHERINE

Suzanne   Florence ···················· Ésaïe

Laurent   Dave   Me   Cyriaque
(m.1987-1995)   (m.2004)   Laetitia   (author)   Charlie
                              Willy   Christelle
                              Reece   Franz
                                                        Marlène
                                                        Elisabelle
                                                        Maggie
                                                        Philippe
                                                        Ange

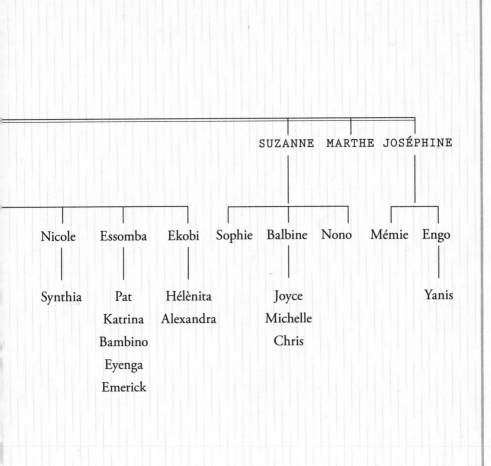

SUZANNE   MARTHE   JOSÉPHINE

Nicole   Essomba   Ekobi   Sophie   Balbine   Nono   Mémie   Engo

Synthia   Pat   Hélènita   Joyce   Yanis
          Katrina   Alexandra   Michelle
          Bambino   Chris
          Eyenga
          Emerick

Layers

HOME, NOUN.
  1 a: one's place of residence: DOMICILE
    b: HOUSE
  2 : the social unit formed by a family living together
  3 a: a familiar or usual setting: congenial environment
    also the focus of one's domestic attention
    b: HABITAT
  4 a: a place of origin
    also one's own country
    b: HEADQUARTERS

MERRIAM-WEBSTER DICTIONARY (2019)

I HAND MY AMERICAN DRIVER'S license to the black guard in the window of the French consulate in Washington, DC. When he calls me *madame*, his accent resembles mine: the impeccable French of double-diaspora children, seeded in the tropics, grown in European schools, and re-scattered in lands more fertile with opportunity. I wonder if his accent changes when he speaks to his mother, the way mine does. I show him proof of my appointment for today, December 4, 2017. Passport replacement. He looks at the license and at my face again. He asks: "Where are you from?"

My features are distinctly sub-Saharan but unremarkable. Protruding brown eyes, broad nose, thick lips, dark skin. The last name on my license, Assae-Bille, reveals nothing about my origins. This throws him—and every African-born Uber driver—for a loop, spiking their curiosity almost as much as it did French whites. They would not be asking if my being from here, wherever *here* is, was a possibility in their minds. For all their shortcomings on race, this is one thing I appreciate about Americans: how in this country, black people have the right to simply declare, if asked, what city is home; how people of my complexion can claim Richmond or Dallas without being pressed a second or third time. Standing on the fiction of French soil in the United States, the rules revert back, the question beneath the question.

I could tell him about the recurring dream, the one I have had for more than a decade now, and that each time feels more real than the last. I realize that I am scheduled to leave for Yaoundé imminently and cram clothes into a suitcase as fast as my arms will let me. But I never make the flight to Cameroon. Some nights, I am trapped in traffic with minutes to takeoff. Or I am waiting in the security line when my boarding pass evaporates from my hand. The layovers grow more elaborate; they pick up where previous nights have left off. My psyche is sly. Sometimes, she whispers: This time isn't a dream, see? We are finally making good on our promise to return. A flight attendant directs me to my row and the seat belt sign comes on. Then the airplane floor splits in two. The fuselage vanishes; our seats hang in midair. I open my eyes and find myself in bed, summoned again by a homeland that doesn't quite feel like it's mine.

I answer the guard: "Poitou-Charentes." I doubt he's ever been to that region. There's no reason to pass through that sleepy mosaic of grapeseed and wheat, where the countryside bleeds into a flat horizon dotted with ruins of forts, and the dwindling villages that once toiled for them. The Poitou-Charentes exists only in reference to other places. It is ninety minutes inland from the Atlantic coast. A jaunt south of the Loire Valley. A short drive from where the Cardinal de Richelieu, the scheming villain in *The Three Musketeers*, once built a magnificent château. For my American friends, I draw a ring in the air for Paris and trace a downward diagonal to indicate: two hours southwest by train. In the twenty years since I left France for good, the government merged the Poitou-Charentes with the neighboring Limousin and Aquitaine, binding the three regions into a supergroup that it renamed Nouvelle-Aquitaine. I will never call it that, though, so in a way, my finger points to nowhere on this virtual map. But I am all too familiar with the knowing smile on the guard's face. This is not what he is thinking of. Indeed, he insists: "Côte d'Ivoire? Centrafrique?"

Growing up, I used to envy my classmates for having the option to explain where they were from in one breath, without caveats or asides. Home was in this or that city, this or that state, often under a single flag. My classmates could see themselves in the faces and names of their parents. Answering the guard's question, the luckiest ones might picture a childhood house where boxes of their crayon drawings were still safeguarded and friends from kindergarten reappeared down the block on family holidays. Even the kids who had been ostracized for their social standing or economic class could identify a place to which they unequivocally belonged.

I yearned for a home this absolute. Mine, however, always felt slightly out of reach. My parents, Suzanne and Laurent, adopted me out of Cameroon at ten months old. I was Suzanne's niece, born out of wedlock to her sister Florence. For five years, they raised me in Châtellerault, a small, majority-white French town that might have been best known for its relative proximity to the Futuroscope media park. In places, Châtellerault was quaint. Its heart pulsed with cobblestoned streets that wound like varicose veins between artisanal storefronts. Much of the population descended from farmers and manual laborers, and now powered the institutions that made up our modest town—*boulangeries* for bread, *pâtisseries* for sweet confections, and *tabacs* for cigarettes. My own dad pushed sand at a factory that manufactured car parts. And while I had long forgotten what life was like on the African continent, already my preschool and kindergarten teachers wondered where I was from. My blackness was a marker that assigned me in and out of teams. The stark contrast against my dad's white skin and differing last name reminded me of having been imported. An outsider in my body and in my own home. But I doubt my mom saw it that way; she herself never carried her birth father's name.

After the divorce, home shifted rapidly. My dad stayed behind while I followed my mom to a village in the Rhône Valley, then to a large public housing project in inner-city Lyon, before the two of us emigrated across the English Channel, to London. I turned eleven in Harlesden, a working-class borough in northwest London, and blew out fourteen candles with my aunt's family in Reno, Nevada. My mom and I passed through houses and apartment rentals and hostels that we left before getting too attached.

The modest farmhouse where my grandparents lived and worked, in a Poitou-Charentes hamlet where nothing ever changed, became the only constant in this childhood. My parents, then just my dad, took me there on Sundays. We ate lunch in the great dining room, a striking highlight on the property. My grandmother furnished her home for her own comfort and practical needs, as a woman with no intent of leaving would. The result was an eclectic but unapologetically *paysanne* home, filled with a warmth that made me feel rooted and safe. A place I never regretted returning to. Perhaps it was this early exposure to beauty, and its direct connection to the farmhouse, that would feed my persistent preoccupation with the physical home.

THE ANSWER I have given the guard is already a compromise, a reflection of what I do each time my origins are in question: reach for the layer that feels most relevant, or representative of me, in the moment. But where in time is home measured? By which parents or neighbors is it defined? By what flaws or virtues?

I condense my answer, say France or briefly England. Depending on who's asking and why, I might tell them that I am from the United States, though this feels dishonest. Even after twenty years on this continent, I struggle to fully claim either Nevada or Washington, DC.

But don't we all do this? Don't you?

Home to me feels as cumulative as a nesting doll. Home is a shell painted with the present: the city where I live and work, the neighborhood where I feel the streets belong to me as much as they do my neighbors, the apartment where I rest my head at night; it is the soil my grandparents tilled to provide for my parents, for me; it is the church body that once shaped my ethics and the beliefs that filled the void when the church could no longer supply answers. But home is also the innermost layer, the envelope in which I navigate the world: my body and skin, my gender and sexual orientation, the names that follow me.

Between these layers are iterations of myself. None of them static, though they are fixed in the moment that I remember them. For those who grew up in a single house, in a single gender or orientation, to a single set of parents, the nesting doll may be sparse in layers. For others, it is packed as densely as mine. But the layers are always there, projecting themselves onto the present and future, informing what we can and cannot call home.

Where we are from, where we *get* to be from, seems inextricable from not only our personal histories, but also the histories of certain people and spaces. In that way, home is a function of what each of us is entitled to and why, tethered to the economic and political forces that shape our lives—forces that include or exclude, give or take away, all the while, often, maintaining the illusion of complete autonomy.

I am reminded here of the first tale many of us are ever read about home, the one that goes like this: Three little pigs leave the familial nest to build their own. Driven by laziness, one brother builds his abode out of hay. The second, slightly less lazy, out of sticks. Only the third has the foresight to erect one out of brick. When a wolf threatens to eat the little pigs, the flimsy houses fall, sending the first two brothers to the brick house. This last one stands and rescues all three. I was too young then to question the implication that good things come to those who work hard, or that home is a reflection of character, and that those who lack it deserve less. Rather, I processed the little pigs' homes through the lens of the narrator: facades reduced to personal choice.

But home doesn't exist in a political and historical vacuum. The location and quality of our housing, the safety of our streets, and their proximity to amenities or economic opportunity are products of policy decisions made above our heads by government bureaucrats, corporate executives, and outspoken neighbors. So is the extent to which natural disasters, global pandemics, and financial crises consistently hit some populations harder than others. Nor can context be divorced from the bodies that we call home—given how much outside perceptions of their worth affect our ability to care for ourselves, to obtain medical support and economic protection, our right to live without fear of sexual violence and the carceral arm of the state.

Our sense of home is thus necessarily tangled with that of others. For some, deciphering its meaning, its boundaries, and its relation to the rest of the world is a matter of survival. But this should not leave us hopeless. As my friend Pete Davis wrote in his book *Dedicated*: "Our roots can lie in the future," binding us and our descendants together in a shared destination, be it a goal or a land.

I find it helpful to remind myself that, for all its layers and complexity, home possesses a certain universality. Our nesting dolls are built from the same DNA blocks and carbon atoms. As we close our eyes and think *home*, I suspect that we all feel *something*, that our minds entertain similar questions in seeking to define it. It's the confidence in this universality that emboldens us to ask complete strangers where they are from. We pry, certain that we will recognize elements of ourselves in the stranger's answer, no matter the distance between our places of birth and present circumstances. I'd like to think the best of these encounters sharpen our own appreciation of home.

This book is my long answer to the question of where I am from. In pursuit of thoroughness, it is also an excavation of my most intimate layers: from my name and body, to the places that shaped me, homes that I passed through and broke away from, the homes that were threatened, that were reclaimed, or that will someday be lost. I want to tell you about the homes that I made mine and about the ones that made me.

As novelist Kazuo Ishiguro wrote, "In the end, stories are about one person saying to another: This is the way it feels to me . . . Does it also feel this way to you?" And so, I share these stories and interpretations as half of a conversation between us—a test, perhaps, of this universality's boundaries.

I hope there is merit, in ever-turbulent times, in continuing to examine what home is to us and what we dream it to be. These stories are thus also an inquiry.

This is the way home feels to me.

Does it also feel this way to you?

Floating Feather Tree

---

5 **a:** a name or collection of proper names
also one's markers of identification

HAVING CHEEKILY ANSWERED THE GUARD with "Poitou-Charentes," I waltz into the offices of the French consulate for my passport replacement appointment. While I have the attaché's undivided attention, I mention an oddity on my birth certificate. I had never noticed it before, but the document lists my biological mother as "Florence" and leaves the line for "Father" blank. This is inaccurate, I tell him. I was adopted by parents of French citizenship— another mother and a father who loved me to the ends of the earth. But neither Suzanne nor Laurent is memorialized here. Surely this is a mistake, does he not agree? The attaché squints back and forth between his computer screen and my birth certificate while I wait patiently, a black winter coat laid across my lap.

I withhold what else I know, what I have known since that developmental phase when toddlers acquire self-awareness, realizing that they are of their parents yet another person altogether, and that these recurring syllables form their own name. A means for the world to relate to them, but also a point of reference in which to anchor their identity. My parents had wanted to be candid from the beginning. My real first name was not Vanessa, as everyone called me. And my real last name was not Jucquois, the last name they'd shared since marrying one year and one day before my birth; it was not Jucquois even though it appeared on my school files and on the booklet in which my pediatrician recorded my progress. Nor was I the biological result of their union. My name was Elisabeth Vanessa Assae Billé and I was adopted.

Synchronizing our last names was never high on their list of priorities. My parents insisted that nothing could lessen our family. Not the set of letters forming my legal name, not my face, and not my skin—far darker than my daddy's. Names, to them, did not make family any more than blood or genes. I was their daughter from the moment they left Cameroon for France with me in tow, that summer of '89. They hadn't built me from scratch but had chosen me as their child. I loved them and they loved me more. I was taught that family was this, but also something else. Family was what we created in intentionally being together. Outsiders only had so much power to define us.

The proof was in the way we bled into each other. I was a Jucquois in my grimaces, in my expressions, in my tics. My parents' slyness was baked deep into my own wry sense of humor. I was the worst of them—short fused, hypersensitive, secretive—and the best of them—proud, loyal, resourceful. Often, the line between my genetic predispositions and their imprint on me seemed blurred. Was this not more the essence of family than a name?

Still, I felt torn. Though we were one family, happy under the roof of our little rent-controlled apartment in Châtellerault, in the Plaine d'Ozon neighborhood, it seemed there were two of me. Elisabeth Assae Billé was a ghost, a memory. Once, she'd been a speculative future in the imagination of her birth parents who'd wondered, while pacing Yaoundé's hills in the days preceding her arrival, which of their likenesses she would carry most. That little girl's home was with them, thousands of miles south. Erased in all manner but paperwork, the ghost lingered. Being summoned by her name felt akin to hearing my genus and species. The description was accurate in a sense; I could answer to it. But the syllables meant nothing to me.

The person I felt most like was the other me: Vanessa Jucquois. Yet, I understood that *feeling* was a fiction. Even when my schoolteachers played along, it was the ghost's name inked in my administrative files. The letters truest to me were borrowed, my identity conditional.

How unsurprising that I would, at the age of almost four, rechristen myself. My parents had picked a bedtime story featuring a little boy named Mini Bill.

I'd felt such a kinship toward this character that, beyond demanding that we reread the book dozens of nights in a row, I refused to answer to any other name than his for weeks on end. My tickled parents had indulged me. Another day, another set of letters.

Rather than anchor me, then, my name kindled a sort of dissociation. I was both girls and neither. Of my parents but not enough.

Was I already searching for a way to rewrite myself in the singular at this rechristening?

ONE AFTERNOON IN '92, when I was not quite four years old, I awoke from a nap to an unfamiliar voice down the hallway. A nameless man stood across from my mom, in the living room of the little Châtellerault apartment. My brain would register the next minutes as if subconsciously aware that there would be no next time, no next visit. The outline of the memory is imprecise but I remember him being a head taller than my daddy and blacker than the country sky at midnight; how he bantered with my mom in a language that I recognized but couldn't decode; how he called her by the secret nickname that only her family knew; and how they laughed like friends who'd loved and betrayed and forgiven, perhaps because nothing else could be done about the summer of '89, other than be better to each other, for my sake.

I watched them with wide eyes, head resting against my mom's hips, and wondered whether the stranger was coming or going, whether we were in the beginning or at the end. My mom caught me staring at the white cat he had brought, a stuffed toy so pretty that it just might pounce to life. She bent down to let me examine it. *This one's not for playing,* she said, then shelved it out of my reach. And, *What do we say?*

I thanked the stranger for the gift.

Our eyes met. His existence had never struck me until that moment but I remembered then that I had come out of another mother's belly. It occurred to me that while my parents had never expanded on the fourth counterpart, the biological equivalent to my daddy, this could be him, I thought. Or rather, I knew.

Without being able to quite articulate why, I felt a consuming urge to hear it confirmed from him. The rush collided against my manners. In this household, we respect our elders. In this household, we do not interrupt adults mid-conversation. We do not ask rude questions. We resist our impulses. Disobeying these sacred rules risks a time-out or spanking. But I needed to know. I had to know. I had to.

No sooner had they paused than I blurted out: *Are you my daddy?*

My mom gasped my name with slow, breathless horror: *Vanessa!*

Immediately, I wished to rewind time. The distinction between fathers and daddies is hard to parse but I was old enough to understand that one word is distant and the other intimate. A man without a name to me couldn't be my daddy. It didn't seem right. I felt the weight of my mistake. Thankfully, my daddy was not home to witness this. But I was mortified at the possibility that he might hear about this and guess, correctly, that in asking my question, I hoped the stranger would say yes, that he was my daddy. To think that I betrayed my dearest parent for a stuffed white cat. It felt unforgivable. A shameful daughter.

But the nameless stranger was not embarrassed. He simply chuckled. Then he was gone—train to Paris, flight to Yaoundé—leaving my question to hang in the little apartment, unanswered, and the ghost to roam, unclaimed.

*

WHATEVER THE STEPS were to match my name to theirs, my parents never took them. *Maybe when you're older* turned into *Maybe.* Then the divorce became final. I was almost six when my mom reclaimed her maiden name, which she had inherited from her grandmother, and which did not match mine either. The two of us moved to the Rhône Valley, in the French southeast.

For the first time in our relationship, my daddy wrote me. Twice a month, I rummaged through the mail until I found the careful handwriting of my favorite person and only pen pal. The letters came folded in envelopes that he addressed to me, his Vanessa Jucquois. I doubt my daddy understood the reassurance that seeing our last name on paper brought me. The letters meant that, even a five-hour drive from Châtellerault, in this country house where neither my mom nor her new boyfriend bore the name Jucquois, I could still be the person that I felt most like.

The letters began with, *Hello my little flea.* Or sometimes, *My darling.* I read and reread them. The updates were banal. Recurring back aches. A pleasant bike ride. Sundays at my grandparents'. I pictured him walking through the door of the empty little apartment, grime under his fingernails from a long day's work. My poor daddy: eating alone, reading alone, and finally drifting to sleep—alone still. The end of the letter was near when I reached the obligatory note about my next trip home. *Loin des yeux, près du cœur*—far from the eyes, close to the heart—he often wrote. Our very own special incantation. I heard it in his voice because he repeated it before we hung up the phone every week, and at the end of my school breaks, when he kissed my head on the platform, as my ride home entered the Châtellerault train station, wheels grinding against the iron tracks, and my chest heaved from crying, this despite my earlier promises to be a big girl about our goodbye.

Hundreds of days would need filling in until our next visit. I learned to summon his face, his hands, his laugh, his smell, his gait. Sometimes, to console myself. Other times, so I wouldn't forget him. I remembered him sneaking me bubble gum from the tobacco shop and pushing me on the swing set by the forest. I imagined all the places we'd go to distract myself from the calendar, which slowed to a crawl while we were apart, and sped up when we were together.

Which is to say that my daddy was the first person I truly missed. I missed my daddy as if it were a competition, as if the rules required my devotion to go entirely to him, lest any be left for the man whose name assumed credit for my entire being. Assae Billé on my French passport. Assae Billé on my school report cards. Assae Billé on the medical forms. Assae Billé everywhere and nowhere at once.

It wasn't fair, I would come to think, that people could brand themselves on others without having done anything to be missed.

THEN, ON A scorching day in Madrid: a discovery at the municipal pool lockers. My two aunts, Balbine and Sophie—first cousins of my adoptive and biological mothers, and sisters themselves—talking animatedly in a fast Ewondo on one end of the bench. On the opposite end, a pair of girls, aged nine and seven and a half, grow noticeably quieter as their ears perk. My younger cousin, Joyce—Tata Balbine's daughter—and I loved collecting the crumbs of French scattered by the women raising us, and recycling them as we combed our dolls' hair roughly, threatening to cut it all off if the dolls kept crying, all the while parroting to each other in gibberish, itself scattered with just enough French to thread a fictitious conversation. We played variations on this game each year that our mothers reunited us, typically for a whole summer month under my mom's watch in France, then for another month, this time in the apartment that Joyce and Tata Balbine shared in Spain. Temporarily relieved from our status as only children, we demanded matching, sisterly uniforms down to our underwear. We laughed and talked and laughed until our mothers begged us for peace and quiet, until we succumbed to sleep, with Joyce pinching my arms and me twirling the bottom of her braids. And in the morning, we began all over again.

In eavesdropping, the substance and particulars mattered less to us than the delivery: the preponderance of hard *z*'s, the teeth-sucking and gesticulations—in other words, the performance of speaking Ewondo. And it *was* a performance. Not that it was inauthentic. Rather, embodying the dialect was a trait that could be turned on and off. At our schools and at their jobs, or in the company of their white friends, our moms and aunts became demure and even-toned. They spoke in a bashful French and laughed with measure. It was this stark contrast that made imitating their true selves all the more fun for us girls. But at the pool, that afternoon, we listened with sincere interest. The women were talking about our birth fathers.

I knew next to nothing about mine. A man carried the last name Assae Billé. Then, that man had fathered me. And finally, that man had brought me a plush white cat that I never named because it was not for playing. Neither of my parents ever said a word about him, good or bad, so the letters of his last name bore no other connotation. I knew of no translation for them. Where Assae ought to have appeared in my mom's crimson-bound encyclopedias was blank space. I felt that to lack roots in Greek or Latin was to lack etymology, or a raison d'être. Assae Billé was a black hole. The stranger and I both were.

But my birth father had to have a first name. And, I figured, for him to have stood in the little apartment, my mom must have known it. Was there a chance then that one of my two aunts might, too? After all, they still lived in Yaoundé at the time of my birth, in October '88. They were as close with my mom and birth mother as Joyce and I were with each other.

I scooted across the bench to try my luck.

Ésaïe, answered one of them. *That's his first name.*

I repeated after her. *Eh-zah-yee*. A name unlike anything I'd heard before.

I made a mental note to look for him in the encyclopedias when I got home to France, but there found no more of him.

⟡

I WOULD NOT discover the meaning of his last name for another decade, this time on a rare trip back on Cameroonian soil, over the 2007–2008 winter break of my sophomore year in college. I had returned to Yaoundé once after my adoption, for a wedding, at age four. Then not at all for the next fifteen years. It was not my parents' fault. More a question of means than willingness. Time, distance, and the expense of international calls made it difficult to build a relationship with the family I had there. If my birth mother had second thoughts about giving me up, I could not say the same. Maman Florence and I rarely spoke and when we did, our conversations felt stilted, vague. She would ask how school was and I would answer that it was fine, that my grades were good, that I liked it—the stuff of distant relatives. I did not know her or our homeland enough to miss either earnestly. Perhaps she feared that it would remain like that indefinitely without a more concerted effort. And so, the moment she came into some unexpected money, Maman Florence insisted on gifting me a flight *back home*, to Cameroon. For five weeks, I stayed with her, on the small property where my late grandparents had built a home and adjacent bungalows for their children.

Ésaïe was no longer alive, but my uncle François, who was his first cousin and the closest he had to a best friend, arranged for me to meet some of Ésaïe's children halfway through the trip. Three lived in the West—from what I heard: Belgium, France, and Québec—but five remained near their mother in Yaoundé. A car dropped me off at their childhood home, in the neighborhood of Kondengui. The second-eldest son, my half-brother Charlie, greeted me at the door. Three of the girls, my half sisters, walked in, sized me up, made small talk, and walked out without saying much. Charlie suggested that we go up the street to buy bottled waters and went inside to look for change. I waited on the front porch near their mother, who sat alone, cleaning fish in a *kaba* dress. She looked up from the bowlful of scales and guts, and asked if I was hungry. I said that my ride home would be back for me before dinnertime, leaving out my maternal family's instruction not to accept any food from Ésaïe's widow. The woman smiled and returned to her task without insisting. I stood in silence, ashamed to share her daughters' features so pronouncedly, to be alive in her presence.

Charlie returned after what felt like an eternity. As the two of us climbed up the small hill, he told me about his father's study. A room of the house that was off limits to the children, and even to their mother, who could no more enter it without Ésaïe's permission. Charlie had gone in a few times. Would I believe that only one child's photo was displayed in there? He paused for dramatic effect. *The photo was yours*, he said.

The teenage girl working the street stand traded us bottled waters for Charlie's money. I listened cluelessly as they spoke in dialect for a bit, wondering why the girl was ogling me so sharply. In this country, people always pegged me as foreign before I opened my mouth. I stuck out like a grain of rice in a pot of black beans. On our way back to his home, I asked Charlie about their exchange.

She asked if you were an Assae, he said.

How did she know?

The eyes.

From time to time, Charlie continued, his father would lock himself in the study and order the children not to disturb him because he was calling me on the phone. I scoffed. *Your father has only called me twice in my entire life.*

Charlie said nothing, his face impassable. We walked in silence awhile and I regretted suggesting that his father was a liar. But what I'd said was true. Ésaïe and I had spoken twice since his visit to the little apartment in Châtellerault, which marked the last time he and I would ever be in the same room. Charlie didn't seem angry with me, though. Pensive was more like it. Maybe I'd reminded him of a side of his father's character that he didn't enjoy thinking about. We were new acquaintances and I was much less familiar with Ésaïe than he was, but we both knew the type of person Ésaïe *could* be. My last name alone was a testament.

His parents had given Charlie and his siblings names that were unique variations on Assae Billé. One of my half brothers was Billé Assae. Another daughter was simply Assae. But none of the children bore the name in the precise order—his order. When the seventh legitimate child was born, two years after me, their mother had insisted on giving her Ésaïe's last name in the precise order that he bore it. Only then had Ésaïe admitted that his last name already belonged to me, his mistress's daughter. Omission and revision were a short leap apart.

Crouching uselessly next to Tata Nicole as she vigorously stirred a pot of *sanga* stew over a ground fire, back on the family property, I wondered out loud, without looking up at her, whether Assae Billé was a black hole in our mother tongue, too. It was summer on the equator, too hot to cook inside the bungalow and too hot for a stew, but my aunt would hear nothing of it. *Sanga* was one of my favorite Ewondo dishes and I was her guest. The dust at our feet turned a melancholic red as the sun set. It was absurd to still care enough to ask, at all of nineteen, when my name was decidedly here to stay. I half expected my aunt to say as much, to dismiss my question lovingly but firmly as white nonsense. But instead, Tata Nicole answered me in earnest. *Of course,* she said. *Assae is for when a feather floats or suspends in midair. Billé is the word for tree.*

♪

IN EWONDO COUNTRY, where my maternal line comes from, names set expectations. Clan to clan, kin to kin. Your set of letters announce: here is the headman from whom this person is descended; here is someone who might share your blood, your values; here is one more person whom you owe and who owes you something, a courtesy, a kindness, a certain degree of trust. This is also true of the places that our ancestors named. Several of the quarters around Yaoundé, the Cameroonian capital, were once villages where kinfolk were concentrated. Many begin with the word *mvog*—meaning *descendant of*—followed by a proper name, which represents bloodlines. And so, the land is inextricable from our identity. A name is a place and a people at once. It is foundational to our definition of home.

Folklore says that three brothers founded the Ewondo clan. To say that we are from the Mvog-Ada quarter, as is this side of my family, is to reveal that our ancestor was the brother whose son counted Ada among his five wives. But it is an instruction, too. If your people and mine are from Mvog-Ada, then we are too closely parented to intermarry. Nevertheless, honor demands that we look out for each other.

Ewondo children can be named after anyone: their father or mother, a beloved relative, an old friend, someone never met but respected, or one missed greatly. Being given another's name makes you a *mbômbo* of that person—a cross between their godchild and their protégé. In practice, having a homonym might mean being doted on the most while visiting them with other relatives. Or even being sent to live in their home. My mom is a *mbômbo* of her maternal grandmother while my birth mother is a *mbômbo* of an infertile great-great-aunt. Our family brims with distant cousins with identical last names while full siblings bear a patchwork of surnames, drawn from the same pool of respected elders. Mangas after my great-grandmother. Essombas for my great-grandfather. Foudas and Ekobenas in honor of late great-uncles. Of my grandmother's five children, only two carry my grandfather's last name.

Among those who are unrelated, shared names forge a bond as strong as bloodline. In generations past, killing your *mbômbo* was forbidden.

Even at war.

∮

THE NAME ELISABETH was a compromise. Maman Florence suspected that it might have been Ésaïe's mother's name, but she was not sure and understood their mother-son relationship to be complicated. Nevertheless, he had insisted and she had relented. The papers could say what they said, no one in her household would call me that anyway. Her siblings and mother much preferred the youthful and spunky Vanessa, recently popularized by the French teen pop star Vanessa Paradis. A name so pretty it still worked when my great-grandmother mispronounced it *Banissia*.

Maman Florence left the "Father" line blank on my birth certificate but gave me his last name in full. Assae Billé: so others would open doors for me as they did for him. Assae Billé: so he would treat me no differently than the six children that he and his wife were already raising. Assae Billé: so the world could not deny our relation. That was my biological mother, a philosophy major and stubborn idealist. Her last name, Atsama, means *disarray*.

One of the forked tongues in the family must have warned her. Fathers disappeared. Her own father, Simon, had left for France in the '60s and raised an entire family—six children!—with a white woman. Never mind what Florence thought she knew about this lover, the family must have thought. People could not be trusted, especially at war. To list him as the father on the birth certificate was a form of insurance. But Florence hadn't listened. She was twenty-five and this was the beginning of their story. Youthful naivete could make anything seem possible. She lay near my cot, convinced that the father would fill that blank line with his immense presence, regardless of whether she revealed his fatherhood to the state. One day, she would tell me, *I kept you as a memento of him*. A decision she never regretted. The forked tongues hadn't witnessed her lover in the maternity ward like she did, on the day he brought his sons. Their mother had stayed home with their three daughters and her dignity but, I would later find out, the boys would forever remember the trepidation of holding me in their arms for the first time. Had their mother consented to this visit? Perhaps the boys were too young to consider, or perhaps it did not matter to them. Their father—our father—had made his decision clear.

I was somewhere around five months old when Ésaïe proposed to my birth mother. She refused him—she, the college student whose tuition fees and books he so generously paid for; he, the government official whose salary at the Cameroonian Presidency would provide for her for the rest of her life, if only she agreed to be his second wife, concurrently to the first. Polygamy was legal but incompatible with her Catholic roots and, anyhow, this was not the life she envisioned for herself. So she had said no. Ésaïe stopped coming by my grandmother's house with formula and cartons of diapers, disappearing altogether. Tonton François now brought supplies of his own volition, self-conscious about what the turn of events said of their family, and perhaps feeling the weight of his role in my birth—after all, the estranged lovers had met through him, while he and Suzanne dated for a brief spell in the early '80s.

Ésaïe hadn't left a note explaining his prolonged absence but his reasons were not difficult to decipher. Millions of men before him had set fire to their households over less. A woman younger, poorer, and less politically connected than he was, with little to offer in return other than herself, had the audacity to withhold even that. And on what basis? If anything, she owed *him*. He would teach her a lesson in humility. This was war.

Here, imagine the possibility that Ésaïe resurfaces at my grandmother's house before the summer of '89, and that his infant daughter awaits him, indifferent to the chasm between one day and one hundred days. The mother forgives his lapse in judgment and the episode is buried for good. Perhaps the daughter even teases him over it once she is older. Ésaïe apologizes to her for leaving, again, though he cannot seem to articulate what exactly he is sorry for. The daughter does not dwell on the matter; the fleeting petulance has not hurt her, not since he has cared for and protected her all of her days. And anyway, this father is her lot, isn't he? There are worse men out there.

In this universe, the daughter has no names to reconcile, no split to resolve. The ghost is no ghost at all, for her parents raise her as amicable exes. She sees herself in their faces, their tics. She speaks Ewondo with her grandmother and French with her friends. Life in Yaoundé is different, some say chaotic, but having a father as wealthy as hers eases the burden. To please him, she elects German over English in the school curriculum. *Look where it got me*, he tells her. From a tiny village in the south of Cameroon to college studies in Bonn. From nothing to the Presidential Palace in Yaoundé. *You, too, can write yourself into existence.* And so, the daughter charts her own life, as meticulously outlined as the plot of a novel. She dreams of becoming the first doctor in her immediate family, trained in European universities. If she ever gets to Germany, she has no doubts that Tata Suzanne and her French husband, Laurent Jucquois, will look out for her from their little apartment in Châtellerault even though she rarely sees them. Long distances make for expensive flights. But Tata Suzanne and Tonton Laurent call on the phone, and around Christmas, ship her dresses from the Tati discount store. Her aunt returns *back home* for funerals; her uncle comes to Yaoundé even less frequently. And after their divorce, not at all. Seeing his face in an old photo album, decades later, she'll strain to remember his name.

But summer comes and Ésaïe refuses to end the standoff.

He does not return. He is not embarrassed. He is not sorry. None of this came to pass. And so, the unraveling from the girl who was intended to be Elisabeth Assae Billé begins.

SUZANNE AND LAURENT landed in Yaoundé midsummer of '89, at the height of rain season. The little girl waiting for them isn't me. I do not mean this figuratively. They have come to pick up my older cousin Nadège, who was promised to them months earlier. Ewondos are not precious about passing children around the family. A child can be sent to help an aunt with a new baby or tutor a younger cousin for a year. They can be taken in while their parent recovers from an illness or after they have passed away. This was how Nadège's own mother, my aunt Ndzié, had ended up in my grandmother's care as an infant after losing her mother, a cousin of my grandmother. The family had turned to my grandmother, who was her last name incarnate: Ngameyong, for *woman of the people*. She was still breastfeeding her firstborn, Suzanne, but produced milk enough for a second baby, and so agreed to take her in. Tata Ndzié was raised as a daughter of the Ngameyong household.

And when she came home pregnant twenty years later—no father listed on the birth certificate—my grandmother had simply made room for one more.

Her baby daughter, Nadège, and Suzanne, overlapped in my grandmother's house and became close in the first years of the child's life; so close in fact, that Nadège sometimes slipped up and called Suzanne *maman*. As the eldest of five, Suzanne had always cared for the children who came after her. She felt protective of her siblings and the myriad of fosters who passed through the house. Yet, the responsibility she felt toward Nadège rose to a higher level.

Suzanne moved to Châtellerault in '87, soon after meeting her would-be husband, Laurent, while on vacation in a nearby town. She was twenty-seven years old. Permanently apart from her niece for the first time since her birth, Suzanne found herself missing the little girl as one might her own child. Nadège, too, felt this loss deeply. Perhaps Suzanne was the first person she ever truly missed.

Suzanne had broached the subject of adoption with Tata Ndzié in the spring. Her pitch was modest. She could promise that the girl would be as beloved in France as she was in Cameroon. Her husband longed to be a father and her in-laws were eager for a child to roam their farm again. She could promise more comfort than either of them had been afforded growing up. She and her husband were struggling to conceive, but someday hoped to give the child a sibling. They were not rich but Nadège would have access to good universities and a French passport to unlock the world to her. Importantly, they would also be candid with the child from the beginning. Nadège would know that another mother had carried and loved her as much as her adoptive parents if not more. Tata Ndzié had agreed to sign adoption papers when Suzanne and Laurent returned to Yaoundé.

A few nights into their trip *back home*, though, the birth mother got cold feet. Suzanne didn't attempt to change Tata Ndzié's mind even as she felt her heart rip inside her chest. An exchange of this nature only works when all parties are willing—a child cannot be stolen or given under pressure. So Nadège would have to stay. Just because Ewondos are nonchalant about passing around children does not mean the separation of parent and child must not feel impossible, or hurt more than anything. Suzanne understood why Ndzié would renege on her end of the deal.

But her younger sisters, Florence and Nicole, were furious. It was unfathomable to them that Suzanne would go home empty-handed. On this same night, the sisters made a pact: one of them would carry out Ndzié's promise and give Suzanne a child. But how? At twenty-two, Nicole was still childless. Florence only had me, her firstborn and only child, aged nine months old. She pondered the option. With things still on ice with Ésaïe, a second child seemed unlikely anytime soon. This left only one solution: I was the one Suzanne must take to Europe.

One condition applied. Everything that happened next had to remain secret. The family knew Ésaïe well enough to foresee that, at the first hint of this plan, he would do all he could to axe it. Ésaïe could be generous, exceedingly so, but only on his own terms. No one took from him what he did not intend to give away. And this was his daughter, his *mbômbo*. All paperwork had to be processed outside of the city. My last name was too precise. A bureaucrat could recognize it and alert Ésaïe that a namesake of his was being removed from the country. The sisters realized that they would have to move fast to complete the procedures before the end of Suzanne's visit. Ndzié's softness had already cost them precious time.

Ésaïe heard that Suzanne was in town with her husband. Before this feud with Maman Florence, he and Suzanne had been good friends. They could still be, he seemed to believe. Ésaïe invited her and her new husband to dinner. She accepted reluctantly, to avoid rousing his suspicions.

Day of, the family was tense. Could someone have tipped him off? Does he know about the friend with the municipal judgeship in a nearby town, the one who will sign off on the adoption discreetly? Suzanne thought to herself: *If he already knows, then there's no point in postponing the fight.*

Ésaïe parked a shiny SUV in front of my grandmother's house and waited outside. Suzanne took the passenger seat and Laurent, the back seat. A duffel bag full of cash sat near Laurent's shoes. He tried to reconcile the image of Ésaïe reaching into the bag to pull out a bundle of bills, with that of my grandmother's packed house, the concrete floor, the spare furniture, the fact that the man paying for their sumptuous meal that evening had not brought diapers for his own daughter in months. Suzanne had forgotten to explain *feymen* to him. The duffel bag is less unusual than her husband thinks. Cameroon is run by men like Ésaïe—the roads may go unpaved and public construction may be delayed but somehow, the *feymen* always get their cut on time. It is the way things work here. That night she slept blissfully. The father of her niece was still in the dark. But Laurent's rage boiled all night. *How can a man have no sense of embarrassment?* he wondered.

With the adoption papers finalized, my first passport ready, and the summer of '89 drawing to a close, my new parents and I prepared for a new life together. The family had initially worried about my transition. I had never seen a white man in my life—how would I react to being raised by one? But their fears vanished the moment Laurent set foot in Cameroon. I had adopted him as much as he adopted me.

We were waiting to board our plane at Nsimalen Airport, the three of us, when my mom spotted another cousin of Ésaïe's at our departure gate. It was a woman she had met before and instantly disliked. As far as she knew, the feeling had been mutual. My mom thought, *Few things would bring this woman more joy than to have Ésaïe ground this plane.*

We migrated to seats farther away from the gate. Though they were not religious, my adoptive parents prayed for one more hour of unfussy baby. I delivered. By the time the cousin noticed us on the flight, we had crossed into Nigerian airspace and out of Ésaïe's political reach. The woman slithered to our aisle. She and my mom exchanged contrived pleasantries. Finally, she got to the bottom of her visit.

But tell me, she asked. *Does this child not look like Assae's daughter?*

Yes. And now she's mine.

IN DC, THE consulate attaché clears his throat. He has solved the mystery. My adoptive parents' absence from the birth certificate can be explained by the type of adoption, he says. A *plenary* adoption would have appointed my aunt and uncle as my sole set of parents, and automatically converted my last name to Jucquois. But my parents had opted for what the French state called a *simple* adoption. The latter was faster to process but had its drawbacks. For instance, it maintained the status quo by merely adding the new set of parents to any existing ones. In the eyes of the French state, I am therefore the child of three parents, even as I carry the last name of an unlisted fourth.

A ball fires up in my throat. I cannot blink or look down because if I do, tears will stream, and I will not know how to stop them. I try slow, quiet breaths until my heartbeat steadies. My shoulders slump, countering my efforts to exude stoicism. My parents have never explained the technical aspects of the adoption that way, but their decision makes sense. Of course they did what they needed to take me home in time. Nevertheless, the dizzying sensation of being divided rushes back, heightened this time by the visual of my adoptive parents' absence from my birth certificate. I feel like a little girl again: stranger in my own name, pulled down by a ghost as I grasp for a means to steady myself.

But my parents are my parents, the attaché says. He is not much older than me but delivers this assurance as if he were comforting a daughter. It is pity, not condescension. His cheeks are flushed, he did not mean to shock me, he says. I assure him that I understand. *Oui, je comprend, je comprend.* As if repeating this like a mantra can make it true.

He tells me that the window to convert my simple adoption into a plenary one has long closed, but if becoming a Jucquois would bring me solace, there may be another way. He pulls out a brochure. *This is a how-to for petitioning the French government for a name change.* For a reasonable fee and a few hours navigating red tape, the state will erase the ghost and, in the process, the man who left me unclaimed.

How satisfying might it feel to clear that history, to submit Ésaïe's memory to my own will, the way he'd so easily submitted women to his. Becoming a Jucquois would amount to a second killing. Because names, and the rewriting of them, have that power. This much was already clear from the other names on my birth certificate. Cameroon: from *Rios de Camarões*, for the shrimp that Portuguese explorers encountered on the littoral, rewritten as *Kamerun* by the German colonists, and again as *Cameroon* and *Cameroun* by the British and French empires after the Great War. And Yaoundé: for the outpost the Germans built and called *Jaunde*, a distortion of the word Ewondo. Whatever names my ancestors had for these lands before the white pen, no one could remember now.

Do I have it in me to do this to him, to us?

After all, Assae Billé is more than our last name. It is the oral history of a place. *Floating feather. Tree.* At once a description of what fluttered away and of what remained. A record embedded with the birds in the skies of my ancestors. Forests that fed generations of my paternal family. The blue-bellied turacos and lanky obeche trees of southern Cameroon. Constants as homes were made, unmade, and remade. Perhaps this was what Ésaïe saw when he spoke our last name, a map home.

The brochure in my pocket promises a severance.

And still, I hesitate.

The Dreaming Is Free

HOME, NOUN. (CONT.)
also a place of autonomy
6 a: a safe and affordable domicile

SUNDAY, 14 DECEMBER 1997

The Duchère neighborhood is in a deep slumber. If you drove past the housing project at this time of day, you might confuse it for the most tranquil hill in Lyon. No police sirens. No shattered glass. No stereos missing, yet. Birds whistle on the concrete windowsills, the same lullabies they sing at my grandparents' farm in the countryside. They're always around, the birds. You just have to listen harder to catch them here.

Footsteps in the kitchen.

My mom likes to say, *The future belongs to those who rise early.* She's never needed sleep wherever we live, and she doesn't think I should need much either. In a bit, she'll knock on my bedroom door and barge in before I can say *Come in*. I squeeze my eyes shut and see my dad's face.

Waking up early is the only thing my parents have in common. For as long as I can remember, my dad has worked the five A.M. shift one week, and the two P.M. shift the next. Still, he's always up by eight A.M. on the evening-shift weeks. I know four facts about my dad's job: that it's called the Foundries of the Poitou; that the factory has two large buildings: one blue and one red

(I can't remember which he goes into); that the men who work there melt sand into parts for Renault cars; and that the foundries make my dad's herniated disk hurt more.

Little rays dance through the curtains, wash the walls in blue. When the sun has risen, the walls will become white again, matching the kitchen, the bathroom, and my mom's bedroom. White for cleanliness and purity. But also: fresh starts. Wherever you were before is gone, and so is whatever happened in this apartment before you. Wite-Out for your life. To me, however, the white denotes nothingness. The absence of choice, of individuality. The walls see the tenants as interchangeable numbers more than people. The rooms in our apartment are cold, as if whoever was in charge gave up halfway through. As if the kinds of people who move into the Duchère, people like us, couldn't possibly mind. But I *do* mind; I wish my bedroom was pink.

Has anyone here ever asked the government for permission to paint? I wonder sometimes. My mom definitely hasn't. Maybe for the same reason that I won't bug her to paint my room pink. After a while, you realize that you may never get yesses, but that there is one easy way to stop getting nos: you take what you're given and you learn to live with it.

I bet the administrators who run the complex from their government-issued desks figure that, if the Duchère gets too comfortable, too bright and too happy, nobody will ever want to leave. Their children will want to call this place home. And so will their grandchildren. Next thing you know, generations will have been raised in rent-free apartments with no future to chase.

It's hard to tell where the administrators would get such an idea. My mom and I couldn't wait to get out of the Duchère, even before we lived here. We used to drive in to this very project from our house in little Couzon-au-Mont-d'Or. It shared the "Mont d'Or" part of its name, French for "Hill of Gold," with a few other small villages in this part of the countryside, where ochre-tinted limestone made the hills glow at sunset. The house belonged to my mom's first boyfriend after the divorce. With two floors, three bedrooms, two toilets, a bidet, a fireplace downstairs, and a living room wall made of stone, it was by far the most beautiful place I'd ever called home.

My window overlooked a courtyard lined with pampas grass and rose-bushes, and next to them, the cars: my mom's silver Citroën, her boyfriend's sedan, and his sports car, which he insisted we call *the Alpine*. When Joyce visited me from Spain, we spent hours huddled under the great magnolia tree in the backyard and used its thick green leaves to wrap our baby dolls in makeshift *pagnes*, the traditional Cameroonian dresses our grandmothers sometimes wore. Beneath the house, railroad tracks fed trains into the Lyon-Part-Dieu station. At night, their humming rocked my bed softly. I liked the coconut trees on the walls of that bedroom.

Couzon-au-Mont-d'Or might as well have been on a different planet. It was a portrait of serenity, the kind of France that people pictured when they spray-painted *France for the French* on underpasses. Danger hadn't struck it since 1993, when a wedge of rock broke off a hill and politely deposited itself some feet away. No one had died in the minor disaster. The wedge still sat right where it'd landed, like a fat slice of ochre-stone cake.

Because the village was even whiter than Châtellerault, my mom and I made excursions into the Duchère to get our hair braided. We parked across from Tata Delphine's *barre*—a block-wide tower—and triple-checked the Citroën's doors before going up to the ninth floor. Tata Delphine would spend the next eight hours patiently knotting extensions into my hair. In the daytime and evening, waves of laughter and shrieks and raï songs and car alarms would sift through the open windows.

I suspect that the walls of Tata Delphine's apartment could've been painted any color—although they were white—and my mom would still poke her head out on the hour to see that our ride home was where we left it. Same Duchère, same trouble—only with a coat of color, to give people the sense that a piece of this hill was theirs.

But I am speculating. Maybe our neighbors don't care about the paint at all. There's no kid my age I can verify my theory with, since my mom won't let me play outside.

Too dangerous, she says.

It's funny. My mom always swore she'd never live here but six months in, it's not as bad as she thought it would be. We live here because three years after we moved to Couzon, she and her boyfriend broke up. Suddenly, my mom was spending weeks searching for rentals in the city, where the jobs were. But the math was not working; it turns out that Lyon is expensive. By midsummer, we were running out of days to lock down an address in time to register me in the fifth grade. (I had skipped the first grade, putting me a year ahead of other nine-year-olds.) Tata Delphine encouraged her to apply for public housing in her complex. The Duchère was nowhere as quaint as Couzon—few places in Lyon were, unless you were rich—but it was built for hard times, and these were hard times for us. This is how we landed in the white apartment.

Lyon, the third-largest French city, was a city of three hills—two jewels and one stone. On the right bank of the Saône was the leafy Croix-Rousse, which was once dominated by silk weavers and still harbored an artisan class. On the left bank was the Four-vière, where 798 steps meandered from the old town to the majestic basilica, from where the city could be observed in her entirety. To the north was the Duchère—developed into a neighborhood starting in the 1950s as the de Gaulle presidency sought to modernize the French standard of living while also accommodating a population boom after World War II. The affordable buildings were called HLMs, short for *habitation à loyer modéré*, and were heavily subsidized.

The Duchère itself was subdivided into three plateaus: de Balmont for the middle class, the Château for the working class, and the Sauvegarde for the immigrant poor. HLMs in the Sauveg-arde were mostly filled with immigrants from the Maghreb and sub-Saharan Africa. In the mid-1990s, 14,000 people lived in the Duchère's *barres*. As the neighborhood deteriorated, the third hill became known for rampant petty theft, carjackings, and drug seizures—like the 1994 police raid rumored to have uncovered 550 pounds of heroin. About 80 percent of the adults residing in the Duchère had no high school diploma; one-fifth were unemployed. The residents who worked didn't earn enough to leave.

ɟ

SHUFFLING IN THE HALLWAY.

Five more minutes until our Sunday really begins. *Time to get ready*, my mom says. *Market day again.*

The car coughs and whistles as we pull out of the parking lot. Neither of us likes frosty weather, even if it means that Christmas is right around the corner. It's sunny out by the time we set up the tent, the folding table, and the products for sale today: hair extensions, hair lotions, hair nets, hair relaxers, smoothing face creams, and lipsticks for every mood.

I recognize some of the merchants. One of them, an older man, has a crush on my mom so he sneaks me a free döner kebab around lunchtime. My mom's market-best-friend, Djamila, is never too far. She grew up in Togo, a country I'd never heard of until I met her. On her table are leather knockoffs in all hues: purses, wallets, boots, even hats. If she were a piece of jewelry, Djamila would be a massive fake ruby. She loves bright red lipstick and laughs from deep in her belly. Usually, you hear her before you see her.

Since summer, my mom has been selling beauty products here and there, on top of her temp job working nights at a nursing home, but the outdoor market is Djamila's full-time job. She has two kids to herself, a seven-year-old boy and a four-year-old girl. I've babysat them before but they're mature enough to watch themselves. I am, too, but my mom takes me to the market with her anyway. Because I spend Mondays through Fridays at boarding school, we spend as much of the weekend as we can in the same place.

I know the markets bring in extra money, which we very much need, but I hate them more than anything in the world. How early you have to wake up for them. How there are so many boxes to unpack and repack. How happy you have to seem no matter what, so people will come to your table even if, earlier that morning, Princess Diana died in a tragic car crash, and you'd much rather cry in bed while flipping through photos of her in *Paris Match*. Instead, you have to stand and wait patiently, smiling.

That's a lot of what the outdoor market is: standing and waiting in inconvenient weather. There's no way to know if a market day will be good or not except by waiting. That's the other part I hate. How we have no control over the outcome because it depends entirely on the goodness of other people. African women must be due for a relaxer. African women must be in the mood for wigs rather than extensions. African women must want to buy at the market rather than a brick-and-mortar shop. If they do not want, then a bill gets paid late here or my grandmother has to skip her treatment *back home*.

It doesn't seem fair.

WE PACK UP the merchandise for the day a couple of hours after lunchtime. On the way home we stop at Tati, the big discount store. This round of last-minute shopping isn't for me. My mom has already bought and hidden my gifts. She'll hand them to me before I go see my dad. It's his turn to have me this Christmas.

Tati is always this crowded and disorganized. Finding two items of the same kind in different sizes requires diving through thick piles of cheap fabric with a slight chemical smell. The whole experience makes me irritable, but my mom doesn't mind the hunt. The prices are right. She pulls out dresses and cardigans in the shapes of her siblings, and she holds shirts up to my chest to eyeball my cousins' sizes. She rechecks the tags and does some computing in her head. Our cart fills up quickly. Next week, the clothes will fly *back home*, alongside handwritten letters and vitamins for my grandmother.

My mom won't deliver the packages to Yaoundé herself. That would mean a plane ticket, the cost of days not worked, the anxiety of being apart from me, quelled by buying more minutes from the expensive international calling cafe, all this on top of gifts for every single person my mom can think of. The math never adds up to "enough money." So, to make her deliveries, my mom leans on other travelers—friends of friends, second cousins of friends, strangers willing to carry her gifts in their suitcases. She hopes to pay it forward someday.

⁕

IT IS ALMOST dark out by the time we park at the Duchère, in a parking spot underneath our *barre*. There's no safe space in what the city has labeled an "urban sensitive zone," but anything visible from the seventh floor will do. Upstairs in our apartment, my mom dumps the contents of her fanny pack onto her bed. I brace myself for this part. Because she tells me everything, I know when my dad has dragged his feet on sending child support, or when changing the car's oil leaves too little for the gas bill. Every franc counts. Some days, like today, I check her tally. When my mom doesn't ask me to help, it means the day was unlucky. Not enough money to warrant a second look. On those days, she asks the ceiling, *What are we going to do?* and my stomach churns with nerves. I don't know what we're going to do. I wish I knew.

My mom keeps an eye on dinner while checking that I am packing my boarding school bag with clean shirts and fresh undies. In my *cartable*—the rectangular backpack that my friends and I all wear to school—I stuff a three-ring binder, lined notebooks, and refill cartridges for my fountain pen.

Boarding school was Tata Balbine's suggestion. As my mom was making her peace with moving into the Duchère, my aunt reminded her that Joyce had been in a private boarding school for a year in Spain, on a scholarship, and that she had adjusted well. After doing a little research, my mom discovered the Internat Adolphe Favre, one of the last municipal boarding schools in France. It just so happened to be a short drive from our *barre*. The downside was that I would be out of her sight for five days a week. That'd give her no way of knowing whether I was surrounding myself with good kids. *You're too influenceable*, my mom often tells me. But I don't see it as a bad thing. To stand any chance at making friends in elementary school—heck, in any school at all— you have to figure out what people think is the right way to act, and then adopt that way as your own, or as much as you can without hurting anyone. It's less faking than reading the room. A whole ecosystem preceded you, one that won't be painted over just because it's *your* first day. So you have to absorb it and do it quickly—the friendships, the games, the jokes, the slang. I mean all of it. You might still get chewed up but your odds of coming out in one piece are vastly improved. Or, at least, that's my theory.

Whether my mom agreed with this or not, *someone* was going to highly influence me that school year. She decided to take her chances on the fourth- and fifth-grade girls of the Internat over the kids in the Duchère. Whatever had brought the girls in, perhaps the idyllic air of the Croix-Rousse hill would change them before they could change me.

We drive away as night drapes the concrete towers. From our side of the river, the colorful houses and buildings on the hill of the Croix-Rousse make it look like a quilt sewn out of bright facades. We wind up Chazière Street until the iron gates appear in the windshield. With its brown brick and severe tiled peaks, the Internat Adolphe Favre building reminds me of a convent. Living there is way more fun than that, though. I'm excited to be back for the week.

The Internat began as an orphanage. In 1881, Jean Chazière, a wealthy native of Lyon, gifted to the city a property he owned on Missionaries Street. The city converted the donation into a public orphanage for girls, which opened in 1891, on the renamed Chazière Street. A public orphanage for boys followed in 1911. Six years later, the city merged and expanded the two institutions into the Adolphe Favre Orphanage—christened in honor of a city hall worker killed in World War I. The orphanage would become a boarding school in 1925. More than a century after its inauguration, the building remained funded by the city and served as a harbor for boys and girls aged around six to thirteen, issued from vulnerable environments and low-income families. Five days a week, with the exception of occasional out-of-town trips, children ate, slept, played, and did their homework at the Internat, while attending the local schools during the day.

*

OUR FLOOR BUZZES with the indefatigable energy of girls in the fourth and fifth grades. Some are unloading their belongings while others are already in pajamas. The adults in charge of watching us greet my mom and me at the door. Each floor has two of them; we call them the educators. Martine is thirty-nine, or two years older than my mom. She has a chubby face and wears her blond hair short and feathered like Princess Diana used to. Her favorite sweater is made of a knitted mesh that looks itchy. We do not push our luck with Martine because when she's angry, she roars and turns redder than a beet. Karine is the good cop. She's twenty-four and mouselike. I've never heard her raise her voice, and she hangs on our every word when we talk. Sometimes, she even lets us negotiate bedtime.

In the morning, our two educators will make sure we have eaten breakfast and wave goodbye to us at the gates, as we head off to Jean de La Fontaine elementary school down the street. I'm in the CM2, the fifth grade. (My best subjects are spelling, cursive, math, and art. I am bad at science, poetry, and history. Also, any activity requiring hand-eye coordination.) In the evening, we will find them on this floor again, waiting for us with snacks and their full attention. From tonight through Friday after school, they will be our guardians and emergency contacts, entrusted to protect our little lives.

My mom doesn't stay long. There's no need for dramatic goodbyes because the week will fly, as it always does. One kiss and we say, *Until Friday!*

MONDAY, 15 DECEMBER 1997

The most fun part of the Internat is getting to live with my best friend. Her name is Anaïs as in Anaïs-Anaïs, the perfume that my mom got me on my eighth birthday. *Every woman has to have a scent*, my mom likes to say. Hers is called Paris and smells much better than what I've seen of the capital. Five days a week, Anaïs and I get to pretend that we're sisters even though her hair is sandy and her eyes are the color of dark-green olives. She's shorter than me and has round cheeks that dimple over the cheekbone. We are the same age but in different classes because I skipped first grade. Like me, Anaïs is in her mom's custody and loves her dad more than almost anyone in the whole world.

One secret: there has to be something wrong with you or your family to be admitted to the Internat. Its point is to make us feel like all is fine and dandy. Most of us live with single moms. Anaïs is here in part because her dad is sick. When it's his turn to watch her, he drinks and drinks until he can't stand straight, and forgets to take her places he promised. This, too, is a secret. Anaïs can't talk about it or she'll cry herself to sleep. Some kids have severe dyslexia or other learning disabilities. Some have siblings who are a handful at home. A few are, themselves, the handfuls.

I live at the Internat because my mom wasn't sure she should send me to the local school. Maybe the place would chew me up. Kids in the *barres* are built tough because that's what you need to survive in an "urban sensitive zone." But my shell is soft from our three years in Couzon. Even though my mom grew up in Yaoundé, in places that were nothing like the Duchère, I think she relates to its kids and their resilience more than she does to me. If she knows how to fight, it's because she had to stand up to bullies growing up, to protect herself and her younger sister—my birth mother, Florence—who was as clumsy and head-in-the-clouds as I am now. She doesn't see that strength in me.

We don't really stick out from the kids at school who live in the Croix-Rousse year-round. Still, you'd be pressed to find any of us volunteering information about our weekends. It's weird, I guess, that we never talk about it. Not even to one another. I don't, despite being a blabbermouth. I've seen the way adults scrunch up their noses at the mention of the Duchère, like it's the sorriest thing they've ever heard. The neighborhood has a reputation for being troubled. But it's also a dead giveaway for being poor. I'd rather not find out what my classmates would do with that information. Not that I know where she lives, but what if knowing that I was from an "urban sensitive zone" made Anaïs too embarrassed to stay best friends with me?

*

MY MOM WORRIES about what our neighbors and their kids are up to. But to me, the patrols are the scariest part of the Duchère. Police officers in dark uniforms monitor the complex as if watching a pot of boiling water. I see them on the weekends, on my way to and from the bakery—the only place I'm allowed to go alone besides Tata Delphine's apartment next door. The officers lean against their motorcycles and glare so intently that I find myself questioning whether I really did pay for the baguette in the crook of my arm. I'd rather run as fast as I can, but I maintain a steady pace, stare straight ahead, and pretend to be invisible.

I'm curious about whether any of my friends from the Internat feel this watched when they go home, but not enough to ask them where their home is.

TUESDAY, 16 DECEMBER 1997

After school, my friends and I head back to the Internat under a navy sky illuminated with bows, snowflakes, and bells. The air smells like roasted chestnuts. My dad calls me before dinner. I pick up the phone in the hallway, tugging at the long purple cord that spirals from the wall. He asks me how school is going, what I'm up to this week.

Soon, I'll be home with him again, in our little town where everything is close together and where all my favorite memories still live—on the streets where I learned to walk, in the studio where Miss Patricia taught us ballet, and in the parking lot where the circus sets up every summer. I wish it was already next week.

To get to Châtellerault, you have to take a high-speed train from Lyon-Part-Dieu station. I've taken this route by myself many times; it's always the same and not scary at all. I'll have to wear a tag for unaccompanied children so the controller will know to watch out for me. Over the long ride, I'll read a *Famous Five*, and work on my paint-by-numbers—the portrait of a dalmatian this time—and I might also count cows out the window while eating my ham-and-butter sandwich. The most important rules to remember are, first, not to talk to adult strangers ever and, second, to listen very carefully for my stop. I know that we are close when the voice announces: *Prochain arrêt: St-Pierre-des-Corps*. The last stop before Châtellerault.

I can already picture my dad waiting on the train platform. He'll be easy to spot despite not being very tall. He's almost bald and wears thick yellowed glasses. He likes to stand with his hands in his pockets. When he gives me a big kiss on the cheek, it will smell like menthol cigarettes and aftershave. He'll hold my hand tight all the way to the car and then peek at me through the rearview mirror to make sure I'm not a hallucination. Seeing him will be the best.

After my mom and I moved away, my dad left the apartment that we used to live in all together in the Plaine d'Ozon neighborhood and went to my grandparents' farm for a bit. But after his sadness had passed, he went back to Châtellerault. His new apartment is near the forest, which has a playground with a large swing set and a slide that turns into a frying pan in the summer. On our walks, I pick wild blackberries off the side of the trail.

I like this apartment better than the one we shared with my mom when I was little. For starters, the bathroom is pink. I have my own bedroom there but always ask to sleep on the pull-out couch so I can watch *Hey Arnold!* from bed first thing when I wake up. This is our secret. My mom thinks TV rots children's brains. When I ask her for permission to watch just one cartoon, she always says, *After twelve P.M.* But without exception, the news is on when I try. After a while, I stop asking her and save it all for school breaks.

My dad shares the plan on the phone. It's basically the same every year but it still feels good to hear it. On Christmas Eve, we'll have dinner at the farm and sleep over—my dad in the bedroom that can be accessed only through the outdoor staircase, and me in the tiny bedroom that was his as a kid. The next morning, I'll tear into my mountain of gifts while he and my grandparents make *oooh*s and *aaah*s. And finally it'll feel like the most wonderful time of the year.

Martine is summoning me to the dining room. I tell my dad, *A très bientôt!*

WEDNESDAY, 17 DECEMBER 1997
France gives Wednesdays off to maternal and elementary school children, so we spend the morning constructing elaborate forts at the Internat. It's easy after you've done it once. All you need are ten loft beds, ten sheets, and at minimum one girl with long arms. (Our bedroom is a large square containing all these ingredients at any given time.) You bring the beds off the walls and closer together. Then have the girl with long arms tuck the sheets under the mattresses to make a ceiling and walls. That's it! When the forts are done, we only allow the boys who swear to be nice and not make fun of us to come inside.

After catching up on homework, we gather in the games room for more playing. I take a Tintin comic to one of the poufs and read until it's my turn to shower. The littlest boarders are finishing their dinner downstairs when Samira, the most popular girl in the fourth and fifth grade, orders us to line up in front of the bathroom mirrors with our chests out. She says the secret to growing boobs faster is to tap them with a cold spoon every night. You can choose to believe her or not, but that's what she did, and at eleven, Samira's already an 85B. The girls who arrived prepared tap their own nipples. I look at the pathetic swelling around mine and doubt there's an 85B in my future.

Still, I sneak a spoon back from dinner.

✕

SAMIRA AND I are great friends but not best friends. She's a massive fake ruby, just like Djamila. Very funny, mostly nice, and a surprisingly good listener. She's kissed boys before and has two teenaged sisters who wear makeup. This alone puts her on my mom's bad side. And that's without my mom knowing about that time with the cigarettes.

The fall trimester was in full swing when rumors of their presence had started on our floor, spread to the boys' floor, then back down to ours. It was so very hush-hush that by the end of the night, it wasn't clear to me that there really were cigarettes, or if there were, that any were actually hidden on our floor. The next morning, though, Samira and I were walking to class when she told me about meeting up later with some girls that I didn't know, so they could smoke the cigarettes in question. She'd swiped them from her teenage sister. Samira said she hadn't asked me earlier because she didn't think I'd be into it. But of course, I was invited. *It's okay if you don't wanna come*, she said with hesitation. *I don't wanna pressure you.* But I was too flattered to refuse. We split up at the ring of the bell.

There were risks to this plan. If Martine smelled cigarette smoke on us, we'd be toast. Grounded to eternity and beyond. Maybe murdered—if my mom caught wind of it. It wasn't even that I cared to find out their taste. I liked the smell fine, but only because it came from my dad and it meant we were reunited and on a nice walk. The thought of setting my own throat on fire made me feel queasy. Still, the invitation was irresistible. I loved secrets and Samira was hands-down my coolest friend. Being invited cemented that I belonged not just at the Internat but also at my new school. How could I say no?

The more hours passed, the guiltier I felt about the plan. Even if my mom never found out, I still would've proven her theory that I was influenceable to a fault by choosing wrong, despite knowing how hard she worked to care for me and the emotional sacrifice she was making in being away from me most of the time. All so I could try cigarettes that I *probably* wouldn't enjoy? It was more than being influenceable. I was being selfish.

At recess, I looked for Samira and told her I was out. She hadn't seemed mad or all that surprised.

*

FOOTSTEPS CLIMB THE stairs, shuffle down the hallway. A pause. The night guard's flashlight roves under the door. Our bedroom is plunged in darkness. A girl giggles under her covers and another shushes her. More giggles. Lionel, the night guard, whisper-yells at us to quit chattering or he'll rat us out to Martine. We know he's too sweet to subject us to her wrath but pipe down anyway. It's getting late. To make myself dream about my grandparents' farm, I force a picture of the fat turkey Mamie will serve on Christmas Eve, how she'll make me try the chocolate *bûche*, even though the only good chocolates are Kinder eggs, and how cool is it, I wonder, that Catholic children—and by Catholic, I mean the real Catholics, not just the ones who were baptized, like me—how cool that they get to wear white robes at Midnight Mass, and sing angelic hymns at the front of the church—or at least that's what Joyce once told me, and I believe her, she'd know since she's so Catholic that, for as long as I've known her, she's worn a gold chain around her belly, like a thin belt holding a pendant of the Virgin Mary, for protection, but from what, I'm not sure, going to Midnight Mass would be one way to find out—and I wonder if my dad would take me, especially knowing that I'll fall asleep twenty minutes in, and that he's an atheist, or that's what he told me when I asked him if he believes in God, to which I responded that, in that case, I was too—and I wonder how old he was when he stopped sleeping in the tiny bedroom—ten? twelve? thirteen?—and I wonder whether Mamie also made the room this cozy for him, with piles of blankets that smell like her bar of black soap: floral and woody—as for that room, how peculiar of her to keep a Santa in the tiny bedroom year-round, that porcelain doll in the red coat with the wire-rim glasses, and on the same shelf, under a glass bell, a shepherd in a woolly coat, the two of them close to each other as if they might be related, although there's no use in asking Mamie just how—she's not a religious woman either, just a really great cook grateful for an excuse to roast a fat Christmas turkey and, as my eyes grow heavier, I consider whether there's a chance, any chance at all, that the Santa in the tiny room is actually the one who puts the presents out by the fireplace or—

Around eleven P.M., a sixteen-year-old boy named Abdelkader Bouziane sped through the Parisian suburbs at the wheel of his mother's car. He was from the Plaine-du-Lys, which looked a bit like the Plaine d'Ozon in Châtellerault. Abdelkader was supposed to grow up so that one day, he and his mother would look back on this night and laugh at the terror that he was, to steal her car keys for a joyride with his older cousin. But that night, the boy blew through a roadblock in Chailly-en-Bière. Questioned later, the police officers would say that Abdelkader was barreling toward the next roadblock, at the Liberation intersection in Fontainebleau, when they fired four rounds into his car. (A forensics report, however, would conclude that the car was moving at less than twenty-five miles per hour.) One of the bullets lodged into Abdelkader's neck and killed him before he could be taken to a hospital. News would reach his complex the next day, and people would notice that the police didn't seem very sorry for what they did. Some would suspect they were lying about the details. And a quiet rage would begin to simmer in the Plaine-du-Lys.

THURSDAY, 18 DECEMBER 1997

Sitting at the desk underneath my loft bed, I wonder what my mom is up to this evening. Is she spread on the sofa like a pancake, the faint scent of geriatric medication and bleach still enmeshed in her hair? Or is she carrying market boxes from the Citroën to the apartment on the seventh floor?

While I hate the markets, it pains me to imagine her working them alone. My soft fingers and stick arms aren't the most supportive, but I'm not the worst person to wait with. I can handle small boxes, and listen while she complains to the ceiling. My poor mom, who'll be alone during the weeks that I'll be with my dad. To think that I haven't asked where she'll spend Christmas. How awful of me. I promise myself to work extra hard at the market this weekend.

It's hard to focus on homework tonight, with so many Santa lists going around. Everyone has one, even the Muslim kids. Mine includes Barbies, a Polaroid camera, one new anything with the Spice Girls on it—literally anything—and a board game called La Bonne Paye that we play a lot here. (It's like Monopoly, but less boring.)

I put a Nintendo on there but that's a long shot. If Santa got me video games, my mom would probably hunt him down and finish him right there in the chimney. By Santa, of course, I mean my dad. No way Santa's real. We're not allowed to say that here in case one of the littlest boarders is within earshot. But no girl on the floor for fourth and fifth graders still believes. If magic was real, we wouldn't need the Internat. Half our lists won't make it under the Christmas tree. But the dreaming is free.

At this very moment, across the river, in the Duchère, the police were bringing the twenty-four-year-old Fabrice Fernandez to the police station. Earlier that evening, Fabrice was playing cards in his uncle's apartment, on the fifth floor of a Duchère tower nicknamed Chicago, when he noticed from the window that his half-brother Daniel was ensnarled in an argument downstairs. So, Fabrice grabbed his other half brother, Alain, to see what was going on. A gunshot echoed. The police appeared quickly, for they were never far. Elsewhere in France, they were nicknamed "guardians of the peace." But on these blocks, teenagers spotted their fatigues and gathered stones in their pockets. They looked the officers in the face and yelled, *Nique ta mère!* (tr.: fuck your mother) before scattering in the concrete recesses of the Duchère.

Daniel was holding a shotgun when the police arrived. No one was hurt. Fabrice's uncle would tell the press that Fabrice tried to stop the officers from arresting his half brothers. Maybe he was hoping for an act of mercy—it was almost Christmas after all. But the officers wouldn't hear it. They arrested his brothers and shoved him to the ground and handcuffed him, with a roughness typically reserved for the young black and Arab residents in the complex. Whites who lived in the *barres* were adjacent enough to these ostracized groups. As the police took him away, the uncle remembered Fabrice shouting, "Look at what they're doing to me, look at what they're doing to me!"

The three brothers were separated at the precinct, with Daniel and Alain in one room, and Fabrice in another, alone with a certain Officer Carvalho.

At 9:36 P.M., Fabrice was slumped in his chair, dead, his wrists still shackled behind his back. At trial, months later, Carvalho would say that Fabrice's last words to him were: "You're incapable of it." The officer would maintain that he had only meant to scare Fabrice when, at 9:35 P.M., he pointed the seized shotgun at his face. That he hadn't meant to shoot him point-blank. But the bizarre aftermath, recounted by Carvalho's own colleagues, beleaguered the mind. They'd watched him stand outside the station, moments later, leisurely smoking a cigarette and filing his nails. Eerie calm notwithstanding, Carvalho swore it was an accident. Yet, pulling that trigger required an 8.5-pound pressure.

In the morning, news of Fabrice's killing began to spread through the *barres* and the rage that simmered in the Plaine-du-Lys leaped to the Duchère.

FRIDAY, 19 DECEMBER 1997

Samira leaves on the back of a motorcycle. Anaïs's mom has already picked her up. While I toss the last of my dirty laundry into my travel bag, my mom grills the educators. *Did Vanessa do the . . . and was she . . . by the way, did she ever find . . . certainly, she is . . . are you sure that . . . well, in January, we'll . . .*

She unlocks the passenger door for me. Ever since we started the markets, she's been letting me ride up front. Usually, she has funny stories for the way home. The market attracts weirdos on both sides of the tables and the older people she watches at the nursing home are characters. This week, though, my mom reports that a young man died at the police station. A tragic accident, the news said.

We cross into the "urban sensitive zone." The air feels taut, as if a strip of cellophane has been stretched over the Duchère. Police officers are posted by the *barre* doors and near the entrance to the commercial strip that houses the bakery. They have come to remind us that the apartments belong to someone else—our lives, too, if we catch them in the wrong mood. The parking lot is unusually full. We loop around the lot a third time before we give up and park in front of Tata Delphine's *barre* instead of our own.

When my mom was just starting out with the markets, she'd bring each box of merchandise up the elevator at the end of the day. But neighbors had their own packages to load and unload, so the elevator doors would get held up for what felt like hours. On those days, we took the stairs. Seven flights after all that standing and waiting. The apartments may be white but the staircases are black, lit by small pockets of flat glass windows. When the staircase isn't empty, kids slip in there to swap tongues and neighbors can be found sleeping off a rough night. Things are sold and exchanged between floors. It's wiser not to hang out in the staircases longer than necessary. After a while, my mom stopped hauling the loads up religiously. Now they spend the night in the trunk of the Citroën under a sheet of tarp.

We triple-check the locks and head upstairs. Tomorrow's a big day. Saturdays tend to draw more shoppers but this is Christmas week. African women will want to look their best and we'll have just what they need. My mom is optimistic. The future belongs to those who rise early, so we go to sleep before too long.

Downstairs, small crews of neighbors have gathered. Had my mom not sent me to school across the river, it might be my friends' older brothers and sisters masked up in the parking lots and on the edges of the commercial strip, throwing stones at police officers and firefighters. A rifle bullet pierces an empty police car. But it's the thunderous clap that wakes up my mom.

Footsteps in the hallway. I stir but keep dreaming.

My mom checks the living room and sees that fire has engulfed the parking lot, swallowing rows of metal with ravenous appetite. Briefly, she forgets about having parked beneath the *barre* next door. Where is the Citroën?

The Duchère is mourning Fabrice. Up north, the residents of Plaine-du-Lys launch Molotov cocktails for Abdelkader. My mom

runs downstairs. Broken glass crunches under her shoes. Around
her, loud pops shake cars in varying degrees of degradation.
Chunks of alloy slide off charred skeletons of metal. Firefighters on the scene examine the broken windows of their own
trucks—whoever threw the stones long gone—all the while yelling
inaudible directions. My mom covers her mouth as she passes
officers in riot gear. Burnt rubber and fuel. Too smoky to
think. She wades through the neighbors. Some are thanking the
heavens while others curse the thoughtless creatures who reduced
their cars, their most valuable possession after their children,
to cinders.

She reaches the parking lot beneath her friend Delphine's
barre and finds her Citroën unscathed. What has she done to
deserve such luck? Though not yet a believer, my mom thanks God
for another day of work tomorrow.

SATURDAY, 20 DECEMBER 1997

My eyes open before the knock on the door. The sky is still too opaque to paint
the walls in blue but the birds have returned. They sing through a faint film of
smoke. My mom barges into my room with a luminous smile. *Market day*, she
says. How I've missed her.

A handful of officers are still loitering by the building doors. They watch
us leave the parking lot. Across the city, administrators for the Duchère are
watching the first footage of the burning. Newscasters ask what only someone
who doesn't live here would wonder: what kind of people would burn their
own home?

It's unclear whether the question is being posed to us or whether we are
merely intended to be its subject. And how we *are* its subject. The Duchère exists
for people like my mom and me. A reality that subsumed our identity the
moment we qualified for the white apartment, our last resort, and made our
home here. The mere act of living in this project makes us the kind of people
who'd burn our own homes. And the kind of people we are is poor. But the
newscasters' question is flawed. The white apartments don't belong to us; no
real property on this hill does. The news cuts to commercials before asking the
better question: What kind of home would make its dwellers burn it down?

My mom has relocated the car from the lot across Tata Delphine's *barre* to a street over. We keep marveling at our luck. *What if we had returned an hour earlier. What if our usual parking spot was open.* My mom opens the trunk. Our merchandise awaits under the tarp. Two miracles in one morning, then. The Virgin Mary who watches Joyce across the Spanish border must've extended her grace to us.

```
The news reports that twenty-seven cars and three trucks were
completely torched in the Duchère. They barely mention the
Plaine-du-Lys. The number freezes at twenty-seven on TV but con-
tinues to climb long after the news channels get bored of
reporting on the ghetto. After each night cracked by loud pops,
the Duchère residents will return to the lots in the morning and
assess the damage, trying hard to mask their guilt and relief at
their neighbors being hit rather than them. The chaos will sub-
side and, the farther the nights of December 17 and 18, the more
people will forget.

    On the one-year anniversary of Fabrice's death, the French
state will send police reinforcements from Paris and Marseilles
to encircle the "urban sensitive zone" for days. Just in case the
pot boils over again.
```

THE CITROËN COUGHS and whistles out of the Duchère, drowning out the birdsong. At the market we set up the table, the tent, and lipsticks for every mood. Judging by the laughter down the block, Djamila has arrived.

Five days until Christmas. Four days until Christmas Eve. Three until my dad kisses me on the platform. But first, I must abide by the promise I have made to myself. Today of all market days, I will be grateful.

While my mom chats up a customer on one end of the table, I offer my toothiest grin to the African woman eyeing our table. One approaches and I know this will be a good market day. *Buy one get one free,* I sing to her. *Most wonderful time of the year!*

But by His Grace

HOME, NOUN. (CONT.)
7 **a:** a place of worship or religious comfort

THE TWO OF US WERE sitting in the car when I asked my dad if he believed in God. I was back in the Poitou-Charentes for the school break—in the spring or summer of 1997, I am no longer sure—and he and I had just come home from the grocery store. His new wife, Lisette, must have been inside. I knew that she was Catholic, and an earnest believer at that. I understood, too, that religion anchored our most decadent family meals, Easter and Christmas Eve. But we were not the type to say grace or ruminate on the existence of God. My parents had me baptized at Châtellerault's little Catholic church for the same reason their own parents had baptized them: it was just what people did, milestones to denote the passage of time. I remembered little of it other than what the photos showed. A chunky toddler version of me dodging the priest—a man who led mass on Sundays and, as it was well known, worked a construction job during the week. My parents, Maman Florence, and godparents watch him sprinkle my forehead with water. And later, the picnic on a grassy expanse.

The vast substance of my religious experience up to that point stemmed from the few summers I had spent visiting Joyce and Tata Balbine in Madrid. I remembered those moments fondly, sitting beside my cousin in my aunt's bedroom, on one of those sweltering nights, as we each tried to commit the

Our Father and Hail Mary prayers to memory, the waxy beads of the translucent rosary rolling between our small fingers. From Cameroon to France to Spain to the United States, the two prayers shared the same beginning, middle, and end. To know them in one language was to know them in all others. Catholic Sundays held no surprise. I found comfort in these rituals and the connections they offered strangers around the globe.

In the car that afternoon, my dad answered that he was an atheist. I replied that, in that case, so was I. Still, something drew me back to the faith. That very year, my dad would find himself spending Christmas Eve in a Catholic pew, my head resting on his lap. Attending Midnight Mass had been my idea. I wanted to see children sing beautiful hymns dressed in angelic white robes. Eager to please me, my dad located a Christmas Eve service in the vicinity of my grandparents' farm. Joyce had been right about the whole thing. The choir was so heavenly that I promptly passed out.

Would this service have marked the end of my exposure to religion had my grandmother, Mamie Catherine, not needed a minor surgery, and had her surgery been performed in France rather than Cameroon, or had she received a transfusion untainted with the virus, and if my family had been rich— Magic Johnson rich or, on second thought, just rich enough to buy her Magic Johnson time?

Then, perhaps, the phone wouldn't have rung when it rang, on that dreary night in October 1998.

We were home, my mom and me, on the seventh floor of our *barre* in the Duchère, when the fax-telephone that my mom had purchased for her market business rang. Cameroon calling, the country code announced. Too late in the day for good surprises, we knew it right away. A woman's voice emerged from the loudspeaker. Tata Balbine's older sister, Sophie. In their youths, she and my mom had been as close as Joyce and me. I listened closer. Maman Florence and Tata Nicole seemed to be standing behind her. Odd, I thought, that it would not be them on the line instead. More voices yet, a crowd. It was difficult to make out Tata Sophie's words under such conditions. She explained that the whole family had gathered at my grandparents' property, in the Ngousso quarter of Yaoundé.

A pause filled the silence on our end. My mom's face collapsed as she realized what a girl my age could not. Tata Sophie had picked the short straw. Mamie Catherine had been sick for what seemed like forever but was now deteriorating fast. The vitamins we sent *back home* were no match for the disease coursing through her veins. Chances that she would live through the night were slim.

Before my mom could ask, Tata Sophie said there was no use in handing the phone over; my grandmother had lost her ability to speak days ago.

Days ago? *Days* ago? Why was she only being told now? my mom asked, her face twisted with anger. Couldn't they give her water? Had they called a doctor? What had they done?

I looked at the clock on the fax-telephone. Saying goodbye in person would require booking a flight as soon as travel agencies reopened in the morning. No plane flew straight to Yaoundé from Lyon, so my mom would have to head north to Paris, on the first train out of Lyon-Part-Dieu station, then seven hours south, to the city where my grandmother would have already taken her last breath. That was, if my mom could scrounge up the money for the ticket at all, money we did not have. I watched her melt onto a chair.

The math never did seem to work in the Duchère.

Her friend Delphine, from the neighboring *barre*, shared the news with their circle of friends. Without her asking, the circle of friends—themselves African immigrants, themselves poor—surprised my mom by pooling enough money to send her home in the next few days. Too late to say goodbye, but choices were a privilege reserved for people of means. Tata Delphine brought the envelope over and babysat me while my mom went to bury my grandmother.

WEEKS AFTER THE funeral, my mom called me into her bedroom. It was a little before bedtime, on a weekend home from the Internat. I found her leafing through a stapled booklet. The poorly hand-drawn cover featured a black man wailing on his knees. A friend had sent her this collection of prayers and religious lyrics from London, though the words were in French. She asked if I would read them with her. I scrutinized her face for any sign of irony. This sudden interest in the spiritual realm felt foreign coming from her. Then again, we had recently consulted a tarot woman and a tea-leaves reader. I gathered that we were there to see if Mamie Catherine would beam some consolation down to us. My mom glanced at me with hopeful eyes.

I lied instinctively. Of course I had no interest in reading the booklet with her. What I wanted, what I needed, was for Mamie Catherine to resurrect, for the grief that shrouded my mom to evaporate, and for the math to allow my mom to pay the rent without a second thought. But how could I refuse her? I knelt at her side while she read out loud, my hands clasped, eyes shut, all the while talking myself into openness to possibility. Were our lives not a cycle of unlucky surprises—for when we were poor, that was the nature of most surprises—followed by scrambling? Over and over. We had so little to lose.

My mom pled with natural élan.

Where do we go from here, Lord?

Where do we go?

When the Lord answered with London, my mom sold our sputtering Citroën and brought me a summer study book to prepare for our next chapter. We were operating on faith. No job awaited her there—but my mom was determined. She would find something, she always did. Nor was there an apartment in our name. But she trusted, too, that someone in the local Francophone African community would house us while we figured things out. I worked hard on my booklet for English beginners as the summer of 1999 approached, completing a couple of pages each day, carefully matching stickers to words, and practicing the art of rolling my tongue to push *r*'s from the back of my mouth rather than my throat. When she had time to spare, my mom helped me with impromptu quizzes on the basics despite her own scant mastery of the language. *Where is the toilet? I have three pounds and seven pence.* I pictured the day my favorite Spice Girls lyrics would reveal themselves to me without effort.

Our belongings went to friends except for the essentials: clothes, photo albums, her Julio Iglesias and Whitney Houston CDs, the pink Nkodo Sitony cassette tape, and the white plush cat that Ésaïe had gifted me. We crossed the English Channel on the Eurostar, our faces glowing with renewed hope in the future. When God did the math, the results could never be wrong.

Goodbye France, goodbye misery.

Soon upon entering England, we met the legal definition of homelessness, which is to say we had no address and not enough money to afford one without help. This precarious status described us, even if the generosity of friends of friends masked it for a time. We first arrived in the neighborhood of Kilburn and stayed with Virginie, an immigrant from the Democratic Republic of Congo (which Africans simply called Congo-Kinshasa). She, my mom, and

I shared her bed, while her nephew, his nine-months-pregnant girlfriend, and his seven-year-old son from a previous relationship slept in the second bedroom. The main drag that passed through Kilburn was lively and bustled with storefronts that sold cheap clothes and electronics. I delighted in popping my head in to see what people were like here (extremely polite compared to in France) and what they ate (a surprising amount of breaded fried fish and chips). On slow days, I killed the time by playing *Tekken III* and *Mortal Kombat* with the seven-year-old on his PlayStation.

After a month or so, my mom and I moved to the neighborhood of Willesden Green with a friend of Virginie's, a woman named Thérèse who had immigrated from the Republic of Congo (which Africans differentiated as Congo-Brazzaville) and married a Brit with whom she was raising a toddler. There was more room there, and we were grateful for the generosity shown to us, but also longed for a space of our own. A caseworker explained to my mom that to obtain assistance from the government, we would have to move out and enter temporary housing. This was the only way, even if Thérèse was willing to let us stay with her forever. We made the jump in the fall, shortly after I started Year Six—the last grade of elementary school in England—at a Catholic public school. But London is expensive, so the waiting list numbered in the thousands. Until our turn came, the city shuffled us from hostels to inns and back on its tab.

Saint Mary Magdalene Primary didn't have a classroom dedicated to foreign kids, which left us newcomers—Katarzyna from Poland, Jude from Zimbabwe, and me—with full immersion as our only option. My parents' divorce had forced me to start over before, but lacking a means to communicate with others was debilitating. Mouths would move. Hands would gesticulate. And all I could do was answer in monosyllables a quarter of the time, if that much. And though British kids were so kind—eager to include me on the playground and excited to help teach me English—that first semester still felt a lot like getting dumped in the ocean without a life vest. I wondered if and how I would survive.

My teacher, Ms. Hayes, spoke in a melodious but hurried British English that inhaled the *t*'s so that sentences became *sen'ences*, and breathed in *r*'s, turning words into *wuhds*, neither of which my language workbooks had previewed. On the first day of school, I stood helplessly as she introduced me to her class as *Elisabeth*. I made out the word France but missed the rest of her speech.

A colony of boys and girls in blue school uniforms observed me with curious eyes. This was my chance to correct the record, to say that I went by Vanessa, but that if they were going to call me by my first name, then it should be pronounced *EH-lee-za-bet*, and that by the way, the French alphabet supplied an accent on the last letter of my last name, which was pronounced *bee-leh* and not *billy*.

Instead, I offered a tongue-tied smile and hurried back to my seat. My new classmate Tara asked if she could call me Lizzie for short. I found the request peculiar, for what kind of nickname was based on the middle of the name rather than its beginning? I had never heard of such a thing in French, but the class seemed in immediate agreement with her. Thinking that a further deviation from Vanessa couldn't possibly make any more of a difference at this point, I answered Tara with the international nod for yes, thereby marking the beginning of a three-year sentence as a "Lizzie."

In the late afternoons, my mom would keep her mobile phone on hand in case a bureaucrat called with instructions to pack up because we had to sleep elsewhere. If no one called, we stayed where we had been the previous night. Whether this was good news depended. Sometimes, our lodging was as charming as the bedrooms that my mom cleaned in her brief stint as a hotel maid. Other times, we spent one more night in a cramped hostel—like the one near Edgware Road, past the posh homes and tall hedges, the one that had a mouse problem, a kitchen that my mom refused to use without deep cleaning it first, and a repeat boarder whose kindness was undermined by the unfortunate scent that overwhelmed the hostel anytime he showered.

Being a tween meant being at the mercy of adults and their judgment. I had no power over my own person, no autonomy. Divorce custody had outsourced the matter of where to be, what to eat, when to sleep, what to watch, whom to see, and where to settle. If this aspect of childhood felt tolerable, it was because it came with a sunset. Children were supposed to grow up and receive the keys to their lives. But after hauling our suitcases between inns and hostels, being jerked around like the silver balls in a pinball machine, I wasn't sure I still believed in that handoff. Poverty superseded age and it swallowed up choices. It turned us into people life happened to.

But at least my mom and I were no longer alone. Our new church, Praise Tabernacle Pentecostal, was located in the northwest neighborhood of

Harlesden. Thérèse, a sporadic attendee herself, had invited us to join her one Sunday. Its congregation was largely Congolese, although two or three other Cameroonians, including a daughter-in-law of the pastor, were regulars. My first Sunday there, I had prepared to fall asleep again, but this place was nothing like Catholic church. Service was, for lack of a better word, kinetic. The faithful swayed and clapped to lively worship music, switching effortlessly between French, English, Lingala, and celestial tongues. I watched in awe as the church enacted belief through the body, stomping, fainting, running, and grasping for the skies. At Praise Tabernacle, prayer was a loud and collective endeavor. Then, when it all ended, women in colorful headwraps served lunch and doughy beignets in aluminum containers.

Pastor Ilunga, the church's grandfatherly and charismatic leader, had become a spiritual father to my mom—a keen ear and trusted ally as she processed her deepest loss yet, that of her mother, while navigating the local bureaucracies in her broken English. I was of little help, as the local language was just as mysterious to me.

This, too, shall pass, the pastor assured us. Not only would my mom be reunited with Mamie Catherine in the afterlife, but God would guide us out of the present storm for He would never saddle us with more than we could bear. My mom took the encouragement to heart. After all, Pastor Ilunga was an elder and a veteran in the British immigration system, having navigated it himself decades ago. She could trust him without reserve. And I, in turn, trusted her wholeheartedly. Besides, in taking on this shepherdly role, Pastor Ilunga had relieved me from the sometimes-crushing weight of being my mom's closest confidante. I tried to summon this gratefulness whenever my stomach began to growl three hours into the Sunday service.

To my great surprise, the inscrutable sounds of the English language began to unscramble. Not six months had passed. Being of elementary school age helped, as did having the saintly Ms. Hayes for a teacher. The rest, I picked up on the playground, from classmates who were eager to let me in, and did not mind repeating themselves often, or patiently explaining that when they said *tell me about it*, it wasn't a cue for me to start the story from the top. Soon enough, I was translating for my mom at parent-teacher conferences.

After a spring of uncertainty, the housing authority found a leafy corner of Willesden just for the two of us. It was a pleasant flat, except for the mold in the kitchen. My mom bleached the black patches and opened the windows wide. Still, the mold persisted. We hated to seem ungrateful—this flat beat the hostels by a mile—but my lungs were sensitive and my mom's cleanliness bordered on compulsive. She mentioned the issue to the authority, hoping a professional would treat the wall in a few months. Instead, the authority offered us another flat, this time on the first floor of a plain Victorian rowhouse in Harlesden, another working-class neighborhood in northwest London. More than a year had passed since we had left the Duchère and felt truly settled anywhere. We were exhausted, ground down by months of uncertainty. My mom accepted the Harlesden flat without first visiting.

This was how we discovered, on move-in day, that while my mom's bedroom was adequate, the second bedroom was in reality a closet the width of my single bed, so small it could only be entered and exited from the left pillow side. A window was carved into the wall that ran the length of my bed, and a shelved nook was cut into the opposite wall—a closet within a closet. But the bed pressed against the nook, blocking the bottom shelves. Thick black spiders perched on the burnt-orange curtains at night and watched me ball up as far away from them as our narrow circumstances allowed.

On the day of our arrival, the landlord, a handsome Jamaican man with exceptionally clear skin, urged us not to report him to the housing authority. We were exhausted, steeled to discomfort, and not ones to complain in the face of God's grace. The landlord and his fudged math were safe with us.

Besides, escaping was as easy as shutting my eyes. I liked to borrow home decor and furniture catalogs from my mom's friend, who collected them in her flawless house in Wembley, and splay among them, daydreaming in the darkness of my closet room. As a kid with a vivid imagination and an aptitude for the visual arts, I had long paid attention to space and aesthetics, to the way things landed and were laid out. But seeing others' visions in these catalogs opened my eyes to a universe of possibilities. Home didn't have to be a compromise or mere afterthought; it could be intentional, a place built on principles. I held on to the hope of someday moving into a home where I could paint the walls, and realize just one of those possibilities for myself. In the meantime, I stacked imaginary bookshelves to the ceilings of imaginary homes in which money was no object, and God's grace protected us from evil.

It was a wonder, I sometimes thought, that my mom and I had gone on so long outside the Christian faith, or that I had once openly confessed to not believing. My dad was still happy in his passive atheism and seemed rather indifferent to our conversion, if he was at all aware—church never came up much in our conversations—but I pitied my past naivety. The proof of God's existence and kindness was evident in our own lives, which had finally found some measure of order. I had not changed in some drastic way but felt comforted to know that some higher power was interested in our success. We credited Him for helping my mom find a good job, driving double-decker buses across the city. And while my French accent drew the occasional giggle from my classmates, I was back to excelling academically. The worst had passed, as the pastor predicted. God always delivered on His promises.

KNOWING THIS MADE the night of the late phone call inexplicable. It was the spring of 2001 and Joyce was living with my mom and me for the school year, while Tata Balbine resettled from Spain to the United States to join her new husband, Noah, a Cameroonian from the Anglophone region of the country. By then I had started Year Seven at the Convent of Jesus and Mary Language College—another Catholic public school, but for and ruled by middle- and high-school girls from Harlesden. Joyce attended a co-ed Anglican elementary school next door. She and I were playing on the floor—almost certainly too old for dolls, at ages twelve and a half and eleven—while my mom and her friend Tina were chatting on the sofa, when my mom's mobile phone rang. It must have been ten or later. We paused our games, alarmed by the time. Was this Cameroon calling? Was someone dying again? My mom listened intently as a saccharine voice rattled in urgent Ewondo on the other end. No, not *back home* calling. This was only her friend Hélène from church, crying hysterically. I felt relief.

Tata Hélène had arrived in London from Yaoundé at the tender age of twenty-two, a few months after us, as an asylum applicant, with the singular mission of bringing her fiancé, Thomas, to London after her own status was granted. I am not sure who first brought her to Praise Tabernacle but once she joined, my mom became a sort of big sister to her, taking her under her wing the way other members of the congregation had cared for us. I understood from their conversations that Thomas did not have French papers, that he could not simply board a Eurostar train bound for London without questions, as my mom and I had. It seemed instead that he would come the *bush way*, through Morocco or some other intermediary soil. My mom had expressed skepticism at this plan. Many tried this route and failed. *You are young*, she would tell Tata Hélène.

What if he never makes it? And even if he does, what life can he offer you? Why not try and meet someone here?

But Tata Hélène's rail-thin frame concealed a bullish stubbornness. She was bringing that man to her and that was that. Despite my mom's misgivings, Thomas had arrived during our first year here, then brought over his three sons from previous relationships. The eldest and I were in the same grade. Friends on Sundays and mostly indifferent to each other at Saint Mary Magdalene, which we attended together until he went to the local boys' school for Year Seven. Pastor Ilunga had married Tata Hélène and Thomas quickly, in a ceremony organized by the church's wedding committee, which was mostly run by the pastor's wife and adult daughters. The committee had set the theme (lilac and white), arranged a balloon arch over the couple's table (also lilac and white), taken care of the food (all Congolese except for what my mom and Tata Tina cooked), and chosen the music (Lingala gospel). I was designated as a flower girl. Once Thomas and his sons arrived, it felt as if they had always been in London, sitting on the Cameroonian row on Sundays, next to Tata Hélène, Tata Tina, my mom, me, and Joyce.

Thirty minutes after the frantic call, the four of us sat in my mom's battered Volvo, in the lot across from the bleak apartment tower where the state had placed Tata Hélène and her family. It was pouring rain. Pastor Ilunga's green Jaguar parked next to us. Tata Tina offered to wait in the car with the kids while my mom accompanied the pastor upstairs. No sooner had she stepped out than we pummeled Tata Tina with questions. Our heads squeezed between the two front seats, we begged her to cough up the *kongossa*, the gossip that had brought us here this late.

If I tell you, you really can't say anything, said Tata Tina.

My cousin and I swore our secrecy.

Well, Tata Hélène was messing around, talking to other guys. Playing the nyanga, *you see?*

We nodded, recognizing that word from dialect. A *nyanga* is a girl who is a bit too full of herself.

So, Tonton Thomas knocked her around a bit.

He did what? I asked.

He punched her.

We receded into the back seat, stunned into silence. Tata Hélène was tall but slight. At twelve, I probably weighed more than she did. A fist to her delicate cheekbones would be devastating. And his sons, our friends. The apartment was small. The boys must have been present for the fight. Had they watched the beating? What had they done when she screamed?

This was not what we expected. Then again, I did not know what we did expect. In his short time here, Thomas had shredded a dress of Tata Hélène's with scissors because he thought she looked slutty in it. Another time, she had been unreachable for weeks because he had tossed her cellphone out the window in a jealous fit. But to keep sitting with us at church every Sunday, even after these incidents, to remain a part of our makeshift family, it seemed impossible to me that Thomas would also be capable of harming our sweet auntie.

My mom jiggled the handle of the car door open. I waited for Tata Hélène's lanky shape to appear in the window so we could complete our rescue mission, but she never did come down. Instead, Pastor Ilunga let himself into the back seat. Joyce flattened her body to the far door; I squeezed into the middle. The pastor felt heavy, pressed against me like that.

We had to hand this situation to God, he said. *Amen?* We answered the cue like good servants. *Yes, amen.* He launched into a proper prayer, spritzing my eyelid and bottom lip with spittle. Joyce flinched as the spray reached her. God would mend Tata Hélène and Thomas. God would permit a resolution and return peace to their home. Pastor Ilunga continued. What was done was done, it was best not to dwell. But we would continue to pray for them, understood? The car said amen and my mom drove us home.

The following Sunday, all was normal again. We sat in the Cameroonian row, with Tata Tina, Tata Hélène, Thomas, and the boys—one makeshift family within the makeshift family of our congregation. Except that nothing felt normal. I grasped that when God did the math, the result could never be wrong. And Pastor Ilunga had never led us astray. It made sense, I supposed, that none of us could see the situation more clearly than him, the man with a direct line to God. I was a mere child, a babe in the faith.

Yet, something gnawed at me.

We had left Tata Hélène behind that night, on the basis that doing so was a testament of His will and grace. But stealing glimpses of the concealer caked on her face, while Pastor Ilunga delivered another passionate sermon, I felt neither from God.

Smells Like Team Spirit

HOME, NOUN. (CONT.)
  8 a: a place of dignity
    also a shared base *or* foundation

I HAD BEEN IN AMERICA for all of two days, that summer of 2002, when I first noticed the pretty little house on Lucky Lane. A mature tree hid half of it, but there the little house stood, behind a backyard fence and redundant wall. Short and capped with an almost flat roof. Its siding, a sort of imitation wood, glimmered queerly in the light.

From my aunt and uncle's house, I watched the chimes on its porch scintillate in the rare Nevada breeze. Lucky Lane was inaccessible from our street, so I'd never examined the little house up close. But I envied it all the same. The cozy size, just wide enough for two people. The singing chimes, so bright and colorful. How nice might it be, I thought, to someday call a house like that home—for my mom and me, as it used to be. Anything for a bed of my own again.

My mom had floated the idea of one-way tickets for America at the beginning of the year, a little heartsick, I think, from needing an international calling card to reach our nearest blood relative. Praise Tabernacle had been good to us, these last three years in London, and in many ways the church had become *like* family. But it also never quite rose to the real thing. The way my mom saw it, having little to our name meant little to lose by leaving England and starting over. If we floundered in America, at least it would be near our people.

I would miss London more than her. I had not known what to expect when I learned that the school I would attend for Years Seven and Eight would be a gendered school, but as it turns out, a world free of boys and their antics suited me just fine. I had made a solid group of friends and my French intonations were vanishing. I was beginning to feel British, a part of the city. That was the beauty of being thirteen. Assimilation came easy. Nevertheless, I had cheered the plan from the outset, thrilled by the prospect of being reunited with my dear Joyce, who by then had left London to join Tata Balbine, her new step-dad, Tonton Noah, her stepsister, Nadishia, and their new half sister, Michelle, in the silver state—not that Cameroonian culture or our family placed much weight on halves. A sibling was a sibling.

Granted, the distance from my daddy would not be ideal. Then again, I heard from him less and less these days. Our visits had dwindled to one or two a year since my mom and I had left France for London. I was not angry with him so much as disappointed in the state of the visitation schedule. Neverthe-less, I resolved to be patient and mature about the wait until our next reunion. It was natural that the farther I lived from Châtellerault, the more each trip back would cost. Neither of my parents had a lot of money. My mom had worked long, hard hours to provide for us in one of the most expensive cities in the world. Meanwhile, my daddy and Lisette had become parents to new little girls, both under the age of three. No one had to explain to me a move to Nevada meant that, for a while, we might have to settle for hanging out once a year instead of every school break. It would not be simple to make visits happen, but I had faith. If my dad had found the means to ensure he and the little girls met Lisette's family in Mauritius, then he would find the means to bring me home. And so, I had heartily encouraged my mom to take us across the Atlantic.

We lived together in Tata Balbine and Tonton Noah's house, one street over from Lucky Lane, on the edge of a ring where houses matched each other like pieces of an assorted doll set. Ours resembled the others in its obligatory two stories, white garage doors, thirsty lawns out front, and fenced yards in the rear. Windows lined with shutters that weren't supposed to shut. Each house finished with horizontal wood panels painted in respectable pastels. A slice of

Pleasantville in the high desert. Seven of us were crammed behind this idyllic facade: my aunt's family of five, plus my mom and me, sharing three bedrooms and two bathrooms.

By the time we arrived that July, daytime Reno was a cloudless oven. Joyce, Nad, and I stayed indoors more often than not. The house was rarely quiet after dawn, starting with our parents, who conducted all communications at peak-Cameroonian volume, a perpetual sort of shout whose mood required a trained ear to discern. To pass the time, we alternated between taping music videos on BET and experimenting with sliding down the carpeted stairs (inside cardboard boxes, then on top of them); we practiced our cornrowing skills on Nad's thick, waist-length hair, and tested each other on American states and their capitals.

Dare look bored for a minute and a floor-length list of chores would materialize. Our parents had no shortage of ideas. We punctuated our play to sterilize baby bottles and change diapers, pull out weeds and clean out tilapia for dinner. At any given time, one of us girls was either hand-washing or dreading her turn at hand-washing the bottomless tower of dishes. In this house, a dishwasher was strictly a drying device. A full house meant short showers and sharing beds. But also, an abundance of laughter and tenderness.

I spent much of my free time that August studying for high school. Not class subjects or even the structure of America's educational system, although perhaps I should have spent a minute on the latter. After all, there had been significant differences between the French and English systems. The former elevated students to the next grade based on performance, permitting some to skip grades while holding others back as long as the teaching staff deemed necessary. This was how I had gone straight from kindergarten to the second grade. The British, on the other hand, stuck rigidly to placing students in grades based on their dates of birth. Saint Mary Magdalene did not care that I had just completed the sixth grade right before arriving in London. I, being born in October 1988, was obligated to attend Year Six—end of story. A modicum of research would have revealed that a new continent might mean new rules, and most importantly, that the British Year Eight was equivalent to the American seventh grade. But such technicalities were not my concern that summer.

What I wanted to know was how American kids talked, what they wore, what their school day looked like. My references were outdated: mostly reruns of *Fresh Prince, Boy Meets World*, and *Sister, Sister*. The last time we had moved countries, at almost eleven years old, I had trusted my mom to prepare me for my first day of school. And she had trusted that the British served a free lunch to all students as was the norm in French public schools. I realized her mistake when the bell rang at midday, and most of my classmates pulled sandwiches out of tin boxes. I tried asking for water but no one understood me. Hunger stirred my belly while the clock crawled to dismissal time. Never again, I thought, as I typed the words *Wooster High School* into my aunt and uncle's desktop computer.

Like so much of the internet in those days, Wooster High's web page was scant and unhelpful. An academic calendar was up with holidays, among them Labor Day in September instead of May 1, Veterans Day around the Armistice, and something called "Thanksgiving." One of the school buildings had a facade painted in scarlet red. The edge of each wall was bracketed by a set of horseshoes and, between them, in shiny white paint: HOME OF THE COLTS. Nevadans had so many words for horses. Steeds. Mounts. Stallions. Mustangs.

One section of the website, dedicated to sports, confirmed what I'd gathered from our neighbors' front lawns and from browsing the offerings at the Meadowood Mall. This was a nation of teams. It lived to sort people into categories to which it could sell corresponding gear. Colts versus Huskies. Reno Wolf Pack versus Las Vegas Rebels. West Coast versus East Coast. Black versus white. My uncle, it turns out, had a whole speech about the latter rivalry. He'd given it to my cousins before. Sensing the speech coming, the girls took a mysterious interest in tidying their rooms and left me alone with my uncle.

"You want to know something," he said in his pronounced Cameroonian accent. "In this America, and you're not going to believe me, but it's my job to tell you, in this country, you have to work twice as hard as white people, do you understand? This is a very racist country. Very racist."

I nodded, unsure what to make of the warnings. It wasn't that I doubted his experience. My uncle had immigrated from *back home* in the 1980s and attended college in Texas, as dark a black man then as he was now. But we were far from the South, and even farther in time from the American cruelty that I'd seen depicted in the TV miniseries *Roots*. In my thirteen and three-quarters years of life, no one had ever called me the n-word. Mentalities had evolved; this was the new millennium!

Nevertheless, I promised to do my best.

One other team rivalry, I realized, dwarfed all the others by a long shot: America against the world. How else to explain the obscene display of red, white, and blue flags in places that made no sense? Front lawns, large poles, T-shirts, license plates, eating plates, hats, baby onesies, adult onesies, windows, cupcakes, water bottles, monster truck bumpers. It was as if America feared that people would forget where they lived, or the long road traveled from their country of origin to here. I wondered if America had developed this insecurity after that awful day the year before, when I came home from school and stared at the British broadcast, mouth agape, refusing to believe the tiny bodies were jumping off the collapsing towers in real time. But Joyce said her middle school already made her pledge allegiance to America every day before the September 11 attacks.

I peppered her with questions. What were the kids here like? What did they wear? What else should I know? My cousin shared everything she could remember. You could bring your own lunch, but there were carts and vending machines to buy food during breaks. A cafeteria offered free lunch if you were eligible for it, as in poor enough, like we were, but the cost of accepting the free meal, particularly in a full lunchroom, amounted to social suicide. So that was out of the question. She wasn't sure *why* it was supposed to be embarrassing. It simply was. You either brought your own lunch or cobbled together the money to pay for it.

Vaughn Middle was, according to Joyce, as cliquish as any American school on television. Guessing that Wooster High might be too, we lay on our bellies and excavated the glossy pages of her seventh-grade yearbook for data to prepare me. Having never seen a yearbook before, I devoured the intel as if it were a teen magazine. Each student and teacher appeared on a designated page, in an individual photo that cited their name underneath—an apt tradition for a nation that could Never Forget. Throughout the academic year, a select group of intrepid students scoured the school to document its layers. If they were thorough, every subculture would be represented, from the smokers' corner to the hard-of-hearing students and varsity jocks. The school sent the final layout to a professional printer, then charged something like sixty dollars for the hardbound time capsule.

I wondered if my mom would have the money to get me one. Joyce said that buying a yearbook wasn't mandatory, but what else would you pass around for signatures the last week of school?

There was a club for everyone and everything: chess, Spanish, model UN, debate, photography, math, Dungeons and Dragons, drama, band, even one for the yearbook itself. The possibilities seemed endless. The only time students wore uniforms was to compete in sports, which were played in seasons. Fall was for soccer (football), volleyball, and (American) football. Winter was for skiing and basketball. And spring was for track and field, baseball, and softball (baseball for girls). In Europe, high school existed for the exclusive purpose of study, but here, it was a conduit for *school spirit*—a sense of pride instilled through fight songs, team colors, and mascot costumes that students wore on game day. Sports were such an integral part of the curriculum that you were allowed, and even expected, to miss classes and exams. The best athletes went on to do the same at college in exchange for free or reduced tuition.

Joyce showed me the popular kids in her yearbook. Since we had them in France and England too, the category needed no explanation. Popularity was usually a byproduct of exceptional attractiveness or athletic talent. A slim crop of students rose by virtue of their charismatic personalities, though I knew popularity was not interchangeable with being kind. We combed the appendix to get a good look at the crushes Joyce had secretly harbored.

Next, she identified the ambitious kids—the ones organized enough to campaign for seats on the student council—and her girlfriends, both the true ones and the renowned backstabbers. We flipped the pages slowly. Here, she pointed out, were the ones who welcomed her despite her weird Franco-Hispano-Cameroonian accent. And there, some of the girls who'd be at our bus stop on the first day.

Two of them, Allison and Amber, were rising freshmen like me. At Vaughn Middle, they'd been popular and popular-adjacent, respectively. Allison, who lived in the pastel ring like us, was an alum of the middle school's volleyball and basketball teams. Amber was into cheerleading. Her home was around the corner from ours, somewhere on Lucky Lane, but Joyce wasn't sure where exactly. She didn't know either of them well. These girls were white; her closest friends were Mexican or black, like her loud and uninhibited classmate Brittany.

I liked Brittany a lot. She was American but, like me, was raised by a single black mom devoted to church—an experience that transcended borders, from the interminable night prayers and three-hour-long services, to the strange phenomenon that was "speaking in tongues." During the summer, Brittany walked over from her end of the pastel ring to ours, and braved the miserable two-mile trek to the Meadowood Mall with us. We went for run-ins with cute boys but mostly settled for Dippin' Dots and trying on stuff at Charlotte Russe. As the end of August approached, we made mental notes of the shoes and shirts we'd have to convince our moms to buy at Meadowood instead of Ross, their favorite discount store. Money being tight, always, we knew to be judicious with our demands.

Other categories of yearbook-people, informal ones, were new to me. *Cholos* and *Cholas*. English-As-a-Second-Language (ESL) kids. There were also Loners and Losers, categories that frequently overlapped. The latter was less self-explanatory. I asked Joyce if accents made people losers.

Were we—

No, she said. Lots of people had accents here. (One-fifth of Reno was Hispanic.) The way you spoke didn't matter ... unless you had a speech impediment. Then you might be a loser.

The list of sins that landed people on the outs was hard to define with any finality. The most obvious losers had trouble making friends, or shared a visible passion for fantasy fiction—dragons, wizards, spells—that preceded and surpassed the mainstream *Lord of the Rings* fare. They were kids who got called creepers because they stared too long or wore the wrong trench coats to school, their vibe more "Columbine shooter" than *The Matrix*.

I wondered if perhaps some people were just born with faulty wiring, the kind that destined them for the edges of society. Innocent heirs to parents who had been losers, perhaps themselves descended from losers. But it was more complicated than that. Loserdom could be reversed, by makeover or a timely growth spurt, just as it could be caught. One vicious breakout of cystic acne, a blowjob to a blabbermouth, or an exhibition of sadness past the social expiration date, and you might find yourself in exile, too. Unless you were exceptionally attractive, in which case, you had immunity. Not all of it made sense. The most important thing was to avoid the stink altogether. Because once it was on you, there was no telling how long it'd linger.

*

TWO WEEKS BEFORE school started, I sat in the registrar's office with my mom and uncle. The woman behind the desk asked if I planned to take honors classes. The point would be, she explained, to prepare me for Advanced Placement (AP) exams my junior and senior years. Each cost eighty dollars, but a good score was convertible to college credits, which promised to cost thousands of dollars more later. Alternatively, the registrar said, I could enroll in the International Baccalaureate (IB) program, which had extra requirements like philosophy and physics. These exams, too, came with fees. Other than electives like Spanish or Art, most of my classes would be with IB and AP kids. She pressed me for an answer. I'd have to commit immediately, in part because of the IB program's demanding math sequence: Geometry, Algebra 2, and Trigonometry. Then Calculus senior year. My mom's and uncle's heads bobbed in synchronicity as the registrar played a round of bingo with their favorite adjectives. *Rigorous. Challenging. Advanced.*

The woman glanced at the records that my mom had brought. Six schools in eight years. Perhaps I might appreciate this last advantage, she said. Wooster High was the only school to offer the IB program in Washoe County, which made it a sort of magnet school. Enrolling would allow me to stay even if someday my mom and I moved farther away.

Four consecutive years at Wooster sounded appealing but I smelled trouble. Setting aside whatever trigonometry was, other than an assured tanking of my grades, this plan guaranteed that I'd be besmeared as a nerd the moment I set foot on campus. Besides, the program presented other impracticalities. The registrar wouldn't know it from my pressed shirt and my mom's pearly smile, but we had little money to our name: just her last paycheck from driving double-decker buses, meager child support from my dad, and what she managed to get for our well-used Volvo before leaving London. In this country, my mom had no working papers. If she couldn't afford to buy me a name-brand backpack, where in the hell would she find eighty dollars to pay for each exam, my junior and senior year?

I was plotting out how to accept the brochure and talk my mom out of it at home, when I heard my uncle exclaim, "Okay, let's do it!"

On the first day of school, Joyce and I walked to the bus stop around the corner. I recognized Allison, the popular girl from the pastel ring, right away. She was around five nine but didn't slouch the way some tall girls did. Her skin was bronzed and freckled, and her hair a natural dark gold. Teeth perfectly aligned. She wore clothes branded with *Billabong* and *Roxy*. We made small talk. She said her brother was an upperclassman with a car but, for whatever reason, wouldn't drive her to school. American families were odd like that.

Amber arrived from Lucky Lane minutes later, with her older sister, Cristel, and Cristel's best friend, Mickie. She waved hello and asked me if I was Joyce's sister. She, too, had been at Vaughn Middle the previous year but was starting the ninth grade with me. Maybe we would have classes together. By then, Allison had returned to her phone at a respectable distance. I wondered if she was shy. She'd greeted Joyce and me, but only because we said hi first, I think. This was more than she gave the Lucky Lane girls. With them, Allison didn't even bother to nod. I thought at first that she was simply engrossed in her phone, but she ignored their presence the rest of the week and every week after that. Stranger yet, the Lucky Lane girls didn't seem offended.

I wasn't blind to how shiny Allison looked next to them. Mickie had thin eyebrows that she penciled over in thick brown, and wore a dark lipstick that made her face paler. Her teeth were crowded, though that didn't stop her from smiling big and loud. Most days, Mickie sported a pair of black jeans faded with wear. Her sweatshirts were loose, as if inherited from larger boyfriends who smelled of stale cigarettes. She was short but took up space. I gathered that how others felt about it was not her problem.

Cristel, on the other hand, looked a little lost when Mickie skipped school, like a shadow in want of a human to trail. I remember that she smiled at jokes on a slight delay. By her own account, Cristel dated boys who treated her like garbage. Her round cheeks and surprised eyes made her seem fragile. That first day of school, I mistakenly assumed she was younger than her sister, Amber.

Since Cristel and Mickie were juniors at Wooster High, I could see why they might think nothing of Allison's coldness. They were preoccupied with older boyfriends whose every motion—calls/no calls, texts/no texts, visits/no visits—generated an immense supply of material to analyze on the school bus. But I remained baffled that Allison and Amber were not friendly. Not just baffled—bothered. It wasn't just that they were pretty-faced blondes who *looked* like they should get along. They were also the same age and had lived around each other forever. Allison in the pastel ring and Amber among the pretty little houses on Lucky Lane.

Every morning, for years, they stood on this sidewalk and awaited the school bus ten feet apart. The two of them shared a ton of friends. And while Amber's clothes were fewer and more worn-out than Allison's—you could tell three weeks into the school year—these girls obviously liked the same surfing and snowboarding styles.

Some mornings I chatted with Allison or Amber, but never with both together. When the yellow bus pulled up, we each gravitated to our actual friends. The IB program isolated me with fellow nerds, which meant no classes with either girl. I struggled to put my finger on why the bus-stop division troubled me so much, despite the fact that their friendship wasn't remotely my business.

Yet, every morning, I watched them ignore each other, and wondered how my study of the yearbook had failed to predict this outcome. It was as if an invisible barrier separated Allison from the Lucky Lane girls, and none of them was curious about what hid on the other side.

§

AS THE FALL semester unfolded, I settled in my new ecosystem, made friends, permitted their accent to start rewriting my own. My new classmates taught me Americanisms. Bins were called *trash*. The loo or toilet was a *bathroom*, and sometimes a *half bath*, despite having no bathtub in it. Rubbers were always *erasers*, unless you meant condoms. As for the little houses on Lucky Lane, the ones I found so charming, they were *trailers*.

And the people who lived in them: *trailer trash.*

In my mind, the word *trailer* conjured images of caravans attached to trucks, or the aluminum container in the middle of the basketball courts where Wooster High made ESL students take classes. But trailers could look like the pretty little houses behind the pastel ring, too. Single-wides that were ten feet across and double-wides that spanned twenty feet. Some older models were as narrow as eight feet.

While working in the affordable housing space, much later in life, I'd learn that, starting in 1976, the US Department of Housing and Urban Development imposed construction standards that vastly improved the fire safety, insulation, and overall shelf life of these "mobile homes." The mandated changes brought the structures closer to permanent housing than their predecessors, rendering them harder to pick up and move in lean times. Only the federally compliant models counted as manufactured homes, though. Older houses, like most of the 187 double-wides on Lucky Lane, which were built in 1971, would never get to be anything other than trailers and mobile homes.

Trailer trash, I soon realized, was a derivative of *white trash*. If you asked people what white trash was, the definition tended to soften. White trash became a person with no *cultural* class, the kind who misbehaved and broke social norms. But the odd thing was, we all knew kids with money who technically had no cultural class, and yet didn't quite fit the white trash mold. They, too, had parents with criminal records, parents who smoked cigarettes indoors, parents who forgot to pay the electricity bill, who had disabilities, who got laid off, who lost custody. Rich kids weren't immune to other kinds of markers for low cultural class either, like catching lice or chipped front teeth. Every year, at least one of them temporarily lost their driver's license to a DUI. My senior year of high school, the wealthy dad of a boy in town—and close friend of several of my IB friends—would murder the boy's stepmom after being ordered to pay spousal support. He then tried to take out the family court judge using a sniper rifle, before escaping to Mexico where he was promptly caught. But no one would call *that* family white trash.

It was doing these kinds of acts while poor that transformed them into failures of character. You could be as kind and polite as Amber, you could join cheerleading, wear the right clothes, and date upper-middle-class jocks, but if you lived at the Lucky Lane Mobile Home Park, there was no getting out of it. You were white trash. Which is to say, it wasn't about cultural class at all. People just didn't like to admit the required components of so-called trash: whiteness, poverty, and sometimes trailers.

The closest equivalent to *trailer trash* in my French hometown were the *gitans*, a nomadic population of Roma emigrated from eastern and southern Europe. I remember seeing them in the grocery store parking lot when I was little. The children, tan-skinned and smudged, ran up to my parents and asked to clean our windshield in exchange for a few coins. I don't think those children went to school. They lived in camps by the pond and behind the municipal gym, near where my dad still lives. Clothes hung on ropes between their caravans. Every few months, local police appeared unannounced and the Roma camps would vanish for a season or two. But in the end, they always returned. There were no banners against them, no hostile signage or ads in the windows.

Nevertheless, I understood from a young age that the Roma were not welcome in polite society. People held their children and wallets closer when they approached. They scowled when asked for money. Storekeepers didn't bother to invent a reason before kicking them out.

But the concept of trailer trash operated differently in America. It wasn't directed at so-called ethnic whites, like the Roma who were brown year-round, or the recent comers whose first language wasn't English. Black people and Mexicans could be a lot of things—at my school: *beaners, wetbacks, ghetto*— but *white trash* belonged to white Americans born and raised in this country. The term was for them and by them. A means to denote the wrong kind of whites, short of stripping them of their whiteness.

∫

REMEMBERING LUCKY LANE years later, I would wonder if there was something about temporary housing, something about caravans and mobile homes, that caused the people who move into them to lose value faster than a car driving off the sales lot. When Hurricanes Katrina and Rita devastated the Gulf Coast in the summer of 2005, my junior year of high school, the Federal Emergency Management Agency placed thousands of storm refugees in trailers across Louisiana, Mississippi, and Texas. I would learn that in October of that year, the Department of Labor found that the trailers were essentially toxic cans, oozing high levels of formaldehyde—a gas that would, in time, cause the trailer occupants to contract respiratory complications and, in some cases, cancer. Yet little was done about it. The government sat on the information, failing to confirm the findings with more tests for close to a year, and leaving the trailer occupants in the dark about the dangers their homes posed for even longer. I had not merely imagined it: the poor were people life *happened to*.

A part of me would always struggle to understand why the trailer was such a disgrace. It is not as if there was any honor innate to the concrete and bolts that connected the pastel ring houses to the ground. Nor was there more dignity to having a property title, when so many titles were a simple formality. Most of the pastel ring residents didn't own their homes outright. The buildings were mortgaged for hundreds of thousands of dollars, pursuant to contracts that allowed the banks to change the locks on the doors if their borrowers fell too far behind on payments—a reality that many unsuspecting Americans would be reminded of in the decade that followed 2002. But even so-called outright ownership was ephemeral. Houses were not buried with the people who claim them. Walls and floors were no more an extension of us than our cars. What housing *wasn't* temporary?

Perhaps the trailer's fundamental sin was its failure to pass. Apartment buildings and mortgaged houses—like the one I lived in with my aunt and uncle—left open the possibility that their inhabitants were squarely within the middle class or higher, that they were able to weather hardship in place or afford a similar apartment or house elsewhere, should they have to. One might never have reason to think otherwise, not until one was inside anyway. But trailers foreclosed that possibility, revealed too much. The ten-foot-wide evidence of coveting a piece of the American dream—a lot in one's name, a stake in the land—and coming up short. The trailer was an admission of the best its owner could do: a $50,000 aluminum box removable during hard times, voluntarily or by force. In many instances, a landlord owned the land on which the trailer was parked. In Nevada, this imbued trailer park residents with legal protections, but in something like eighteen other states, people assumed the burdens of both ownership and tenancy. This made them responsible for the upkeep of their trailer, yet at the mercy of a landlord's rules and whims.

The trailers' mere existence was a threat to property values. Developers walled rows of them away from freshly painted rings of subdivisions. Realtors downplayed their proximity. With financial equity at stake, the market wasn't going to pretend that trailer residents possess the right kind of class. And with social equity at stake, Allison wasn't going to pretend that Amber did either. I was safe to acknowledge, though. Living in the pastel ring masked my poverty and excused my blackness. It allowed me to pass.

AMERICANS LIKED TO say that everything sounded more intelligent in a British accent. The compliment was meant to be facetious. But something about the way I spoke caused my classmates to approach me as a blank slate. It allowed me to exist outside their preconceived notion of what a girl my color was or could be. I had an idea of what they pictured. Carefully curated versions of France and England had been projected across their TV screens and history books, just like a version of America had been projected across mine. Paris was the Eiffel Tower and baguettes. London was the movie *Love*

Actually and sights of Buckingham Palace. I was presumed to be an extension of those sanitized depictions.

I could've corrected the record: confessed that there were poor people in Europe and that at times, my mom and I were among them; that we'd lived in public housing, where the walls were white and the police patrolled us like feral strays. I could've told them about the northwest London borough where double-decker bus drivers raised their children. But I feared that admitting these truths—educating my classmates about where I had come from—would shrink me into another sort of caricature to them. A team of my own. They'd cease to see me.

Nor was it lost on me that my accent, a French-washed British, legitimized my presence in these elite classes. Entering the IB program at Wooster High, as a black person, required a certain unusualness. And I was an unusual black person. If the registrar had shown the same zeal in inviting other black students into the IB program, from around town or even from my freshman class, the results were not apparent. The only other black student in the IB program's class of 2006 was my friend Caitlin, a mixed-race, middle-class kid whose parents were schoolteachers in the county. People often joked that, like me, she "sounded white"—a remark intended as a compliment.

For all my anxieties about fitting in, I was, in the end, fortunate. My classmates were good kids: smart, thoughtful, curious, surprisingly well-rounded for teenagers. As I acclimated to this country and its plethora of cultures, they were as patient and accepting of me as the kids who had welcomed me at Saint Mary Magdalene, and later at the all-girls school in London. Still, I suspect that beneath their openness lay the incorrect assumption that we were alike, that I was no more complicated than a darker foreign version of them, an upper-middle-class transplant worthy of a chance by virtue of living in the same pastel ring as Allison. The IB program was full of kids zoned for the Galena High and Bishop Minogue High zip code, where the median income was $91,000, double Reno's overall median income. Most of them couldn't have guessed that, our freshman year, I shared a house with six relatives and slept in same bed as Joyce, or that my mom couldn't have afforded to rent a trailer of our own. I wouldn't have wanted them to know. I needed to pass.

ƴ

WE WERE DEEP in the ninth grade by the time I discovered which team American life had sorted the Lucky Lane girls into. I continued to say hello in the mornings, a little embarrassed now to understand why Allison maintained a glacial distance until the yellow bus arrived. There wasn't anything fair about the stink. If it tagged you, then you were it. All anybody could do then was hope it didn't linger forever. A long shot if the stink was the place you called home. I was grateful mine hadn't crossed the Atlantic with me.

I wondered, sometimes, how these first mornings might have played out if my summer study of the yearbook had revealed the Lucky Lane girls as the *wrong kind* of unusual. Would I have greeted them with the same warmth? And what if their luck was reversed—Allison in the trailers—would *they* have chosen to look right through her? I couldn't say for sure. Teenage cruelty can be boundless.

Toward the end of freshman year, I followed my mom and stepdad into a modest rental zoned for Reno High and later, an older house near Damonte High. Both homes were in zip codes surrounded by enough wealth that kids at school didn't bat an eye when I mentioned where I lived. Without a bus stop to braid our lives together, segregated by the IB program, the Lucky Lane girls and I lost track of each other. Our friendship stalled with shallow but pleasant exchanges on the edge of the pastel ring. We would appear in different sections of the yearbook.

Still, I thought of these girls every once in a while, and of those early mornings—vestiges of a more innocent time. My first summer in America, when trailers could simply be pretty little houses.

Hello, Goodbye

Home, noun. (cont.)
9 **a:** a father

CALLING ÉSAÏE ON THE PHONE was my idea. I was fifteen years old and tired of waiting. It was a slow Saturday after lunch and my mom and I were home alone while my stepdad, Dave, worked a shift at the post office. I ran out of my bedroom, giddy to find my mom and execute my plan. If she could find a number for him, even an old one, or if there was no other option, then a number for his cousin François, then *I* could call Ésaïe. Cameroon was nine hours ahead. He might still be awake. And I had enough savings to cover the international calling card if needed. I was willing to pay her back for the minutes. My mom said she might have something. I watched her disappear up the stairs.

To this day, I'm still not sure why it took me so long to think of calling him. For years, I'd peppered my mom and aunts who lived *back home* with questions about him: had he been spotted around Yaoundé lately, had he asked about me, and did he have our home phone numbers—the French ones, the English ones, then the American ones. The women answered vaguely, loath to feed or dash my hopes. But confirming that he knew where to reach me was enough to feed my expectations. I waited for him to call, convinced that it was only a matter of time. My mom waited with me, all the while saying nothing to me about her own biological father—who was not, as I still believed that particular day in 2005, the same man who fathered my biological mother Florence, but who was instead a wealthy pharmacist in Yaoundé, a man whose name she didn't carry but whose face matched hers—nor did I suspect this family history, for my mom never referred to Mamie Catherine's children as half-anythings. She waited and waited, all the while keeping to herself the memories of the pharmacist and his chauffeur driving past her on the street, and refusing to stop for the schoolgirl waving at them. My mom had learned young that some fathers didn't want to be missed.

She returned holding her red agenda, a faithful notebook in which she had amassed a roster of handwritten digits. One of the yellowed pages had a number for him. Too amped up to consider how long this information had sat in her drawer or how long she'd braced herself for this very moment, I urged my mom to dial him right away. She listed a litany of reasons why he might not answer but input the long number on the calling card anyway, then his phone number, starting with the 237 country code. The dial tone rang on speaker.

My mom raised an index finger to her mouth. I pledged silence with a nod despite the unfairness of the restriction; this was both my idea and my call. But the alternative was nothing. I could survive another five minutes of waiting.

Making a good first impression on one's father felt like an odd endeavor. Of course, we had met, but I did not remember him, and the three-year-old he remembered was nothing like the teenager I was now. I had no sense of where to begin, no sense of what he pictured when he thought of me, if he ever thought of me anymore. Perhaps he imagined that I resembled his five legitimate daughters (two more were born after me). But any real likeness to them seemed impossible to me. Their parents were still married. He was the only father they'd ever known. In contrast, I had two birth parents, two adoptive parents, and now two stepparents. Yaoundé held their whole childhoods. Mine was split up among an industrial town in the French west, a hamlet in the French southeast, then Lyon, at the time the third-largest city in France, followed by the English capital, and these days, a casino town in the American west. Our layers were continents apart.

Where we were raised mattered. Growing up, I found that each place where I lived demanded a piece of me in exchange for acceptance. Adopting a new tongue was only the first step. There were norms to absorb, ways to behave, to think. Assimilation revised your person as it expanded your vocabulary. This was even more the case if you were, as my mom deemed me, a *highly influence-able kid*. On a surface level, France and England had shaped the language I used to express myself, the foods and shows I liked, the contours of my behavior around strangers and adults. On a more fundamental level, these countries formed an expectation of the kind of basic services I was entitled to from the government—no doubt that sort of thing seeped into who one became. And while I easily reverted to being Vanessa Jucquois while visiting my daddy, I felt layers apart from the curious three-year-old Ésaïe met in the little apartment. The farther I moved from Châtellerault, the farther I saw myself drifting from this iteration of me. Already I sensed America rewriting me.

But perhaps there was a limit to the mutation of our bits. A layer beneath our accents, aesthetic preferences, and expectations that predisposed us to turn into our future selves such that, whatever shape our layers ultimately took—which is to say, whether I was raised in the global south or in the West, by birth parents or adoptive and stepparents—my person would have always felt fragmented, and split from her father. I suppose there's no way of knowing for sure.

Ésaïe picked up the phone and seemed to recognize the voice on the other end right away. His voice sounded more high-pitched and cheerful than I anticipated. They spoke in Ewondo. I listened closely, feeling around for references that would let me follow the thread, but my mom left no crumbs of French behind. Her tone sobered. I waited patiently for my cue. Then, in French, clear as day, I heard him say: *no, no, no, no, no.*

My heart sank. I wondered briefly whether this could be disbelief and joy on his part. This was supposed to be a nice surprise. But the apology in my mom's eyes and the tone of his voice said otherwise. She let him weep with a sort of guttural sorrow. They went on in dialect a while longer. After he had calmed down, the two of them hung up. He hadn't asked for me. My mom translated at last: *He said he was not ready. He is very sorry.*

She put her red agenda away. Alone again, I replayed the conversation in my head. Had he known he was on loudspeaker? Should I have interrupted their conversation and forced him to acknowledge me? And was it too late to start over?

Two weeks later, the phone rang after one A.M. on a weeknight. My mom's chest must've pounded with alarm, thinking of family *back home*. But it was him, Ésaïe, calling for me. She slipped the cordless phone under my fort of covers. I held it up close to my ear. He spoke in French, in long sentences, and rarely paused to ask questions. I was disappointed by his lack of interest in what he'd missed since gifting me the nameless plush white cat. But this was just the beginning, I told myself. In time, perhaps, he'd show interest in me. Anyhow, I was too sleepy to do more than listen.

Ésaïe told me about his own father, an old man at his birth, and about his mother who was significantly younger. He told me about the night she walked out on him and his father when he was just a child. Decades later, I could still hear his resentment for her lodged deep in his throat. Her abandonment had driven him to make a name for himself. Coming from nothing, he'd become a man he was proud of.

The next morning, I woke up thinking about this grandmother of mine, of what kind of home it must've been for her to abandon it and her son so abruptly. But Ésaïe had been hazy on the details. We'd said goodbye without him mentioning her name. My maternal family guessed that it was the name he'd insisted on giving me: Elisabeth.

*

THE SECOND TIME Ésaïe called me, the conversation went no better than the first. It was the middle of the night again. Too late for anything he said to permeate my brain. But I felt happy to hear his voice, warm under my covers, knowing that he had thought of me, that he had sought me out. But then, weeks passed. I was disappointed even if the prospect of speaking with him felt less urgent. I figured he'd call me late at night sometime, when he had more to share about himself. A part of me looked forward to the day our conversations would flow more naturally. Perhaps the exercise of filling in the blanks would draw us close. And when it did, the distance between Elisabeth Assae Billé and Vanessa Jucquois would thin. Weeks turned to months. Junior year became senior year. And still, more silence.

The spring of 2006 opened with the unexpected death of Tonton Ekobi. People said he had been fine the day of, catching up with friends at a bar, before suddenly feeling sick and vomiting black matter. The family presumed a poisoning. Other signs pointed to complications from hepatitis C. But this was Cameroon, we would have to settle for uncertainty. As my mom prepared to bury her youngest brother *back home*, I wondered if this might mean that I would receive news from Ésaïe soon. Though he had been closest to Maman Florence and my mom, he knew all of Mamie Catherine's children well. I could not imagine a world in which he did not come by the Ngousso family house to pay his respects. Perhaps the tragedy would remind him that tomorrows were not promised. My mom and I talked on the phone during her trip, but the cost per minute was exorbitant, and I knew the loss of Tonton Ekobi had devastated her. I hadn't wanted to take up any of our brief time with trivialities like whether Ésaïe planned any more efforts to connect with me. Better to ask when she returned, if she did not bring it up on the phone earlier.

On her first afternoon back from Cameroon, I rested on the edge of her bed with eager eyes. A large suitcase sat unopened across the room, my mom too jet-lagged to bother with it yet. I was excited to have her home, having missed her company and cooking. My mom caught me up on everyone from Maman Florence to Tata Nicole, my cousin Nadège, now well in her twenties, and the army's worth of little cousins who came behind, including the two little girls that Tonton Ekobi left behind. So many new faces, yet so few names to remember. My mom recalled what she could. Who she had stayed up with, reminiscing all night. The wailers who came to mourn my uncle. Those who showed up with the sole mission of stuffing their bellies. A funny story recounted to her. Until eventually, she ran out of updates.

I stopped myself from bringing up his name, if only to spare myself the indignity of asking first. Chasing after him had me out of breath. My mom was astute, though. She knew what I wanted to know. I wondered then why she circled the matter. We were close, with few secrets between us. Was she ashamed of revealing that his interest in me had again waned? That he hadn't asked about me? I could handle it.

My mom cast her head down, averting the questions in my gaze. Only then did it become obvious. It was now on me to spare her. Summoning a cool voice, I said, *He's dead, isn't he.* And my mom nodded.

It had happened during her trip, but the precise date was unclear to her. She and Maman Florence had attended Ésaïe's funeral with Tata Sophie. There wasn't much to add, so my mom veered into speculation. It had to be sorcery. She asked if I recalled that he used to be in a Rosicrucian sect. The onset of this mysterious chronic illness had coincided with his attempts to defect. If it wasn't sorcery, then how come doctors in France and in New York City had been stumped by his degeneration?

I triaged the information. Ésaïe had been sick. Ésaïe had been on American soil, a six-hour flight away from Nevada. Ésaïe knew he was dying. And even then, he hadn't cared enough to send for me. I asked my mom if I had understood these basic facts correctly. She swore that she'd learned about the trip to America after his death. Whether I did or didn't believe her, what did it matter now?

I allowed myself a tear, but not for him. This end felt unfair. Too close to the beginning. I was owed answers that I would never get. This was his fault. Yet, a part of me felt relief.

With him gone, perhaps I could finally stop searching for myself in him.

The *D* Word

HOME, NOUN. (CONT.)
10 a: a domestic household
also a marriage

PART I

1.

My mom had been with Dave for a few years when Ésaïe died. The two of them had met at the end of my freshman year and taken the plunge my sophomore year, in one of Reno's iconic downtown chapels, on a chilly Saturday in January 2004. My new stepdad and I were good pals. He reminded me of my daddy in some ways. Less because he was also white, although he was—an American born and raised in the Pacific Northwest—and more because he was a gentle soul with little interest in the disciplining aspect of parenting, making him a perfect yin to my mom's yang. And while their childhoods were drastically different, my mom and Dave were on the same page when it came to honoring their Christian faith wholeheartedly.

And so, we spent their honeymoon church-shopping. On Sundays, Dave would print out MapQuest directions to some congregation in the Reno-Sparks metro area while I made a mental game of guessing our destination's vibe based on its name. *Bible* meant uncomfortable pews and dusty hymnals. *Fellowship* was earnest if a little outmoded. *Christian* was redundant and a telltale sign for long-windedness. I could not tell you why but *Emmanuel* was black. *Southern Baptist* might involve fainting spells. And deceptively secular names like *the Summit* signaled chill young pastors in faded jeans and a youth group comprised of popular kids.

The moment service opened, we crossed items off our individual checklists. Church had to be animated but not bizarre. Wednesday Bible study was a must; youth group a plus. There had to be music—preferably contemporary. Tonality and talent optional. The congregation couldn't be entirely white, black, or elderly. And money could only be mentioned moderately, if at all. (My parents were suspicious of prosperity gospel peddlers and any sign of largesse from church leadership would send them running.) There had to be a safe parking lot, and central air for withstanding the searing summers. Start time had to be predictable and closing time reliable. Most of all, the head pastor had to be just right: neither unreasonably emotional nor so dull as to make us wish for the Apocalypse mid-message.

My first pick was Living Stones, a large congregation near the University of Nevada's flagship campus in downtown Reno. It was the kind of church that understood that churchgoers were consumers first, swayed by appealing graphics and deserving of a semi-professional worship team. I loved it because most of the crowd was young, closer in age to me at fifteen than to my parents in their mid-forties. In other words, Living Stones was as cool as church could get. Perhaps for this reason, it did little for my parents.

I was open to alternatives. If it were up to me, we would have simply gone to Little Flower, the Catholic church one block from Wooster High, with Joyce, her parents, and siblings.

But my parents were a firm no. *Bunch of pedophiles*, they liked to joke.

2.

They finally decided to stick with Harvest Fellowship. And being that I was a teenager with little choice in the matter, if we were to be honest, I settled on whatever worked for them. Harvest Fellowship was a small congregation, part of the Church of God, a denomination descended from snake handlers in Cleveland, Tennessee. But the head pastor, a father of three in his mid-thirties, wasn't nearly as eccentric as his spiritual predecessors. He was kind and energetic, a former college baseball player, I learned, and less intimidating than Pastor Ilunga. His wife, a blonde woman with a pinched nose, played piano for the worship team. The youth pastor led the singing, with two youth group leaders—obvious siblings—on drums and guitar.

3.

We had not been coming for long, the Sunday that I walked into Harvest Fellowship, noticed the boy on guitar tune his instrument, and felt an inexplicable conviction. I would marry him.

4.

I saw him at youth group on Tuesday nights, when he was not out delivering pizzas, and I saw him at the church's annual Labor Day weekend getaway, on the California side of the mountain pass, where a wealthy married couple from the congregation had a second home, and got the youth group a generous deal on the cabins surrounding Frenchman Lake. I also saw him on the annual trek to Riverside, where we all went for the Winter Fest teen festival.

The boy was three and a half years older than me, and nineteen on the day we met. He was tall with dark brown hair and eyebrows, and the most earnest smile. He was a good son to his parents and a good brother to his sister and stepbrother. Soft-mannered and sweeter than most teenage boys I had ever met. By this I mean that he was the sort of person others dialed first when in need of jumper cables while stranded on the side of the highway. I was a good girl, too, grownups said, but the boy was different.

There was no rebellion in his marrow. Our church interpreted the Bible to forbid smoking or drinking, so the boy never smoked or drank. He believed in God with unwavering fervor.

Yet, the boy was pleasant to be around. Never one to lecture or scold. This made him a safe ear to confide in. And for his apparent shyness, I was shocked to find that he was funny. How could a person have a movie quote memorized for every occasion?

What I liked most about him, however, was his enduring crush on me. I knew that liking him for this reason was wrong. As were the gaps between us. I was in high school and although the boy was not in college—not his thing, I gathered—he was of college age. On top of that, I was a youth in his youth group. But, hard as he tried to hide it, I saw the way his gaze trailed me, and the way his body oriented in my direction whenever I entered the room. There was no fooling me; boys and men had desired me before.

When my friends said it was creepy for someone his age to be into me, I pretended to agree. But to have someone be this taken by me, year after year—and to know that, should the chance arise, this someone would fall in love with me—it was flattering. No, it was more than that. It felt like power.

Certain that he'd wait for me, I vacillated between exuding the warmth of a thousand suns toward him, and shelving him, for months at a time, while I nursed other crushes at school. Justin: the football player who'd never notice me in a million years—an unmistakable part of his appeal. Kevin: the light-skinned pothead with the long cornrows, who lately went out of his way to run into me. Cassady: the green-eyed varsity swimmer who made me a mix CD when I turned seventeen. And, when the mood struck me: the boy on guitar.

5.

Junior year, spring 2005—a final straw.

Without consulting me, my mom offered my daddy an out from paying her child support. She meant the gesture as a mercy; raising young children was expensive and having remarried had eased the financial burden of caring for me. She could live without the checks he sent her. But the offer, and his swift acceptance, wounded me.

My dad—my *daddy*—had finally done it. He had completely divested from me.

But had he not loathed my biological father for doing just this?

I felt like a fool for ever believing that he could consider me his real daughter, for allowing myself to love him so fervently.

6.

October came and went. My daddy did not call me on my seventeenth birthday.

I wondered, sometimes, if he ever considered the fact that contacting him was not as simple as dialing his number from our house landline. Each minute cost a small fortune and my mom and new stepdad had bills to pay. I could not bring myself to ask them for help. It was not lost on me that my dad was already sending next to no child support, or that he had shown no interest in buying me a ticket home since my arrival in Nevada. In such circumstances, was calling me not the least *he* could do?

Still, I rationalized his disappearance. It made sense that his heart would beat differently for my half sisters, children from his own flesh, true stewards of his last name. A part of me was even grateful to be replaced. Being a good daddy was his greatest talent. To see him deprived of the chance to do it would be awful. This was not to say that I did not envy the girls' unlimited access to him. But I would have happily shared, if given the opportunity. Not to mention that I had been desperate for sisters growing up. Having awaited their arrival with impatience, I relished every minute of our short time together, from stroking their hair as they woke up, to watching my stepmom, Lisette, make their bottles, and curling up with them in front of my favorite morning cartoons.

Three years had passed since my dad had offered to fly me home. I worried that the longer he iced me out, the more likely the youngest girl would have no memory of me. Soon enough, the eldest would forget me, too. My dad was not just robbing me of himself. He was robbing me of the chance to get to know his girls, to build a relationship with his wife, and to see my grandparents. It was for this compounded slight that I resented him the most, more than missing my birthday.

7.

The youth pastor at Harvest Fellowship liked to tell the story of the man who found himself stranded at sea. Rescuers arrived in turns, offering him a hand, a rope, a boat. But each time, the man refused the help. His God was coming to deliver him. Anytime now, the man swore, they would see. On and on the man waited, until finally the rest of his food, potable water, and luck ran out. At Heaven's gate, the man asked God why He had abandoned him. To his surprise, God scolded him. Who did the man think had sent him the hand, the rope, the boat?

THE STORY FIRMED my resolve. No one, not even God, would catch me flailing passively on account of my faith. The stakes were too high. I was familiar with the brink: the shame of coveting more than my parents could afford, the guilt of asking for new track-and-field cleats when credit card bills were piling up on the dinner table, the feeling of being one surprise away from bankruptcy. And this, when things were going relatively well. Of course, we had been poorer than this, my mom and me.

It was settled then. I was going to break this cycle with a foolproof plan. In my meticulous drawing of adulthood, the Outline, I would leave this high desert to study medicine at the University of Washington, and live out my twenties in a sophisticated apartment. Someday, I would marry a man who considered me his sun and moon. We would decamp Seattle for the suburbs in time, to nest in a house with a dog-friendly yard and three bedrooms, two for our children, who would never lack for anything, and this would be the only childhood house they would ever know. I would build a home with a foundation so solid, so deeply rooted, that no surprise could shake it into disarray.

If God so willed, of course.

8.

The boy and I made out in his car. By then, he was twenty-one and my high school graduation was soon enough for us to start dating without raising eyebrows. I had found other things to like about him aside from his worship of me. For example, I appreciated that my ambition did not bother him, even though he seemed completely devoid of any himself. And that he accepted my Outline in its entirety, or what he understood of it, for I withheld from him a core belief that not even God could wring out of me. Loving a man so fervently that a woman's survival might depend on him was a mistake, a mistake that I had seen too many women make in my short life. My Outline would have no tolerance for heartbreak. And who could truly hurt me with only half my heart?

*

WHEN THE BOY said he loved me, I said it back.

I was convincing.

9.

I learned that while the University of Washington had happily accepted me, it also had no real intention to welcome me to campus, barring an unexpected windfall of money on my end, considering that it did not offer merit scholarships to out-of-state freshmen, and that the federal FAFSA form (short for "Free

Application for Federal Student Aid") had set my expected contribution at $18,000 a year, which was, I was fairly sure, more than the money in my parents' and stepparents' bank accounts, combined. And so, in the fall of 2006, I enrolled as a biology major at the University of Nevada flagship, with a full-ride scholarship that was contingent on maintaining at least a 3.75 GPA, and that covered tuition, but not fees and books, let alone gas to get to class and lunch to get through class.

I stayed home to save on rent and supplemented my income with twenty to twenty-five hours of work a week. I answered calls for a cellphone company. I folded underwear at Victoria's Secret. I picked Christmas gifts at an Amazon warehouse at night, where I experienced for the first time the disorienting sensation of falling asleep on my feet. (Friends? What friends?) I worked at the customer service counter at Dillard's department store, and there, mastered the art of wrapping gifts fast and pretty for elderly white women. I researched global food shortages for a professor in the political science department. (Parties? What parties?) I sorted paper at a personal injury law firm, which was run by a temperamental, middle-aged paralegal whom I could routinely hear yell and pound her desk through the walls, while the solo practitioner—whose name actually graced the practice and appeared in late-night TV ads—spent his weekdays snowboarding in Lake Tahoe. (The paralegal would fire me shortly after deciding that I was grossly incompetent for refusing to succeed each period with two spaces.)

I switched majors three times. The excuse I gave my disappointed mom was that I was bored with biology and the endless game of memorization, though this was a half-truth. The other half was that I was mediocre at this subject, which was both unbearable to my ego and a threat to my scholarship.

Political science, on the other hand, came to me easily. The professor who taught my 101 class had even volunteered to become my mentor and advisor if I chose to write a thesis. I began to consider a career in law, not because I knew anything about lawyers beyond reruns of *Perry Mason* and *Ally McBeal*, but because the nature of my new major had placed the political and legal process on my radar, and introduced me to a cohort of students who were planning to take the LSAT.

My parents did not know very many people for whom jobs were more than a paycheck, a hassle they powered through to cover rent and groceries. Nor had my own family produced any lawyers. Besides the absentee snowboarding lawyer, the only other real lawyer in my vicinity was a neighbor for whom I had babysat in high school—a federal public defender who summarized his job as "representing gang members" and "losing every single case." None of that said much about what the work entailed, which to me left open the possibility that the law might be a good fit: rigorous, challenging, advanced.

After praying to God for discernment, I admitted to my mom that the Outline had changed for good. I would not be applying to medical school.

My mom pouted. I was taking the easy way out, she said, which was not wrong. Law school was the path of least resistance and I was tired of resisting.

My mind was made up.

10.

ME: I think we should break up for a while.

HIM: No, we're not doing that.

ME: Okay.

11.

My sophomore year, the local paper reported that the Nevada legislature was considering deep cuts to the program funding my scholarship. Changes could be imminent although I couldn't discern a timeline from the article.

I was teetering enough as it was. My scholarship could be used at any state school, but even Truckee Meadows Community College cost thousands of dollars per year. It seemed too risky to take out student loans for a degree that I was not sure would guarantee a job—because who even got a stable job with just a bachelor's degree these days? If less than my entire tuition was covered for the next two years, then I might have to drop out and work full time for a while, as some of my high school friends were doing. Not all of them had returned thus far.

But perhaps there was another solution. The math was exacting but not impossible. If I overloaded my next two semesters, and signed up for summer classes, I might be able to exit this hamster wheel in three years.

The more I thought about it, the more I felt this was the only choice. I assumed God would agree. After all, He would not saddle me with more than I could bear.

12.

(Sleep? What sleep?)

13.

I typed *how to study for the LSAT* into the search bar. This was how I discovered that one could prepare for this standardized test, and in fact, a multitude of standardized tests, with the assistance of $1,200 courses and books that compiled past entrance exams. I felt stupid for having taken the SATs cold. Had my high school classmates always known this?

The LSAT in-person courses were out of my price range anyway, but I could manage the books. I ordered a dozen and dedicated the summer of 2008 to studying for the test. What crumbs of time remained I split between church, family, two part-time (unpaid) internships in the Reno offices of a Republican congressman and senator, and my boyfriend, in that order. But I was lucky. My boyfriend was understanding and patient. I could always count on him to wait for his turn without guilting me for putting the Outline above all else.

14.

Several of us were standing in the middle of Harvest Fellowship, holding hands for the prayer that typically preceded Wednesday Bible study, when my boyfriend's stepdad opened with an exhortation asking God to keep Barack *Hussein* Obama out of the White House. It had become clear that for many at Harvest Fellowship, the young politician's meteoric rise signaled the end of times—not in a figurative way, but in a palpable, Antichrist-is-coming-as-prophesied way. The concern seemed far-fetched to me. Every year, it seemed, some preacher predicted the end of times, and every year, the times went on. I felt no compulsion to defend Obama. I myself had knocked on doors for Senator John McCain. Still, something about the man's peculiar prayer rubbed me the wrong way.

15.

Pamphlets from interested law schools began to pour into our mailbox soon after the results of the October LSAT dropped, inviting me to apply at no fee. The sudden attention felt like a trick. Duke, NYU, Chicago, and these other places were out of my league. Could these invitations somehow be a sham? Or was there really such keen interest in black students with my *profile*? The implications made me uneasy. I had worked hard for my grades and was near the top of my class. I had not signed up to be anyone's charity case. But if God sent me a raft, who was I to refuse it?

16.

Obama stumped on campus in a last-ditch effort to swing Nevada. Curious about the cult around him, I decided to go, without telling anyone. This was a historic run, a fact that I did not need American citizenship to grasp. No other Western home of mine, not England and certainly not France, had ever come this close to electing a black head of state. What was the harm in hearing him out?

I pushed past fellow door-knockers for McCain, who had showed up with protest signs, and burrowed into the crowd.

Obama commanded the stage, his white sleeves rolled to the elbows. He promised us the future, hope and change. A world that we, millennials, felt we deserved. The UNR crowd erupted in cheers. How handsome and compelling he was—moving at times.

If *this* was the Antichrist, then the nation would fare just fine.

I must have been the least-devastated member of Harvest Fellowship on the night Obama won.

17.

I was working a shift at Dillard's on the day Harvard Law called. The internet forums where applicants lurked to keep apprised of admission developments had warned that this would begin to happen, now that it was January. I was not holding out much hope. After all, this was Harvard Law, and I was just me. (Also, Stanford and Berkeley undergraduate colleges had swiftly rejected me out of high school.)

Nevertheless, the call came. I tried to hide my shock, but it was Martin Luther King Day, a holiday weekend, which made the prospect of such a call all the more improbable to me. The dean sounded curt and evidently irritated. I hung up, worried that my lack of confidence had blown the preadmission interview, but a few weeks later, a thick crimson binder arrived in the mail. I was in.

My mom and I agreed that we could only really afford to visit one of the schools that had admitted me. I wanted to hold out for Stanford Law, which at least waitlisted me this time around, and, in the alternative, thought we ought to see Berkeley Law, the more realistic choice if we were honest with ourselves. But my mom insisted on Harvard Law. We flew out to Massachusetts a day before Saint Patrick's Day weekend of 2009. I realized, upon my arrival, that few other students had brought their parents along. Then again, few were too young to drink.

I returned to Reno feeling so-so about the trip. It boded well that Elizabeth Warren, the dynamic professor who taught the class I chose to audit at random, could bring a subject as dry as contract law to life. I also liked many of the prospective students. But Cambridge was wet and frigid. The school campus itself had a certain gravitas that was missing from UNR, and while I would not miss the latter, which had been a lonely experience, I feared that a place as self-important as Harvard would chew me up in ways I could not yet fathom.

I had not seen Berkeley but heard that it was warm, and guessed that I would adjust to the East Bay quickly. The border between Nevada and California was porous and the two states shared some common culture. But Harvard was offering to pay for 75 percent of my tuition with grants, almost double Berkeley's assistance package. I still balked at the numbers. Living expenses included, a year at Harvard was estimated to cost $67,000. I would have to borrow the difference. Meanwhile, the new University of Nevada law school in Las Vegas would give me a full ride if I chose them. I was tempted. But it was *Harvard*, my mom reminded me, my mom, who had stood hours at the outdoor markets in Lyon, driven double-decker buses in London, and changed hundreds of diapers in her home daycare so I could someday weigh this very decision.

18.

ME: What if we just lived together?

HIM: But then we'd sin. (Have sex.)

ME: Probably.

HIM: No, we have to be married.

ME: Okay.

19.

I announced my engagement.

My family—my mom, stepdad, aunt, and uncle—asked if I was sure. Getting married and moving across the country in the same year seemed a bit precocious, that was all.

But I was *precocious,* I said.

Still, they said.

Well, I argued, *our family always put God first and education second.* A rule I had abided by faithfully. How could they treat me as if I had failed on both counts? I was at the top of my class and graduating a year early. I was headed to the second-best law school in the country. I was not planning to shack up with a stranger. They had met the boy and claimed to like him. And what was there not to like? My fiancé was an unblemished Christian who had never pressured me to break our vow of celibacy. He had not gone to college but he was responsible and supported himself by repairing computers for a small local shop. We had dated chastely, extremely chastely, for three years. Why did my age matter now? Why was perfect not good enough?

Still.

20.

We married in August 2009, shortly after my college graduation. My daddy did not fly in from France. Then again, he never really bothered to call or write me anymore. I trained myself to forget, though on special occasions, I found my eyes darting to my phone, willing it to illuminate with his phone number.

21.

The first time felt like getting pierced open with a spear until my husband penetrated me. I cried with pain. We went again and he was satisfied. We went again but I was not satisfied. I marveled at how effortless it was for him, every time.

My own body refused to accept him or register his presence in me. Why did it hurt but then feel empty? When would sex morph into pleasure *for me*? Could God send a raft for this?

My husband slept peacefully. I pulled out my phone and searched for *annulment.*

PART II

1.

We signed a lease for a first-floor apartment in Belmont, Massachusetts. It had good lighting and laundry by the mailboxes, but cigarette smoke filtered through the poor ventilation system, nagging me with low-grade headaches.

Friends warned me that moving in together might be rough, an adjustment, they said, but sharing a home turned out to be easy. Little changed between us. We hadn't fought before and didn't fight now. What was mine was his, and what was his was mine, but neither of us owned anything of value, other than my 2001 Camry and some IKEA furniture—kitchenware and a table and a sofa—none of it comfortable to sit on, or interesting to look at. It was stuff to get us through the next three years, and nothing I planned to take home with us on a cross-country trip back West. These were starter sets, the sort of thing one purchased out of necessity rather than love.

2.

I created an email address appending my middle initial to his last name, a first step toward adopting his last name, which I told myself I was postponing because filling out paperwork caused me anxiety, and not because my internal chorus was yelling that my future law school diploma should credit the woman who earned it, and not the man who supported her Outline.

3.

I left our apartment after a quick lunch, on a Monday in late August 2009, careful to time my bus route as to arrive on campus early. I opened the auditorium door to find all seventy-nine of my sectionmates already settled in comfortably. Had I misread the orientation day email? Not a great start, then.

I scanned the room for any seat that might spare me from a walk of shame down to the front of the room, where a blond-bobbed woman was standing authoritatively next to a large screen, a remote control in her hand. Professor Carol Steiker. Former clerk to Supreme Court Justice Thurgood Marshall. Ex–public defender in the prestigious DC office. And my section leader. These days, the professor taught criminal law to 1Ls and an intense course on capital punishment.

While she cued *To Kill a Mockingbird* on the screen, I made a beeline for the one free spot at the end of a back row. It was technically free though the young woman in the next seat over had draped it with her jacket and purse.

I was struck by the woman's delicate features, her wavy brown hair and fashionable glasses, pressed shirt and impeccable makeup. Nothing about her appearance seemed accidental. In contrast, I had not put mascara on since my wedding and still ran late. I assumed the woman would be a bitch. Not out of malice. But everyone knew the prettiest girls always were. Bracing myself for a hostile eye roll, I asked if I could sit by her. The woman smiled and relocated her belongings without a fuss. Professor Steiker dimmed the lights.

HER: I'm Gabriela but I go by Gabi. I can't believe you slept through all that.
ME: I don't think Professor Steiker saw me, do you? It was so dark . . .
HER: Oh, she *totally* saw you.
ME: Oh my God.
HER: I mean, it's whatever! I didn't see you this morning.
ME: There was a morning thing?
HER: Girl, yeah! It was in the email. (She stuffed a notebook into her bag and grabbed her jacket.) I'm going to the bathroom. Do you need to go?

I didn't, but unenthused by the idea of starting afresh with another stranger, after my humiliating grand entrance, I decided to follow her. We strolled past a row of colorful lockers, down a tunnel that connected Pound Hall to other school buildings.

She asked where I was from.

Nevada, I said, but not really. More like from France by way of England, except that I am Cameroonian. Or rather, was born there.

Gabi shared that she had lived in Miami as a kid. And before that, Nicaragua. (I liked how she pronounced it with an uncompromising *r*.) Her parents were from poor families but had immigrated to the States to study medicine and succeeded here. They were since divorced but, like me, she was close to her mom and stepdad. I figured this might mean that while Gabi was well-off, she understood the difference between being broke and being poor.

We carried on from behind separate bathroom doors. She had gone to *the* Ohio State. Good to know, I thought, there were others like me here—state-school types.

I paused, my bum hovering over the toilet seat, unsure of the etiquette on audibly peeing mid-conversation. Gabi hesitated, too, but quickly resumed her sentence over the trickling in our respective stalls.

We burst out laughing. Maybe we'd be friends after all.

4.

I froze in my seat as Steiker lasered her attention to my row. She eyed her assigned seating chart and called out the first name. Adam, she said. The student to my immediate right perked up. I breathed a silent sigh of relief. Adam stuttered for what felt like an eternity before getting to his answer. The class giggled, though not viciously. His words then tumbled out at once. I was awestruck by their intelligence. There was no way in hell that I could've done as well. Only by the grace of God had Steiker spared me from embarrassing myself in my first 1L class ever. This was not misplaced modesty. Princeton had taught Adam a different language than UNR had taught me.

After class, I said hello to the woman on my left. She was a brunette with long, elegant limbs and the air of someone who knew she belonged at Harvard Law. I learned that her name was Lauren. She had graduated from somewhere named Middlebury. I asked where that was. The subtle trace of astonishment in her tone made me realize the stupidity of my question. But I had never heard of Middlebury before, nor of Williams, Swarthmore, Bard, Wake Forest, or the constellation of other prestigious liberal arts colleges represented in the class of 2012.

And now I wondered: Had all the elite school grads arrived much more prepared than me?

5.

Our class brimmed with bona fide adults who, like Adam and Lauren, had worked in the real world before landing here. Some had toiled at environmental nonprofits or worked as paralegals at prestigious white-shoe firms in New York, which they called *the* city. Others held obscure jobs in "venture capital" or "consulting," neither of which made sense to me even after I Googled them.

Then, there were the quirkier backgrounds. Some had been professional ballet dancers or orchestra members. One student, Matt, had spent a decade harvesting seaweed off the Maine coast before deciding to become a lawyer. And my new friend Mike had managed a small record label in California. Each conversation could lead to a new surprise. At a bar one evening, my friend Krista was discussing one of our sectionmates, who had just walked away to get a refill. The snippets I had caught made his former job sound like nothing I had heard of before.

> HER: John was a Green Beret.
> ME: What's that?
> HER: You really don't know?
> ME: No, what is it?
> HER: Well . . . it's actually kind of an embarrassing job to have in the army. It's just like really low-ranked. Probably best to not bring it up around him, actually.
> ME: Oh, okay. I won't.

6.

With my expenses covered by grants and a mountain of student loans, I found myself reacquainted with spare time—a gift I was determined not to take for granted. The work of graduating at a breakneck pace, while constantly worrying about money, and about pleasing God, and about being a good role model to my younger cousins, these things had all combined to burn out any ambitions that I might once have harbored about this place. I felt older than my twenty years.

I wanted to have fun, to be free to act my age, go to parties and escape during spring break, meet people who had nothing in common with me, people who had no gods, people who had many gods. I wanted to hear eccentric ideas about the world and decide what I thought of them without a care for what my parents or pastor might say.

Unbeknownst to my husband, I decided to become a Yes Person, a concept that I must have picked up somewhere on the internet. The plan was working out well so far. In one month, I had made more new friends here than in my three years of college. There were so many interesting brains to pick here. At around five hundred students, my 1L class was one of the largest in the country.

I realized that the moody weather during Admitted Students Weekend had not done Cambridge justice. With its ancient maroon bricks, meandering vines, and tree-lined streets, the town felt like a cross between the colonial America of history books and the European cities of my childhood. It was smaller in size, and pleasant to navigate on foot. I had not noticed how much driving daily, which was obligatory in my neck of the West, had isolated me from interacting with strangers face-to-face, how much I had missed being surrounded by greenery. Some of my new classmates predicted that my infatuation would wear off after the first nor'easter and seven months of winter. There would be long school days ensconced in darkness. But I wanted to love it here. My mind was made up.

7.

Having likely divined my politics from my age and wedding ring, my friend and sectionmate Keri kindly invited me to events put on by the Federalist Society. The student group went by FedSoc. Though it was conservative on fiscal and religious issues, its tent was surprisingly wide, and certainly, much wider politically than my church had been in Reno. FedSoc also promised the best free "non-pizza" lunch talks on campus, and access to its renowned bank of study outlines. And every academic year, it hosted an overnight trip to the spring symposium in DC, where students could watch stars in the conservative bar debate the zeitgeist. It was rumored that certain Supreme Court justices had made an appearance in recent years.

I joined the group the fall of our 1L year. Some common FedSoc views I agreed with, and others I didn't. Of course, I thought, state takeovers could lead to socialism, communism, fascism, and cruel dictatorships. But I was less adamant in my skepticism of government than most members. My mom and I had benefitted from state assistance here and elsewhere. I could not have made it to law school without social housing to keep me warm at night, free school lunches to ensure I never went hungry, and subsidized eyeglasses to see my homework. The welfare system had protected me in critical times.

My relationships with FedSoc members developed easily despite our few political differences. I appreciated how few were shocked or judgmental upon learning that I was the sort of evangelical Christian who had guarded her virginity until marriage. Being among Mormons, Zionist Jewish people, and devout Catholics made me feel like less of an anomaly. That openness resonated more with me than the aggregate of their convictions.

Meanwhile, Gabi had broken up with her college boyfriend and begun to date our handsome sectionmate a few weeks into the first semester. For her, this new relationship meant spending more time with his close friends, a group that included Adam, Lauren, and Mike, and which Gabi and I called "the Libs" between the two of us. We did so not pejoratively—and anyhow, all of them were proud Obama voters—but to distinguish them from my FedSoc friends in conversation. For me, Gabi's new relationship meant making an effort to spend time with a group of people I found lovely but intimidating in their obvious competence. The majority had arrived at law school in their mid and late twenties, and were thus on the older side of our class. They seemed overwhelmingly committed to public service, if not right away, then after a short stint at a private law firm.

I was impressed by the detail of their own Outlines, by the confidence with which they strode through these halls. Where the Libs had a clear sense of purpose for being at Harvard, I was just beginning to understand the immense range of work that lawyers could perform in the world. If we spent enough time together, the Libs would find out that I had been a fluke, an accidental admit. I feared, too, that in time, the depth of my religious background would come to light.

It was an odd concern, I realized. I was supposed to be proud to be a Christian, proud of my God. But the thought of admitting what I believed, or rather, what the Christianity of Harvest Fellowship required me to believe, made me nervous. The potential consequences felt as severe as they once did in high school; once the revelation emerged, it was hard to know how long the stink would linger.

I did not lie, but hid crucial aspects of the America I had come from, beginning with the fact that my stepdad sometimes played creationist DVDs at home, and that he kept a shotgun in a closet upstairs. I did not tell my new friends that I was supposed to accept the coming Rapture and inevitable rise of the Antichrist—that is, if the Antichrist was not already governing from the White House. I said nothing of my staunch opposition to abortion, and avoided discussions of gay marriage, even as our campus buzzed, that semester, with debates over whether the Supreme Court should strike the Defense of Marriage Act as unconstitutional, and whether the president should repeal Don't Ask, Don't Tell from military policy.

I didn't terribly oppose gay marriage. It seemed more important that people get to be happy. But even this truth, I could not express freely. Doing so would betray my Christian ideals.

8.

My husband left early in the mornings to fix computers in a Boston suburb. I took the seventy-three to Harvard Square. Our apartment was a fifteen-minute bus ride and ten-minute walk from campus. We reconvened for dinner. Each evening, I asked about his day and each evening, he said that his day had gone fine. There was not much to report. His job was a job. A reason to be near me first, and a paycheck second.

He missed his family and the people of our church, which had been his second home since he was a little boy. But he was not complaining. He knew we would go home soon. Someday, our three years in Massachusetts would feel like a speck of sand. Besides, he was certain life would improve as soon as we made friends who shared our evangelical faith. I had not wanted to spend our honeymoon searching for a place of worship but we had tried one large, nondenominational church with a young congregation in the Boston area. He liked one newlywed couple that we had met there. A handsome and perfectly inoffensive couple, whom my mind instantly dubbed Barbie and Ken. It always took some effort for me to remember their real names. I felt guilty about it. The couple had been nothing but considerate and inclusive toward us. They seemed so in love with each other, too. My husband thought they might be a good influence on our young marriage. And he would have been right if only I did not find them, and their church, so tragically boring.

I often found my mind wandering to a different Outline: an alternate history in which I did not feel obligated to lie about wanting more devout friends, in which I arrived in Cambridge alone and unmarried, in which the possibility of returning West was an option and not a foregone conclusion. And suddenly, the walls of the apartment felt closer in than before. Yes, I told my husband. Life would improve soon enough. I was sure of it.

9.

What was a *trust fund*, I asked. My classmates explained in hushed tones. It was a stockpile of gifted money, usually deposited by a rich family member into a person's bank account, a person such as this classmate over here, or this one there, and released when the beneficiary came of age, or was otherwise deemed ready to use the money according to the donor's will. A trust fund was how several of them, more of them than I realized, were attending Harvard Law without taking on a cent of debt.

My mouth hung open. Where I came from, children sent money to their parents and to *back home*—not the other way around. I had been poor at times, or poor enough to qualify for the housing projects in Lyon, but by Reno standards, my family was somewhere between working-class and lower-middle-class. We had debt but, I thought, who didn't? I had gone to high school with teens raised in greater need than me, teens raised by parents who didn't have the credit to charge the advanced math calculators on Visa cards, teens raised by foster parents under the watch of a distracted state apparatus, girls like Amber and Cristel from Lucky Lane, or my friend Christina who lived with a father who drank too much, and who had gone to hairdresser school because college was not on the table. Families like mine were the norm in Reno.

Here, though, I was an exception. My adoptive parents and stepparents had not gone further than high school. My mom ran a home daycare and my stepdad repaired postal machines. As for my dad, he still worked at a car-parts factory while my stepmom was a long-term temp, a hallway monitor, at a French middle school. Together, they were a sharp contrast to my class-mates' parents—lawyers, surgeons, professors, corporate executives, and federal judges. Some were descendants of civil rights royalty, the black American college students who had marched for freedom in the '60s and '70s, and gone on to prominent positions. Some of these parents were senior officials in the new administration, on a first-name basis with Barack. Many had degrees from Harvard, Yale, Stanford, and other Ivy League schools. A handful came from cities where the buildings bore their family names, or had ancestors whose names appeared in leather-bound encyclopedias. A number of these parents had hired nannies who looked like my mom to care for my classmates.

10.

The topic of this Property class was public easements and, among other questions, whether beachfronts should be private. I raised my hand. The way I saw it, I said, beachfront property had to be worth a lot of money, money that *someone* had put up. It seemed evident that the high cost reflected more than the nice view. If the beach felt private when the owners bought the place, then it must've factored in exclusive access, privacy, and convenience. Even if the beach wasn't formally part of the lot listed in the property deed, I argued, it should belong to the buyer.

I was picturing, as I made that comment, a house overlooking a pristine stretch of sand, somewhere in San Diego. I had never been but someone I knew and loved had, for drug rehab. I was visualizing a person on the beach, spread lethargically across the sand, their clothes oozing with the stench of alcohol and urine, surrounded by friends in a similar state, as this loved one had been found before. I was realizing that a public easement would give them a *right* to be there, to impose themselves and the consequences of their sinful choices on others, to worry people who had stuck to their Outline and were now seeking a quiet life.

No, I continued. How was it fair for people who hadn't signed up to care for strangers, who had paid, a lot, for a certain degree of remove, to have to nurse strung-out people in their backyard?

When class ended, a couple of Libs gently let me know that my argument had bordered on callous.

I pretended to understand and to be sorry. But for days after, I pondered the alleged offense.

Was it the suggestion that people with substance abuse issues might inconvenience others? But they *did*. I'd seen it with my own eyes and, I was willing to bet, more up-close than they had. Besides, I wasn't suggesting anyone any harm. All I meant was that they weren't entitled to party on a private beach.

Or, I wondered, was it my suggestion that rich people actually paid with the intent not to share? But that was true, too. The wealthiest in Reno—those well aware of trust funds, those who could pay for law school tuitions in cash— lived on hills overlooking the Truckee River and in the lavish estates around the Montreux golf course, at a safe distance from my parents' home, and even farther from the city's trailer parks. It wasn't always an exclusive strip of beach, but the rich did thrive on exclusive access. Private schools without a teen pregnancy problem. Short commutes to the snow. Unencumbered views of

Central Park. The tranquility of the Hamptons. Places where my classmates and their parents had summered.

If I had to guess, a significant fraction of our 1L section had benefitted from being born into the right teams. Yet, none of them seemed to consider their own childhoods callous.

Nor did I think they should. Their privilege was what so many immigrants were fighting for when they crossed half the world to settle in this country.

So what had I missed?

11.

Gabi lived within walking distance of campus, in a spacious apartment that she shared with another law student. The place cost more than mine, but being close to campus allowed her to make and break plans at the last minute. She could stay out late and walk home with friends who lived in her direction.

Once at her apartment, no one interrogated her about where she'd been and why she was there so long, why she'd studied at the library and not in her living room, why she was eating dinner with me and not her boyfriend, whose house the party was at again, what she had consumed there, and why she hadn't answered her texts faster.

Telling my husband when I would be home was a simple courtesy. And I knew my mom meant well when she asked me to check in daily so she would know that her only child was alive and well. Yet, the smallest of expectations had begun to feel like an encroachment on my independence. I envied Gabi's freedom.

I often called my mom on my way back from the library. It was better to do it late than not at all, unless I wanted another voice mail chiding me for being evasive. I dreaded dialing her after eleven P.M. Eastern. The conversation always opened with: Wow, Ness. Again? As if she was tracking my comings and goings on a personal calendar. She'd sigh at my irresponsibility. It wasn't safe, she maintained, despite knowing little about Cambridge and even less about Belmont.

HER: Who are you with?
ME: I'm not alone. (There were people. Women jogging in reflective vests. Men walking their dogs. Mass. Ave. was well-lit at this hour. So, technically, I wasn't lying.)

HER: But you're not with Gabi? She's walking home alone, too?

ME: Uh-huh.

HER: *Akie ă Zámbo wama.* You girls are *not* okay. Is your husband coming to get you? When? Why not? Are you still walking? Why? I don't care if you're tired, I'm not hanging up until I know you're safely home.

Once, after we talked, a package labeled in Dave's slanted handwriting appeared in my mailbox. Inside was black pepper spray, sealed in a hard plastic container. His version of a fatherly love letter. I had asked if he was even allowed to mail that. At which he'd laughed.

12.

A month or so into the semester, at a house party with the Libs one night—without my husband, who skipped these things on principle—I set out to find out if Adam believed in God.

Adam shrugged. Sort of, he said.

So did he still consider himself Jewish?

Adam said he did. Being agnostic, or even concluding that he didn't believe in *everything*, wasn't a deal breaker for being Jewish, and participating in rituals like the Seder dinner on Passover. In his denomination, Reform Judaism, asking questions was encouraged.

I was perplexed. In my church and parents' house, questioning the existence of God was sacrilegious. I wouldn't dare. Faith wasn't supposed to run on proofs and tests. No one was ever called a Doubting Thomas as a compliment. In fact, I was fairly sure the thought of questioning God alone amounted to a sin. Pastor Ilunga and the leadership at Harvest Fellowship warned of doomed endings for those who lived wicked lives. Eve had been banished from Eden. And Lot's wife, petrified into a pillar of salt.

But when I looked at Gabi, who trusted her own instincts, I only saw abundant goodness. Mike, who didn't believe, had moral convictions that I admired. And my dad, the atheist, was still one of my favorite humans in the world. Was it so certain that, if the phone hadn't rung when it did that night in 1998, and I had been raised in a home without God, my soul would've been lost?

13.

There was a plan for my twenty-first birthday: a joint party for me and two sectionmates also born on October 11. So my section wouldn't have to pick between friends that night. Our section would meet at a bar in the square. I told my husband that he was invited, though I omitted the fact that the joint party was my idea.

He asked if I planned to go.

Of course, I said. How could I not? Sheepishly, I told him that also, I planned to drink. I had before—one night, during which the Libs had hidden me in one of their bathrooms, thinking the cops had been called on the party— but my husband didn't know about that.

He was livid. I realized quickly that this was not just about the party, but that it was about everything. About how it had taken less than six weeks away from our roots, from our church, for me to turn my back on God. How he could tell I was milking homework as an excuse to skip church on Sundays. How I was making zero effort to meet Christian friends and, in fact, seemed to be going out of my way to befriend people who would brainwash me: Gabi, who was a lapsed Catholic; Keri, who was Jewish and therefore didn't accept Jesus Christ as the Messiah; and the Libs, who, from what he could tell, were entirely secular. My stupid birthday plan, and it was stupid, said my husband, was proof that my mom was right about me. I was too *influenceable*. A willing participant in my own demise. He'd have nothing to do with it.

14.

We were in the car and my husband was driving.

I was still going to the party and he was still bent on convincing me to stay home.

At the height of the impasse, my husband reached over and pinched my thigh hard.

He was not sorry.

15.

On the day of my joint birthday party, my husband and I went to a theme park, just the two of us. We rode roller coasters and had fun, the most fun since our wedding. And I remembered, that day, why I had liked him so much.

Home again, my husband asked if I'd changed my mind. I said that I hadn't and asked if he had. He said nothing. I sensed in that moment that the weight of the question had shifted back to me, and it was on me to take back my answer. Last chance to do the right thing, to put my faith first and honor my husband.

A pang of shame coursed through me.

I *wanted* him to stay here while I slept at Gabi's. This was the only way I would have fun tonight, without searching his face for approval.

At last, my husband said that no, he hadn't changed his mind.

Gabi opened the festivities with a comically large bottle of apple-flavored Bacardi, which we sipped from as we dolled up with a few other girls. We walked over to the bar. The room was full of my new friends, who were eager to shower me with drinks. I'd be flirting with a classmate when someone would shout happy birthday and poof!—a beer or wine or a gin and tonic would pop up in my hand. Being a Yes Person, I accepted each drink graciously.

I was sitting on a stool and either the room was swaying or I was, when Mike joined me. He leaned over as if he had a secret. (I still loved secrets.) When he had my attention, he launched into a little demonic singsong: *There is no God, Vanessaaaaa.* Why did it make me laugh so hard?

We reconvened at Gabi's apartment later. Her boyfriend, our friend Mike, and a handful of friends followed. I promised the driver that I was good, I would *not* throw up in his cab. The Bacardi bottle was replaced with Chinese takeout. I had not yet opened my Styrofoam box when I projectile-vomited from the sofa. I watched the stream land neatly in a plastic bag across from the coffee table. I slurred: Wait, did you guys see that? (Unfortunately, they had.) And someone whispered that I was going to die tomorrow.

Gabi tucked me into bed.

I woke up around six, brimming with energy. Gabi was asleep. I cleared the food containers, swept her living room floor, and rode the seventy-three home. The apartment was empty. The law school shut down for Columbus Day but my husband's job hadn't. I lay down for a quick nap, thankful for the solitude.

When I woke up several hours later, my head felt like it was filled with lead. I also felt nauseous and lethargic. I tried to piece together my morning. How had I been in perfect form this morning? Was it possible that I had woken up drunk?

Every whiff of green apple sent me straight to the toilet bowl. I crouched there for most of the afternoon. Nothing would stay down. My husband returned home in the evening. By then, the worst had passed.

HIM: How was your night?
ME: It was really fun!
I began listing the night's itinerary. His face sunk.
ME: . . . but I paid for it this morning. I've never been so sick in my life.
I summoned a contrite look. A strange smile crossed his lips.
HIM: Good. Hope you learned your lesson.

16.

On the day that first semester grades were posted, toward the end of January of 2010, I sat inconsolable in the cafeteria. Gabi and Mike took turns comforting me. The most incomprehensible part of all this was that I liked law school despite being tragically bad at it. I had no explanation for what happened. I'd skipped two grades as a kid and hadn't earned a C since my freshman year of high school, a predictable outcome of being placed into Geometry without having taken Algebra 2 first. Now two terrible marks tarred my transcript. No one would ever hire me. One look at my grades and they would *know* I didn't deserve to be there. I was finished. The Outline was dead.

Gabi and Mike tried to put things into perspective. It wouldn't matter in the long run, they said. I'd do better next semester and come up with a plausible explanation for this fluke. I was here, I had already won. The Harvard name and network opened doors. That was the entire point of coming here.

My husband echoed my friends at home. This semester wasn't an indictment of my intelligence. I was one of the smartest people he knew. It was all right not to nail things the first time around.

But what did any of them know?

Gabi and Mike were only 1Ls. Their families had money, connections. They could afford to fail. And if I was honest, my husband's support meant even less. He hadn't gone to college. He didn't understand what it meant to be defined by school grades. He'd never cared enough to be characterized that way.

A light switched off inside of me. It felt like not being able to get out of bed and being constantly on the verge of tears. It felt like wanting to go home but not. It felt like constantly being out of breath.

I had no choice but to stick it out, though. What else was there to do? I had one semester of loans in my name, and another had just materialized in my bank account.

I dragged myself through the interminable winter.

As the spring approached, the school's career office pushed our class to finalize summer plans. I thought it might suit me to represent people who were struggling financially. I'd joined the Tenant Advocacy Project early in the fall, at the encouragement of Dan, my sectionmate, a Lib, and a friend. Dan was so passionate about housing that he was getting a concurrent joint degree at the urban planning school. I'd told him a little about my interest in housing insecurity, which I'd written about in my school application, and which stemmed from those hard first months in London, as my mom and I waited for the city to home us. Eleven years of age was old enough to absorb my mom's stress and feel the embarrassment of lacking a permanent address. Ten years later, just talking about that hard stretch still made me choke up. I might not be convinced that rich people *had* to share beach space with the public, but I wasn't a monster. Everyone deserved a roof over their heads.

The Tenant Advocacy Project had assigned me the case of a black mother on limited income, whom the Boston Housing Authority had overcharged on rent for years. Another student had worked on the case over the previous summer. My task was to bring it to the finish line. Under the supervision of a licensed attorney, I had represented the mother in her hearing. The tenant had been awarded thirty thousand dollars by the housing authority. This made me feel useful. Perhaps I could be helpful again this summer.

17.

I applied to a nonprofit to represent indigent people in Los Angeles, and by March 2010, had accepted an enthusiastic internship offer from them. Gabi and Mike were right. My first semester grades hadn't mattered. I was set for the summer. Slowly, the days began to grow longer, thawing the black snowbanks along Mass. Ave.

I thought the light would switch back on then. But little changed. I felt increasingly restless at home, resentful of my husband, angry with my own body. Something was wrong with me. Women my age were supposed to desire sex. For so long, I had held on to my purity, saved all of myself for my husband, yet the idea of him touching me now turned my skin cold. I watched him sleep like a baby, so happy to share my bed, to be my husband, and someday, the father of my children. The sight of him made me want to cut out my womb.

I looked up *asexuality*. But the definition didn't quite fit. It wasn't simply that I didn't want sex. It was that I didn't want sex with *him*. All these parties I went to, all the flirting, there were inevitably men there. Some of them lingered in my mind. Would I ever act on it? Was I the kind of person who'd set her own home on fire? Months ago, I would've scoffed at the idea. Now I tried to bury it.

As the second semester unfurled, I hid behind a wall of excuses: homework, school parties, menstruation, exhaustion. Anything to avoid him. I fantasized about breaking up. Accidentally dropping my wedding ring in a drain. Escaping to a room near campus. Sleeping alone, waking up alone.

If I strung together the minutes that Gabi spent listening to me complain about my misery, my uncertainty, my confusion, the words would total at least one lap around the earth.

Where to even begin? I'd never broken up with someone. The last time I'd asked, my husband, then-boyfriend, had simply refused me.

The chorus in my head tallied grievances about my character. I was such a coward, they said. My parents had given it a respectable seven years before divorcing, and here I was, giving up after what, seven months, spoiled millennial, brat. Did I need to be reminded? I had wanted this until I didn't. No husband deserved someone this self-centered. He was kind, supportive, funny, hardworking, and so in love with me that he'd followed me to this place. I thought of the people who would be furious with me, and disappointed. I *should* feel guilty for even thinking about it. Not to mention that getting married and divorced in the span of a year, under the age of twenty-two, would (rightfully) make me a walking red flag. Who would want to date me? Who would ever want to marry me again? Ah, the next husband. There was the real me. Already plotting the next exit into my Outline.

I called my mom to talk. As open as we were with each other, sex was always off the table when I was growing up. The first and last time the subject had come up openly was the month before my wedding, at my inaugural Pap smear. The whole thing had ended abruptly as I screamed with pain. My body had sealed shut; there would be no exam that day. The gynecologist had invited me to come back after I was sexually active, when things were more open. I couldn't remember what my mom had said at the time.

She picked up the phone.

I told her something was wrong.

HER: Have you tried relaxing with a bath beforehand? You always
    stress yourself out so much.
ME: I can try.
HER: Have you prayed about it?
ME: Yes.
HER: Good. I'll pray for you, too.

Gabi dismissed the voices crowding my head.

I couldn't live my life to please other people, she said. It wasn't sustainable. And since when was divorce a black mark? To the right person, it just shouldn't be. There was nothing inherently evil about breaking up.

She asked: What did *Vanessa* want?

I pondered the question seriously. These last six months had shaken my worldview more than I ever anticipated. I had grown up watching and listening to conservative outlets like Fox News and the Christian Broadcasting Network paint people like the Libs as unserious and unintelligent, a naive generation who thrived on protesting American wars and defended sinful lifestyles without understanding the stakes. But that caricature hadn't panned out. My friends were smart, interesting, considerate. I admired the way unfairness offended them and drove the principles they believed in.

What did *Vanessa* want?

In the immediate, more than anything, I wanted to be alone. Long term, I supposed that I wanted what everyone else wanted. I wanted to be happy. And if it had to be within a romantic relationship, then I wanted to be with someone who valued outcomes at least as much as they valued process. Who could evolve and challenge my beliefs. Who would seek to change my mind with reason rather than threats of eternal damnation. Who had high expectations of themselves. Who measured success by something other than compliance with the Bible. I wanted, no, needed, a partner with a passion and ambition of their own, but a real passion, and not, as it increasingly felt to me, the self-serving mission of converting others to Christ.

What did *Vanessa* want?

I wanted to be with someone other than my husband.

It was time to tell him.

I was not doing well and it was serious.

When the initial panic of this confession lifted, my husband sprang into action. He returned from work one day and said that he had set up a call with the Harvest Fellowship youth pastor. The youth pastor knew us both. We could trust his judgment. He would understand the pressures of young love, having himself married his high school sweetheart. Three children later, they were still happy. My husband was confident. The youth pastor would know how to fix me.

More important to me than his track record in the marriage arena, the youth pastor had always seemed like a deeply practical man. I thought him smart, too. Capable of setting aside his emotions in difficult moments. Maybe he could help us brainstorm a plan—a decision tree came to mind—to figure out whether the marriage was salvageable.

I agreed to the call.

The youth pastor picked up the phone at the time he had set with my husband. I was to call him and, my understanding was, speak to him alone about my feelings. But I had hardly said hello when he handed me to his wife. I had met her, of course, and even gone to her home while we lived in Reno. Still, I barely knew her. As far as I could tell, we had nothing in common. Our handful of conversations had been brief, superficial. Whatever she knew about the kind of person I once was, she had learned through her husband and mine.

I felt ambushed.

HER: Marriage can be hard, it can be *really* hard. You have to hand it all to God. Things *will* get better.

ME: I was thinking we could live apart, he and I. For a little while.

HER: Don't do it. You *cannot* do it.

ME: But what if I keep feeling this way?

HER: You just can't talk about divorce, Vanessa.

I hung up, dejected.

My husband was beaming. *This* was the validation he'd craved. He wasn't crazy for wanting to fight for our marriage. It was *me* who was being erratic and irrational. He reprimanded me again. This was on me for abandoning church. I had to understand that the only way our situation would get better was if I got back to God. Stepped away from my new friends. Rethought my priorities.

I had nothing to say because I knew he was right. The church had taught me to pray in moments like these, to trust God to lead me out of the darkness, away from temptation, and return me home safe.

But what if I did not want to go home? And what if God had pushed me into this tunnel in the first place? Was it not too convenient that God's desires for my life aligned perfectly with what Harvest Fellowship wanted me to do? What was in it for them? Mike had been right about my first semester grades not mattering; could he be right about God, too?

I loathed myself for asking.

These weren't innocent questions. I might be able to fool my husband and others, but I understood what they meant: my mind was made up. I was bypassing God's math. Feigning uncertainty about what I needed to do to postpone our families' and church's disappointment in me.

What was I supposed to do next?

Gabi was flabbergasted by my call with the youth pastor's wife. The whole thing made no sense. Of course I could leave this man, she said. Women left men all the time. Our own moms had rebuilt their lives and were happily remarried. I'd supported Gabi as she broke up with her college boyfriend, months ago. Did I not remember talking her through it? Encouraging her to do what was right for her? Had any of these church people even inquired into my needs, into my mental health through all this?

She could not tell me what the right answer was, but here was her pledge. Stay or go, she would not abandon me. I could count on her to be there through whatever came next.

I put my faith in those words, and in her, Gabi, my best friend of six months, a girl only twenty-two years old.

18.

I tried to game out the options before me.

Soon, I'd find myself in LA, where I didn't know anyone, while my husband awaited my return here, in Massachusetts. Maybe I'd make friends, but that wasn't guaranteed. It was possible that this new solitude would provide clarity, that I'd realize that I needed to move out of our Belmont apartment. I'd tell my husband. He'd alternate between reasoning with me and guilting me into staying with him. Lonely evenings in LA would soften my resolution. In the worst of scenarios, and, I suspected, most likely, I would entertain the possibility that someday, our marriage might satisfy me. I might even agree to another conversation with the youth pastor's wife. Let him fly in from Boston to plead his case in person. Without Gabi around as my backbone, I'd roll over. He'd say, You can't leave. And I'd say, Okay.

This was why, I decided, I couldn't be trusted to figure things out while stranded in an unfamiliar city. I would need to be near people who cared for me more than they cared for him.

The Public Defender's Office in Reno was still filling its summer class. I sent them an application, interviewed, and when they made me an offer, I told the LA nonprofit that, regrettably, my plans had changed at the last minute. I needed to go home.

Summer had not yet begun but already I realized that twelve weeks apart wouldn't suffice. I needed more space to think. And I wanted to live closer to campus 2L year. Without him.

To my great surprise, my husband didn't shout or cry or pout when I explained this. In fact, he was so unfazed that I wondered if he had heard me. I intended to move out. We would not live together in the fall.

He assured me that he had heard me loud and clear. But I was headed to Reno, he said. Couldn't I see? This was a win to him. He *wanted* me back with my parents and under the watch of Harvest Fellowship, as far away from Gabi and the Libs as geographically possible. He was hopeful again: summer would set me straight. I was not so sure.

I submitted my name to the school-wide system for finding roommates. I reminded myself that an application wasn't a commitment, and for that reason, it was okay not to tell him about this part. I was just covering my bases. And besides, we had talked about it days, or was it weeks, ago. This was the new Outline.

On Memorial Day 2010, I flew back to Nevada.

19.

My husband had already called me several times that day. But it was my third day in Reno and I had set boundaries for the summer, before leaving Cambridge, and he had agreed to these boundaries. I could not let him violate them this early. For this reason, I had ignored the calls. But when he called again after dinner, I answered, wary of a potential emergency. It was almost midnight in Cambridge.

> ME: Hello?
> HIM: The landlord needs to know if we're renewing the lease. It's urgent. I'm emailing it to you to sign.
> My pulse quickened. I had dreaded this moment but hoped it would come later. I was not ready. But I could not wake up another day at his side. I would not.
> ME: We talked about this. I'm not signing that lease.

PART III

1.

My husband quits his job. He puts the furniture in storage and drives cross-country to his parents' house.

Is this chivalry?

The thought of seeing him makes me nauseous with worry. On the opposite end of the country, I could pretend he didn't exist, refuse his calls without being afraid that he might just show up uninvited. I don't see how I am supposed to think with a clear mind with him in the same time zone.

Summer hasn't begun but already, it is ruined.

2.

The marriage counseling pastor's name is Bobby. He is white and in his early thirties. We sit in his study, against the window. My husband describes the current situation.

She wanted to get married as much as me, so we got married. She went to law school. She became a different person. A person who does not seek God. She wants to leave.

This is all fair.

Pastor Bobby turns to me. He wants to know. Before this conversation goes any farther, am I willing to take the *d* word off the table?

I ask the pastor if he means *divorce*.

He says yes. The word is so corrosive, do I see, so damaging, that it must not be spoken between spouses.

That goes against everything I've learned about negotiation so far. I respectfully decline.

Pastor Bobby asks whether I'd drop out of law school if it was the only way to save my marriage.

So, I ask him if he has any idea how hard I worked to get there.

He smirks and leans back in his chair.

It's all downhill from there.

MARRIAGE COUNSELING WAS my husband's idea. I was only willing to go if the counselor was mutually agreed upon and had a professional degree in therapy, a neutral party who wasn't attached to either of us, or to God. But my husband had been adamant. The counselor had to be a servant of God. In a past that feels forever ago, I had wanted him to be more assertive. He thinks now that I meant assertive *like this*, but it's too late. I am past caring. So here we are, in Christian counseling.

My husband is blinded by hope. He does not see that I have agreed to this only to get the session over with. To soften the blow of my made-up mind. I think that if the pastor can see how close this marriage is to the cliff, he'll do the mercy killing for me. I might even be forgivable if it seems like I really tried. When people will ask me if I went to counseling before destroying my marriage, I will be able to say that yes, we did, Christian counseling even, and it didn't work for us, so you must see how dire things were.

My husband let me pick the church. Living Stones, I had told him. The cool church downtown.

⟊

PASTOR BOBBY WANTS to know from my husband how he feels about me. The answer is obvious. He still loves me. Madly. The pastor inhales sharply. It's my turn.

I can see it in his face: bedroom questions, incoming. I expect him to have my husband step out, so I can speak frankly, but the pastor dives right into the muck.

> PASTOR BOBBY: How's the sex for you?
> I hesitate, out of respect for my husband's ego.
> ME: Not very good.
> HIM: Why is that?
> ME: You really want me to answer that in front of—
> HIM: Yeah, come on. How is it?
> ME: Seriously?
> HIM: Yes.
> ME: I think it's not . . . I think it's not big enough for me.
> HIM: Wow! Wow! (He leans back in his chair again, more dramati-
>   cally this time.) Pardon my French but *wow* you are an
>   emasculating bitch. (Yes, he really says this.)

My husband has lost his tongue. He can't look at me, so he just sits there, existing. Pastor Bobby turns to him as if I have become invisible, and says there's nothing else he can do with me. He'll spend the rest of the session with my husband, if that's all right with my husband, whom he keeps calling *brother*. Without dignifying me with a glance, he tells me that there's a chair in the hallway. I am to wait out there until they are done.

I go to my time-out. My heart is pounding and my cheeks run hot.

My phone rings in the parking lot, as my husband unlocks the car doors. It's my mom. She wants to hear about the session. How did it go? Did it work?

Angry tears stream down my face, leaving streaks of white salt. I tell her that it did not go well. And I swear that I'm never coming back to this fucking place.

She is enraged on my behalf. What's this guy's name anyway? Who the hell does he think he is?

All this time, my husband says nothing.

3.

It's been a few days since the counseling session, and in two weeks, I am scheduled to fly to central Texas to visit Gabi. I'm counting down the days. I'm in a generous mood on the day my husband calls. I cover the weather, how my week is going, how my parents are doing. I know why he's really calling. Our anniversary is coming up. I am just praying our call ends before he brings it up, so I don't have to turn him down.

But he insists.

Who knows when he'll see me again—especially if I get my way? It's just a movie, he says.

I say that I'd rather not because I don't want to lead him on. I've made up my mind about moving out. But I'm the one breaking up the marriage. That comes with sacrifices. So I give in. Just for a movie.

My husband picks me up from my parents' house. When the movie ends, he says that we should have dinner. I say that I'd rather not, but he pushes. It's just dinner, he says. Besides, the movie doesn't count as quality time because we didn't talk for two hours. I give in. Just for dinner.

There's a steakhouse near the theater, but he drives to the one close to his parents' place. I'm not stupid, I tell him. He has to take me home right after dinner. I don't want to come over. This is already outside the bounds of the original deal.

Fine, he says.

But after dinner, he begs me to come up. Just for a little bit, to hang out. Please.

I say that I'd rather not.

But we're so close, he says, and he doesn't want to take me home yet. In a few days I'll be gone and he'll still be here. Then, who knows?

He's my ride home and I'm the monster. I guess I can come in, I say, but I won't have sex with him. Does he understand?

The house is empty. And now we are in his bedroom. It hasn't changed, but the two people who stood in it a year ago are unrecognizable. I used to want a house like this one, to read by his side, to tidy up in a rush before our friends visit, to bathe our children before their bedtime. And the gentle boy used to care about what I wanted.

When he starts undressing me, I don't stop him. This is the sacrifice for breaking up a marriage. I must pay. He slips on a condom. I am on my back and he is fucking me and I want to go home but at least it feels like nothing. A couple more minutes, I think to myself. Then, this will be over for good.

When I open my eyes, the condom is rolled up on the bed. I push him off me and tell him to take me home immediately. The car ride is silent. He isn't sorry.

I pray my next period comes on schedule. For the first time in a long while, God delivers.

4.

My new apartment is in Somerville. I share it with two Chinese students who teach in other Harvard graduate programs. It's on Beacon Street, across from the Star Market and the quaintest little pie shop. It's a pretty walk to class, too.

Before classes start, late August 2010, my friend Kendra and her husband, Tim, kindly offer me a ride to pick up my mattress and sofa from storage, where my estranged husband dropped them before returning to Nevada. The other Libs and Keri are good to me. Gabi lets me sleep over when I feel blue.

At a party one night, I'm flirting with a friend when he tells me he's available for anything I need. He leans in so our shoulders touch and his breath is close to mine—*anything*. He has a nice face and I like him, so I say: Maybe when this is over.

5.

On the phone, my mom avoids the *d* word. The whole thing rattles her. She thinks marrying my husband was a mistake and keeps reminding me that she told me so, that she was right, again and again. Yet, she refuses to affirm that she supports my decision. Yes, she and my stepdad have gone through divorces before. Yes, they are the happier for it. But those decisions are different, they preceded their commitment to God. To encourage me now . . . it'd betray her Christian ideals.

I have just turned twenty-two and live alone. For the first time in my life, I feel like an adult. Which makes it all the more stupid that I need to hear my mom say that she'll still love and support me, that she won't shut me out, her only daughter, if I file the papers. But I need it, I do. I plead with her and still, my mom won't yield.

In moments like these, I wish that I was more like Gabi, whose relationship to the church is less intimate. The idea that any woman would deserve to be in a miserable relationship because a book says so is utterly foreign to her.

I think I agree; I'm not sure.

My recent track record makes it hard to trust my own instincts anymore. But Gabi has enough certainty for the both of us. She offers the reassurance that my mom won't. And I have faith that she means it.

6.

My husband is sending me long messages that waver between the fact that he loves me and the fact that I'm narrow-sighted, selfish, and flat-out wrong for leaving.

He logs into my email and reads pages of conversations with Keri. I find out through the screed of fuming texts that follows. He is livid. How dare I use the *d* word with her? Have I no shame?

I change my password.

He heard that a band that we both like is playing a show in Boston soon. Should he visit me then? Delicately, I talk him out of it.

The semester is in full swing. It's easier than 1L year but still a lot of work. For class credits, I represent poor clients at the school's legal clinic in Jamaica Plain. For fun, I go to house parties and school balls. Being a Yes Person is easier without a husband.

Except for when he finds a photo in which I am tagged posing next to a boy (and several other friends) at a law school dance, and he demands to know what's going on. I tell him that I don't know what that's supposed to mean, and that nothing is going on, because it's true.

The days are shrinking again and finals are looming. I'm grateful for the three thousand miles of space between us. It's easier to breathe.

Except on the night my husband posts on Facebook that he's sad and worried about me. Against my better judgment, I read each of the comments. His aunts chime in. His sister. The older sister of the youth pastor's wife. Parents of teenagers in the youth group. Others, too. Some are vicious. It's a feeding frenzy. One would think I had asked them, *the people of Harvest Fellowship*, for a divorce.

How many are hoping God curses me into an unnamed pillar of salt? How many will ever wonder why the options for Lot's nameless wife were marital submission or death by petrification?

I think: Here's one more church I'll never come back to.

That night, I want so badly to tell my husband that nothing will get me back. But it's in my interest to remain cordial. Divorce can speed through the Nevada courts when spouses file jointly. No questions asked, no faults admitted. But first, I must convince him to profess, in writing, that he, too, wants to let go. The negotiation requires me to hold it together. I close the tabs and go to sleep.

7.

Unbuilding a home takes paperwork. Funny how skilled I can be when motivated. The court wants me to split our assets into two columns, his and mine. I give him my car, which is already with him, and which I paid off, and settle for most of our worthless furniture. A small penance, I realize, for the pain I've caused him.

My husband maintains that I'll regret it but, in the end, signs my life back to me.

My mom says the magic words at last. She'll be here. I should do what's right for me. I believe her, too. Within twenty-four hours, I have filed the papers with the court. But for a long time I will wonder, why did I have to convince *her*?

A family judge ends my marriage with the stroke of a pen. Gabi is there the day after, and the day after that. The friend who'd do *anything* for me spends the night in my apartment. In the morning, I am still me. No pillar of salt in sight.

Spring blooms in Cambridge. The light has switched back on. My grades improve. On weekends, I kiss others without bothering to marry them. Summer plans crystalize. I think that this time, I'll try to be helpful in DC and New Orleans.

After that, the Outline is a white page.

EPILOGUE

On Sundays, I sleep in—God's math no longer being my problem. My ex-husband can have Him in the divorce. I keep waiting for their mutual absence to ache, for the darkness to grip me again, for salt to harden and break me, but the doom never manifests.

Not only am I not sorry, I am happy.

But the image of an evangelical flock I once upheld is gone. I think of Harvest Fellowship, Living Stones, and the millions of churches like them, and see a people with stunted empathy, a people that claims the moral high ground, but is petrified in dogma, unable, or perhaps unwilling, to consider why their ministry's core principles sound so cruel when spoken out loud.

In reclaiming myself, I begin there—with what beliefs there are to disavow.

Where to go next?

I've never been less certain, but for the first time, I look forward to being surprised.

The Speculator

HOME, NOUN. (CONT.)
11 a: a community
   also a neighborhood

A SIDE EFFECT OF MY uprooted childhood was a fascination with the physical home that only flourished as I entered high school in Nevada, which was on the cusp of a statewide real estate boom. The future was expanding to the south of Reno and in the adjacent town of Sparks, where the desert was being seeded with imitation-Tuscan homes. To entice buyers, sales agents placed free real estate guides at the entrances of grocery stores around town. The low-end printouts were nothing like the glossy decor and furniture magazines that captured my imagination as a tween. Nonetheless, I never failed to grab one on my way out the door for later study. I skipped past the cheap manufactured homes and trailers on raised foundations to get to the classy stuff. Underneath each photo square, a block of text distilled the top amenities in shorthand. *Jacuzzi in master. Four-car garage. Steps to Kings Beach.* It was hard for me to imagine how anyone could be unhappy in a house that had everything. If you could afford the seven-figure price tag, there was probably nothing you couldn't buy. That my parents would never be rich, and, by my guess, neither would I, was no damper on the fantasy.

But something else about the free guides piqued my interest as a teenager. The grid of listings was evidently governed by the same set of rules that determined the cost of each house. These rules went unexplained, but their effects could be grasped and even predicted with careful study. Reading the guides from front to back, I learned that houses could be identical without being equal: if two houses were substantively similar but one was zoned for Hug High and the other for Galena High, their costs couldn't match unless the second house hid some terrible defect. Even though the precise reasons for these discrepancies eluded me, the Reno metro area's housing market came to feel intuitive over time. Its rules reminded me of gravity; I couldn't explain Newton's Law, but I understood that an apple shaken from a tree would always fall to the ground.

In the earliest aughts, the free guides told a story of prices with nowhere to go but up. A contagion of optimism, and loosened standards for borrowing, meant that everyone suddenly had the chance to buy low, sell at a profit, and repeat until they got rich.

A month before my mom and I moved to America, President George W. Bush stood at the pulpit of St. Paul African Methodist Episcopal Church in Atlanta and delivered a passionate pitch for expanding homeownership among minorities:

> I believe there is such a thing as the American Dream. And I believe
> those of us who have been given positions of responsibility must do
> everything we can . . . to make sure the dream shines in all
> neighborhoods, all throughout our country. Owning a home is part
> of that dream, it just is. Right here in America, if you own your own
> home, you're realizing the American Dream.[1]

My parents pulled the trigger in late December 2004. One cold evening, a school night, the three of us sat in a small conference room across from their real estate agent, a petite blonde who wore her hair in two infantile braids. She explained how to claim a piece of the pie. You had to put in an offer and wait for other bids. After a deal was made, there would be a litany of fees, for a physical inspection, a title search, taxes, and other closing necessities. Dave had gone through this process in the '90s, but this was my mom's first time. She knew the house by Huffaker Park was the one the minute she stepped inside. I could see her chart the possibilities as we checked out the den, dining room, and upper floor. This was the American Dream, then: a loan approval and a house that two parents could agree on.

The agent delivered her spiel over my melodramatic sighs and eye rolls. Embarrassed by my little performance, my parents asked me to spit it out. This deal seemed like trash, I said. The asking price, which hovered around $315,000, was absurd for this particular house. For starters, it was twice my age and looked it. Its most basic features were outdated from top to bottom. And that was before we got to the garish stencil frieze that unspooled from the kitchen cabinets to the walls of my future bedroom, which was smothered in a demoralizing lilac. (The seller family's matriarch had clearly undergone a DIY phase.)

I lacked the vocabulary to talk about market demand or identify a housing bubble, but I knew that *something* was shifting the rules in the south of the city. Whatever that something was, it was causing the freshly built developments in Damonte Ranch and Double Diamond to tumble in price. For $70,000 less than the asking price for this house, my parents could own a never-lived-in house with greater square footage near a mountain, a golf course, and the brand-new public high school. So why was this lady pushing so hard for the older house? (I had not been apprised of the mechanics of commissions.)

My parents listened sincerely while the agent's jaw clenched tight. It was her word against mine. She was an experienced professional, and I was a snotty sixteen-year-old with a quirky obsession. We moved into the Huffaker Park house a few weeks later.

⟋

YEARS LATER, ONE sunny afternoon in 2007, I watched through the window as our neighbor crossed the street and walked over to our home. Brandi was a broad woman with freckled arms and a kind demeanor. Her house was bigger but more densely filled. Aside from her husband and two kids, Brandi also lived with her mother, her grandmother, and two colossal Rottweilers that I'd seen the toddler girl brush like dolls.

Brandi handed a brochure to my mom. A guy in the mortgage business was giving a presentation at her place soon, pitching loans that could lower everyone's monthly payments. Several neighbors had already RSVP'd. My mom said she'd think about it. The day of, though, she and my stepdad stayed home.

They were not finance whizzes but they believed that if a thing sounded too good to be true, it probably was. This miracle loan reeked of bad surprises. They were sticking with their no-frills, thirty-year mortgage.

I now suspect that the broker was peddling mortgages with adjustable interest rates, which were the rage in the mid-aughts. The lender would guarantee a locked interest rate, typically for the first two to three years of the loan. The rate would be on the lower end, allowing for smaller payments. But there was a catch.

After the locked period ended, the interest rate would reset on a schedule. The timing depended on the loan you picked—in some instances the interval could span one year, three years, or longer. The next interest rate was calculated based on a number of factors, including the risk that the borrower would be unable to repay the loan. If the risk was deemed to have increased for any reason, the monthly payment would rise sharply.

Borrowers often bet on one of several scenarios coming to pass *before* the balloon date. Perhaps their finances would drastically improve, making it easy to cover the higher amount. Some planned to refinance the loan instead, which is to say, negotiate a cheaper rate with the lender, as they'd seen many friends and family members do over the years. Others yet saw a market headed ever upward, and banked on selling long before the higher payments hit.

It was a reasonable gamble. In Reno, all of us, whether poor or rich, were only a few degrees of separation from someone who had become a successful house flipper. I had heard that Mr. Victor, the contractor who had tiled the Huffaker house's first floor for my parents, lived in a mansion that he was now renovating for the next buyer. Dave's own parents couldn't have picked a better time to upgrade from their last home. It was a seller's market, through and through. People suddenly had college savings accounts, new garages for new cars, more bathrooms than made logical sense.

Cultivating wealth was supposed to be simple. Buy low and sell high. Invest the profits into the next down payment. Retile the bathroom or splurge on a double oven. Watch the equity build up. Then, flip the house. With enough patience, you were bound to someday wake up in your ideal home.

Faith in the American Dreamers was universal, from the president who relaxed the lending criteria at the government level, to the real estate agents who insisted on showing houses a hair above their clients' budgets, to the lenders who studied the Dreamers' bank statements, computed the numbers, and nonetheless funded their enormous home loans.

Who among the American Dreamers could have predicted that jobs would suddenly disappear, that thousands of their fellow homeowners would default on their loans at once, that construction projects would grind to a halt, investment firms would flounder, and credit would evaporate—all shrinking their odds of selling and, with any luck, just breaking even?

I never discovered which of our neighbors entrusted their future to the broker from Brandi's house. But a few months later, Brandi and her four generations of family moved out, their home repossessed by the bank. Neighbors began to vanish in the night. Some abandoned their house keys in the front door, hopeful this would deter debt collectors from tracking them to the ends of the earth.

The loss spread like a virus. I remember foreclosure placards mushrooming around Huffaker Park. In a vicious cycle, each vacancy and tax sale lowered the value of the house next door. If the neighbors could still afford their loans, they were now likelier to owe more on their houses than the houses were worth on paper. No bank would agree to refinance under such conditions. Buyers held off. Why put in an offer today when the house might be cheaper tomorrow?

My parents had done everything right. The house was overpriced, but their loan itself had been within their means. They were proud to be owners and cared for the house with love. The stenciling was scraped off and the carpet torn out. The first floor was childproofed so my mom could operate a small home daycare. We repainted the walls and planted tiger lilies outside. By the time I left for law school in August 2009, the house was prettier than ever. Nevertheless, outside forces had concluded it was now worth half the purchase price. Like many of their neighbors, my parents were facing a financial cliff. Being underwater meant paying for a house without building equity or security for the future. They might as well have rented and externalized maintenance costs on a landlord. But it wasn't as simple as leaving the keys in the door—unless they could work out a deal, their lender would count on getting repaid in full, no matter how little money a sale could bring in. The ideal home had turned into a financial nightmare that would haunt them for years.

*

THE GOVERNMENT CLAIMED to be on the case. The summer before my second year of law school started, Congress authorized $475 billion in bailout funds. The money flushed corporate giants like Chrysler and AIG with quick cash, but slowed to a trickle for homeowners, and people continued to lose their homes at alarming rates. A new federal statute, the Dodd-Frank Act, promised to reform the financial sector and created a new federal watchdog, the Consumer Financial Protection Bureau or CFPB. Professor Elizabeth Warren had left Harvard Law to erect this agency in DC.

Meanwhile, the Department of Justice and state attorneys general were making a big show of opening investigations. They were going to expose the root causes of the crisis. There was talk of potential criminal charges and fines assessed, and hope that people like my parents and their neighbors would be made whole. But where had this zeal been when bankers were running their industry like the Wild West? How had capitalism—purportedly the greatest economic system in the world—let down millions of American Dreamers?

At a law school house party one night, my friend Dan wondered: Had I considered working for the federal government? Given how much I cared about housing insecurity, HUD might be right up my alley. On top of administering the country's public housing stock and housing vouchers program, subsidizing affordable housing, and dispensing disaster relief, HUD also enforced antidiscrimination laws and prosecuted violations of its program rules. Had my mom and I moved to the United States earlier, HUD might have been responsible for putting a roof over our heads. Whatever had put the country in this big mess, my friend said, the department would have a role in undoing it. The mission drew me in immediately. Dan was right, this was where I needed to be.

↗

I GRADUATED LAW school in May 2012, feeling even more optimistic about the future than I had the summer my mom and I immigrated to England. After a decade of estrangement, I was in touch with my dad again. On the day of my law school graduation, my mom and Dave had surprised me with a flight to see my godparents, who were still close friends with my mom and lived eight minutes from Châtellerault. It was over this short trip that I had seen my dad. Mending our relationship would take time, but things were different. International phone calls and plane tickets to France were still costly, but HUD had offered me the job of my dreams in their DC headquarters. I could save up and come home more often. There I was, my own person, no longer married and no longer a child whose mother required her to check in with her every night. My decisions were all mine.

That summer, Gabi returned to Texas to study for the bar exam and prepare to clerk for a federal district judge, while I drove a U-Haul down from Somerville to the suburb of Arlington, Virginia. My destination was a house next door to a joint army-navy base and an immense cemetery where JFK was buried. By the time I arrived, Brian was settled into the large bedroom upstairs. The basement was taken by his friend, a military lawyer also named Vanessa, and her cheerful sandy Lab, Bruce Wayne. No one had fought me over the cheapest bedroom. It was the smallest but there was ample space for me.

I hardly believed my luck. Friends had warned me that finding affordable housing in the DC-Maryland-Virginia metropolitan area—"DMV" as people call it here—could be a nightmare. But this arrangement had landed on my lap. Our landlord, another law school friend of Brian's, was temporarily stationed with the US Marines in Japan, and didn't care to make a profit. Brian was here to clerk on the federal military court. We weren't close but had become friends after being placed in the same 1L section and participating in FedSoc.

I had seen Vanessa at parties and around school, but had not met her formally until Brian introduced us in the fog of commencement events that consumed our last week on campus. At six feet tall, with a thick mop of blond hair, Vanessa was impossible to miss. She had been a Division I athlete in her home state of New Mexico and could out-pushup almost every man in her life.

The three of us got along well, but Vanessa and I quickly became each other's favorites. She was earnest but not a scold, and never a culture snob, which allowed us to bond over awful TV shows. I was fascinated by her habit of rotating church denominations on Sunday mornings, just to hear what each had to say. She always went alone and without fanfare. To my bewilderment, her ritual wasn't compelled by a fervent commitment to God. If she did believe, it wasn't obvious to me despite the many hours we talked about the subject. Rather, she yearned to understand others. What wisdom they had to offer she welcomed, what didn't seem right to her, she left in their pews.

Though my relationship with God was on a permanent break, I appreciated her openness to others' spiritual philosophies.

We spent the month of July cloistered indoors, living and breathing our study manuals, as our respective state bar exams approached. When our brains started jumbling sentences together, we broke up the day in the kitchen. I stuffed my face with popcorn while imploring Vanessa to teach me criminal procedure—by far my worst subject and her best—in exchange for my tutelage on mortgages and property law—by far her worst subject and my best. I didn't need to ace the bar exam, I just needed to pass it, so that HUD would convert my status from temporary to permanent employee after a year.

ON MY FIRST day of work at HUD, in late August 2012, the coordinator, Dara, showed me to a windowless office that, until recently, had moonlighted as a closet. I was to share it with two colleagues in my class of junior lawyers. I became close friends with one of them, Jacy, a messy-haired brunette who rode a motorcycle and spoke French with an African accent despite being white, a result of her time in the Peace Corps in Benin. HUD had assigned us to separate divisions: Jacy to the group that enforced the Fair Housing Act, and me to the obliquely named Administrative Law division. But none of our supervisors had room for us on their floors.

That was always HUD, a behemoth of ironies. The brutalist headquarters, with its strange curvature, was an iconic feature of southwest DC. Only the architect had failed to account for the large number of bureaucrats who would eventually populate the building. Instead of bright and modern, its hallways were dark and poorly ventilated, earning it the epithet "ten floors of basement." Shortly before my class started, a ceiling collapse had prompted a wave of office relocations—in the building of the organization tasked with ensuring that public housing agencies maintained their units in habitable condition. Dara apologized for the grim welcome, but I didn't mind sharing a closet.

MY DAY-TO-DAY WORK in HUD's administrative law division was captivating, if somewhat remote from the agency's core mission. After Hurricane Sandy proved that northern metropoles wouldn't be spared by climate change, ambitious technocrats at the department decided to run a prestigious competition to gather ideas on building more resilient communities. I spent hours advising them on the confines of the law. Some days, a political appointee might reach out with a question about whether appropriation laws permitted her to redirect funds to a certain project, or about the possibility of serving as a temporary director in one of HUD's many divisions without Senate confirmation, and off I'd go, scurrying into the treatises. I enjoyed the variety and ambiguity of the work, the academic nature of it. It came to me naturally. Besides, whether the client took my advice or not, I could go home every night knowing I'd accomplished my primary job: covering the office's ass with a clear and concise memo.

But what I cared about most was the possibility of guaranteeing safe and affordable housing to all, and at times I strained to articulate a clear link between my work and HUD's responsibilities to the public. There had to be a kind of satisfaction, I imagined, in pointing to a tangible structure and being able to say one's labor had contributed to housing families in economic precarity. I craved that connection. From what I'd heard, the action was in the department's regional and field offices, which buzzed with the deals that turned the agency's lofty mission into reality. Each junior lawyer would have the chance to rotate through the department for a week, as part of our training year. I decided to ask Dara to let me spend part of the next summer where the deals were.

*

THE MILITARY GAVE Vanessa orders to deploy. It was the fall of 2012, just a few months into our young, but deep, friendship. We knew this was a distinct possibility from the beginning. Still, I was saddened that my friend and her sweet dog were leaving so soon. Brian, Vanessa, and I set out to find her replacement, combing through the incoming emails to spot contenders and eliminate red flags. We'd interviewed a quarter of our list when the Craigslist deities beamed Taryn down to us.

Minutes after she left our house, Vanessa and I pleaded with Brian to offer her the basement room. We'd liked her energy the moment she sat down. Taryn was a recovering journalist from Tucson, Arizona, by way of Seattle, Washington. She seemed kind and easygoing. I looked forward to annexing her as my friend. Outnumbered, Brian gave in. Vanessa shipped off to basic training and Taryn moved in with her little black cat Haruki.

Our hunch proved right. By the spring of 2013, it felt as though Taryn and I had been friends forever. Meanwhile, my relationship with Brian was disintegrating fast.

Brian might have been the most self-disciplined person I knew. I had a general sense of his habits at school, but seeing them on a daily basis cemented this realization. Brian went to bed early and rose at dawn so he could exercise before going into work. He was punctual and rarely ate out, or did anything in excess. It was possible that he had adopted this orderly lifestyle to make himself appealing to the navy, for which he aspired to work. Then again, being on the straight and narrow seemed in his nature. To my benefit and Taryn's, Brian's organizational skills extended to managing money. We relied on his convoluted spreadsheet to tally our expenses and credits. Without it, Taryn and I would probably shrug away our house purchases until one of us went bankrupt. Brian was, in that way, a decent friend and helpful roommate.

However, the rotting evidence that piled up in our kitchen sink after Brian's careful meal-planning, and the ring of grime that accumulated around our shared bathtub unless I intervened, suggested his stay-at-home mom had always picked up after him. The thought of doing the same for another adult revolted me, but I cleaned up after him anyway. My will to resist had been ground to dust at the sight of days-old pots of spaghetti, as I worried that gnats and ants would get to them first. I took turns scrubbing the bathtub with myself. After a few times, I would nudge Brian to take the next round. He would assure me that he would clean up. And I believed that he might, for in many ways he was highly reliable. But in the end, it was me, kneeling by the tub with yellow gloves and a bottle of bleach. I loathed to be perceived as a nag, but asked again. Brian would say *all right*. And *all right* would not materialize into action. We tried a chore rotation. But that, too, crumbled faster than one could say I-blame-your-Southern-upbringing-and-intact-two-parent-household.

What enraged me most about this banal conflict was Brian's comfort with our dynamic. The boys-will-be-boys audacity of it all. I tried to temper my feelings. Perhaps I was overreacting. Was it really his fault that I'd inherited my mother's compulsion for cleanliness? How could he have known? At the same time, could Brian not see that my anatomy made me no likelier to enjoy chores than him? No, it wasn't justifiable.

Anger bottled up inside of me until one afternoon, I shot him and Taryn a dry email from work: I was exiting our dysfunctional chore rotation. For my own sanity, I would clean my own dishes as quickly as I liked them done and let them handle the rest between themselves. (The bathroom was too much of a lost cause to warrant mention.) I knew Taryn would understand. She had seen the dishes and at least had a personal bathroom attached to her bedroom. I just hoped that Brian would get it, too. After all, he prided himself on being a principled libertarian. This was simply a firm display of individualism on my part. But in retrospect, the email was too curt, too nakedly upset. That night, Taryn watched quietly from the sofa as my conversation with Brian devolved into an argument.

I was breaking up the "house's community," he said. Not only was he deeply offended that I would refuse to clean his hypothetical future dishes, he was "hurt" by the decision.

I laughed in his face, nearly choking on his entitlement.

*

I BEGAN MY detail at the DC field office, near Union Station, the summer of 2013. I was eager and hopeful. The Obama years were a tremendously exciting time at HUD; one couldn't take a step without tripping over some public-private partnership. Bureaucrats on the public housing side were kept busy by a renewed commitment to addressing the multibillion-dollar backlog of maintenance costs that had allowed 1.2 million public housing units to fall into disrepair. HUD couldn't make Congress fund its public housing budget adequately, not even during that glorious two-year period when the Democrats held the House and Senate on top of the White House. And the department's hands were tied as far as building more units: the Faircloth Amendment, signed by President Bill Clinton, froze the number of federal public housing units at the number in existence on October 1, 1999. So the administration had turned to the private sector to raise the capital, launching programs like the Rental Assistance Demonstration pilot, which created provisions for privatizing public housing in hopes of offsetting the costs of maintenance.

To help stabilize the housing market after the crisis and encourage developers to take a chance on affordable housing, HUD was also investing millions of dollars in insurance for projects with a multifamily housing component. All over the country, fresh construction carried the agency's stamp of approval—a guarantee that if the developer defaulted on its loan, the government would pick up the bill.

What HUD's work looked like in practice, though, hit me with an icy splash of disappointment. Rather than taking the lead on many of these multifamily housing deals, HUD intervened on the back end. This gave it little say on the ultimate design and amenities, or even on the prices renters would have to pay. Contracts between the private actors and HUD were predrafted and mostly nonnegotiable. It was also unclear to me if a deal could be halted once the wheels were set in motion, even for good reason. As the summer went on, I felt a growing suspicion that the government's transactional lawyers were primarily paper pushers, cogs entrusted to check items off a list and babysit developers as they filled out forms. Did this even require a law degree? I doubted it.

I suppose the dullness of this work might have been bearable if the results had aligned perfectly with HUD's mission. But even this was questionable. One afternoon, fellow junior colleagues and I were taken on a tour of beautiful unfinished apartments in the Shaw neighborhood, affordable housing built with HUD subsidies. Upon seeing the rent chart, we realized that we ourselves couldn't have afforded to live in them.

It was impossible not to obsess about housing in DC. Rents were rising all over—but then again, the city had been suffering from engineered housing crises for a century and a half. DC was built on layers of displacement, speculation, and migration. As historians Chris Asch and George Musgrove have written, there would not have been a District of Columbia had English colonists not first spent a century decimating the native Nacostine tribe through "war, disease, and subjugation." Decades later, descendants of these colonists would reproduce the cycle, waging a different war on the local black population.[2]

DC's first white-only communities appeared during the 1890s, and by the turn of the century, the developer Francis Newlands was building Chevy Chase. The neighborhood's central draw was that no black Americans would have the right to buy or rent there—a guarantee the Chevy Chase Land Company was willing to enforce in court.

After the US Supreme Court declared "separate-but-equal" accommodations constitutional in 1896, in the landmark case *Plessy v. Ferguson*, more developers and landlords followed the lead of Chevy Chase. Restrictive covenants flourished. Suddenly, a third of DC's population found its free movement constrained. The proliferation of segregated housing fed an artificial shortage. That cycle of engineered housing crises would roll into the next century, as de jure covenants eventually gave way to displacement via "beautification" and "urban renewal."

By the time I arrived in DC, new and longtime DC residents were at the mercy of gentrification. A study by the National Community Reinvestment Coalition concluded that between 2000 and 2013, DC experienced the highest "intensity of gentrification" in the United States. Between 2009 and 2011, around 30,000 newcomers had moved in, a majority of them white.

I had noticed that national newspapers were reporting on older neighborhoods as if they were expeditionary finds, a habit that some residents derided as *Columbusing*. An overstory of cranes canopied the city, but never to seed additional public housing. President Obama's smiling face joined murals of Bill Cosby and Chuck Brown on the alley side of Ben's Chili Bowl, the iconic restaurant on U Street. A couple of blocks away, the first of seven Busboys and Poets restaurants—their tagline: "Inspiring Social Change"—offered vegan scrambles, live slam poetry, and reassurance that the neighborhood's vicious crack epidemic was firmly in the rearview mirror.

In the era of hope and change, no enclave seemed safe from the creep of gentrification. Last I'd heard, white people had even been spotted east of the Anacostia River, in the blackest and poorest part of DC.

*

HOW BIZARRE THAT the dishes always sprung to mind ahead of other catalysts for the end of my friendship with Brian. Maybe it had to do with the fact that during our worst arguments, we tended to physically drift toward the kitchen. That was where we were standing, one afternoon, when I mentioned in passing that a mutual friend of ours, a white woman, had once remarked that I was essentially "white on the inside." She'd said this without malice, and I wasn't upset with her at the time. The point I was making, in recounting that story, was only that the older I got, the less I found this kind of comment endearing.

While most of my law school classmates knew that I had grown up in France with a white dad and white grandparents, few other than Gabi knew the extent to which being a black dot in a white sea had messed with my self-esteem as a kid. I had to learn to appreciate my blackness, to see my skin for its worth rather than as comparable to whiteness. I did not explain this to Brian. Nor did I fault him for not guessing the roots of my sensitivity. But what I struggled to understand was why, in that moment, it was so important to him to defend the merits of the remark, or volunteer his definition of blackness to me, with all the sensitivity of a sheltered, libertarian white man from Tennessee. The more Brian doubled down, the more convinced he became by his own argument. It didn't seem to bother him that under his definition, I was no longer black. Or maybe that was the point.

We argued again in the wake of the murder of a young black woman named Renisha McBride. My then-boyfriend Alex and I had just returned home from a nice fall outing and were in high spirits that afternoon. We found Brian and Taryn chatting in the kitchen. The subject quickly turned to McBride, whose name was all over Facebook. She had gotten in a car wreck earlier that morning, November 13, 2013, and knocked on the door of a house on a residential street in a suburb of Detroit. The homeowner, a middle-aged white man, had answered with a shotgun in hand. He'd blasted it through the screen door, killing McBride instantly. I found this news deeply upsetting. Black America seemed to be passing through a season of death, starting with the killing of Trayvon Martin a few yards from the home where he was staying—though perhaps the season had begun much earlier and I was only now noticing. Either way, I was tired of being reminded, death after death, that lives like mine didn't matter.

The question at the forefront in our kitchen was whether, like Trayvon Martin's killer, the man who fatally shot McBride, should go unpunished. Under Michigan law, the homeowner could claim self-defense, but only if he *honestly and reasonably believed* that killing McBride was necessary to prevent his *imminent death, great bodily harm, or sexual assault*. My roommate considered the question a no-brainer. Of course the homeowner's fear was reasonable. I couldn't believe my ears. In no universe could an unarmed, injured nineteen-year-old woman begging for help embody such great danger. Unless, of course, her blackness counted as an aggravating factor.

I thought of myself, of how disheveled I could be, head-in-the-clouds enough to misplace my house keys and need to be let in during the middle of the night. I was not African American, but lived under blackness in this country. The distinction between me and McBride felt slim; I could have been her. In retrospect, the talk my uncle Noah gave me when I moved to Reno had been frank but gentle, a limited warning about the dangers of being black in American schools, and later in American workplaces. Belatedly, I finally understood that the warning extended to other parts of American life. We also had to work twice as hard to stay alive.

I remembered the firearm that Brian kept in his bedroom. I asked him. Would he have been that afraid—the *imminent death, great bodily harm, or sexual assault* kind of afraid—if it were me instead of McBride at the front door that morning?

And Brian answered: "Probably."

∮

SOON AFTER THAT fight I began scouring local apartment listings. At any given moment, that fall and winter of 2013, my browser was open to listings in the city and to the home decor website Apartment Therapy, which I'd discovered through Jacy. She shared my deep interest in how and where others lived. We had gotten into the habit of scrolling through endless listings and sending each other the best finds. Maybe in five years, I'd have enough saved to leave Arlington for my own apartment in DC. I admired the staged interiors, speculating about a future that I couldn't remember ever not chasing. Dream job. Perfect romance. Tightknit community. Didn't it all begin with the ideal home?

But DC didn't make the search easy. Luxury apartments went for luxury prices. Meanwhile, the cheaper housing stock was rife with code violations. Jacy lived in an art deco building up in Mount Pleasant, a weird little sublease fitted with a single sink so close to her bedroom that we refused to believe it was up to code. My boyfriend Alex lived just south of her, in a rent-controlled walkup near Malcolm X Park, in Columbia Heights. I had spent a lot of time there since we began dating in the fall, after meeting on a dating website. The rental was large and sunny but infested with a scurry of roaches. In the winter, the central heating puttered out, dropping indoor temperatures to the high fifties. Alex was a saint about it, rarely complaining. I admired his no-frills personality, which I found delightfully consistent with both his politics and appearance. He was a Marxist and a vegan, with wavy brown hair that brushed against the middle of his back. On occasion, strangers greeted him with, "Hey, Jesus!"

I was much less of a good sport about the cold. A quirk made me feel it more acutely on one side of my body. The discomfort made me irritable. But for the babies on the lower floors, the temperatures were life-threatening. Tenants told the supers, the supers told the landlords, and the landlords shrugged off the complaints. A critical mass of the tenants in Jacy's and Alex's buildings were undocumented immigrants from Central America, so the landlords didn't *have* to care. Where else would they all go, the shiny buildings rising on Fourteenth Street?

The sales market was just as strained. Every week, it seemed, another affordable unit vanished from the real estate listings. *Under Contract. Sale Pending. Sold.* In Petworth, the average raw profit on house flips reached $312,400 in 2013, which had earned Petworth the crown for "best neighborhood in the country to flip" that year. A condo would sell, and the following week, a near-identical replacement would appear. Two streets down, same square footage, same appliances. Only for $10,000 more. *Under Contract. Sale Pending. Sold.*

WE WERE EATING lunch in the HUD cafeteria one day when Jacy told me about a city-administered program that sounded interesting. She, too, was looking for new living arrangements. The one-sink apartment, it turned out, was an illegal sublease—a fact that she'd recently discovered by way of an eviction notice.

The premise of the program was simple. City government would put down up to 3 percent of a home price for any household that made less than $126,000 a year and for any property within the DC limits. In exchange, the home-buyer would commit to staying five years. A carrot to retain a yuppie tax base that often decamped for cheaper pastures after a few years.

Though this sounded too good to be true, and though I hadn't lived in a single place for that long since kindergarten, and though my savings were modest, a roach-free apartment for one seemed like a real possibility. Our first raise from HUD, to $75,000, was coming soon. I'd been frugal, saving up $7,000 in my first year. A pittance in the grand scheme of things, but for me this represented my very own safety net. The prospect of handing it over to a real estate agent was harrowing. Still, I began squirreling away money even more diligently and kept my browser tabs open to units for sale.

I told myself that I was just looking, even as I returned to the online listing I'd seen for a condo in Petworth—a charming one-bedroom for sale near Grant Circle. I'd barely visited the neighborhood, but remembered how many of the faces at the Georgia Avenue metro station resembled mine. I'd had the feeling of melting seamlessly into its pot. Something like home.

I was taken by the images of the condo despite their clumsy staging: the imposing armchairs, the awkwardly sized dining table, and the eggshell color that shriveled the walls. If it were up to me, there'd be an antique credenza in the living room, contrasted against a metallic bookshelf. The pendant lights in the kitchen would be swapped out for something more modern. And I'd put in a loveseat with clean lines in a fashionable neutral. Each of my virtual visits to the listing brought a fresh coat of paint: charcoal gray, forest green, a moody navy.

I expected the condo to disappear. This city teemed with people who were wealthier than me, with parents and grandparents whose own lucrative housing investments now allowed them to conjure large sums of money into their children's bank accounts for adorable condos like this one. I deemed it foolish to get my hopes up.

Oddly, though, the condo sat on the market through Christmas. New Year's Day of 2014 came and went, with the condo still available. Reading this lingering as a sign, I made an appointment to go see it.

Though I wasn't aware of it on the day of my visit, this corner of this neighborhood, and the garden-style building itself, were testaments to the city's cycle of crises. The Petworth of the 1920s and '30s had been idyllic. Residents were proud to call it home and participate in civic life. Describing the locals' fierce loyalty in 1939, the *Washington Post* wrote, "their Home and School Association, their churches, and numerous other groups are geared for trigger action when the 'threat of invasion' is breathed . . . No Washington section has more community consciousness, nor works harder to keep it. Petworth is distinctively Petworth."[3]

Perhaps it goes without saying that "distinctively Petworth" meant proudly segregated. Residents leaned on institutional support to maintain this ideal. The Washington Real Estate Board refused to sell homes to black families in segregated areas, and barred real estate agents who bucked the rule. This regime only began to crumble with *Shelley v. Kraemer*, one of the budding civil rights movement's first victories in the Supreme Court. As of 1948, it was unconstitutional for states to enforce restrictive covenants.

Two years later, a black DC postal worker named Samuel Harris bought one of the row houses on Grant Circle. Where white neighbors would once have pooled their resources and sued Harris out of the purchase, now the community settled for harassment and threats. This didn't deter Harris's sister, Jane Harris, and her husband from settling next door to Harris in 1951. A third black family, the Lewises, moved in down the street.

As middle-class black Americans bought property once forbidden to them, a white panic seized the city. Sensing opportunity, real estate agents urged white homeowners to sell fast, all the while flipping their homes back to black buyers at inflated costs. Meanwhile, the Federal Housing Administration—a HUD predecessor—signaled its support of the ring of white suburbia quickly forming around DC with home loan subsidies for those who were fleeing the city. Twenty years after Harris's arrival on Grant Circle, the city had gone from 65 percent white to 70 percent black. Local radio DJs started calling it Chocolate City.

The condo building that I wanted to see was charming now, but for a long time had been an eyesore and a symbol of those troubled days. Code violations had haunted it for years. The elderly owners, Rufus and Delores Stancil, had entered the landlord business in the years following DC's spending spree to revitalize Columbia Heights and other areas underserved by the city. Officials hoped that improving local amenities would entice investment and reverse the white flight. With the opportunity to sell high imminent, in the 1970s, landlords began to evict tenants at jarring rates. Thousands of former rentals sat empty, awaiting developers who would rehabilitate them before selling them, usually to well-off white professionals. The city's rates of displacement and homelessness soared.

Tenants and local organizers pushed back through creative direct actions like rent strikes, squatting, lobbying to transfer properties into land trusts, and even hunger strikes. The movement eventually won tenant protections codified in the law and, in 1978, the passage of the Speculator's Bill, a tax aimed at curbing the ravages of gentrification.

While discussing the anti-speculation tax in a 1975 hearing, the DC council member and future mayor Marion Barry asked: "How do you stop the
speculator without also stopping the bona fide builder or restorer who provides
decent and sound housing at justifiable prices?"[4] The speculators bought low
and sold high, without having changed so much as a lightbulb. Slumlords like
the Stancils thrived on scarcity. But developers were supposed to be different.
Developers were the city council's hope for restoring DC to her integrated
glory, elevating her as a beacon of economic prosperity—a hope for America's
white-deserted cities. But in the end, they found enough common ground with
the speculators to rally against the anti-speculation tax, to ensure that the final
bill was first defanged and then, three years later, taken off the books entirely.

The Stancils eventually lost the Petworth building in a tax sale in the fall
of 2011, opening the door for a developer to gut the property and start over.
Kitchen islands made of silvery-white stone. Wood floors and cabinets stained
in dark mahogany. Long windows along the street-side wall. Sparkling bathroom tiles and tubs. White walls for a fresh start.

*   ⁂

I COULD SEE my breath as I got out at the Georgia Avenue–Petworth Metro
station. By midday, the sidewalk was mostly free of snow, but pools of water
had frozen overnight and left behind coins of treacherously clear ice. I headed
in the direction of Grant Circle. The real estate agent, Katie, parked near the
front entrance and let us into the building. I looked around the quiet lobby,
spotted the mailbox for the unit that had captured my desire. The building
was not yet fully occupied, Katie explained.

The condo was even more beautiful in person. At six hundred and ten
square feet, it was tiny but smartly laid out, and so it felt spacious and airy. I
left the tour exhilarated. My browsing checklist had never been onerous. The
neighborhood had to be walkable and enjoy decent public transportation. I
needed to feel safe, and so refused to be surrounded by affluence or neighbors
frightened by my skin color. A majority-white neighborhood was out of the
question. To me, the best communities were diverse. They were committed to
welcoming new faces without forcibly displacing long-term residents. I saw this
potential in Petworth.

The ideal home would be, above all, a place that I never dreaded returning
to. I hoped for an apartment with the bones to become beautiful at a price that

wouldn't jeopardize my first foray into financial stability. The cheapest unit in the building was priced at $280,000, while the third-floor condos hovered around $400,000. The one I cared to see was listed for $310,000, close to what my parents had paid for the Huffaker Park house, only for a third of the space and no yard. The city's down payment assistance would lessen the risk of financial ruin. Still, teenage me would've laughed.

On the day of the signing, I took the morning off and met Katie at the condo again. By then, I'd attended a mandated class for first-time homeowners and gathered a truckload of paperwork to convince the lender that I could be trusted to make mortgage payments despite the $125,000 in student loans looming over my credit report. I had spent hours on the phone pleading with the clothing store Old Navy and its third-party debt collector to remove a phantom debt from my report—the bill had never been sent to me for payment—with no success, until a last-ditch effort in the form of a complaint to the Consumer Financial Protection Bureau resolved the issue. With the phantom debt finally off my credit report, the bank approved the home loan.

My parents sounded moderately excited on the phone. This was a big debt, the biggest I had ever taken on. Was I sure about this? How small was this place again? I tried to reassure them. The condo was a steal, relative to other offerings in the DMV. My estimated mortgage payment would be around the equivalent of a luxury rental in the city. I was prepared for the cost to feel heavy at first, but this would be temporary. HUD compensated its attorneys on a lockstep system, so my salary was set to increase with each coming year, easing my mortgage burden. Nothing was guaranteed, but these conditions made me confident in my decision.

I took the home inspector's word that the water heater was functional and wired two-thirds of my savings to the developer before committing five years of my life to DC, unlocking the free money offered by the Open Doors program.

And so, this was it. My own piece of the American Dream. I paced the condo, taking in its smells, its eggshell walls, the soft light beaming through the bedroom window. Six hundred and ten square feet of possibility, though with the staging furniture gone, the condo felt larger. I'd have to fill it from scratch. Besides a mattress and an IKEA sofa past its prime—both relics of my failed marriage—my belongings were few.

We waited for the developer's attorney to show up. "She's from Petworth, you know," Katie said, as if to reassure me about my choices. The attorney, a black woman in a smart suit, arrived with a stack of legal documents. I signed and initialed without dwelling on the fine print. This deal was too far along for me to change my mind, and anyhow, the terms of the contract were nonnegotiable. This was what I wanted, wasn't it? Katie handed me the keys with a proud, motherly smile: "Congratulations! You did it!"

I took the train from my condo to the HUD building. *My* condo. I didn't know what to feel. Some of my law school friends had made big announcements on occasions like these. They posted photos of the keys on Facebook and posed by their new front doors on Instagram. Our mutual friends would validate them with hundreds of likes and comments, cheering them on for claiming their piece of the pie. But I couldn't do it. Once at the HUD building, I told no one about my morning, save for my parents, Jacy, and Alex.

The truth was, I was afraid. Afraid of having drained my self-made safety net into an impulsive purchase. Of becoming attached to a place that could be taken from me with one bad surprise. Of jinxing my luck with open joy.

My anxieties were not unfounded. I was, for the first time in my life, squarely in the middle class. A public-servant salary had granted me the financial independence my parents had dreamed of for me. But this stability hinged on my wages; it was ephemeral. Months earlier, my roommate's girlfriend, also a lawyer, had been walking down the street when a car swerved into the sidewalk and struck her. She'd survived the freak accident but suffered the aftereffects of a severe concussion, at times struggling to work. Had this happened to me, I wasn't certain that HUD would've kept me on after my fourteen-month trial period.

Then there were the furloughs. In October 2013, a budget impasse between Democrats and Republicans had shut down HUD and other parts of the federal government for sixteen days. At the time, none of us knew whether we'd be paid back for our involuntary vacation. A longer shutdown might cause me to fall behind on my mortgage. I had no plan B. No secret trust fund to bail me out and no more savings to rescue my family. Being a junior lawyer made me disposable. Last hired, first fired. This home was one more thing to lose, on top of my health insurance.

For my parents, the so-called achievement that was homeownership had generated money worries, and dozens of sleepless nights. I'd seen it break up other families—people lost everything in a matter of months. The financial collapse spared few, and from 2007 to 2010, the median net worth of American families had dropped by 40 percent. But of course, black and Latino households had not entered the recession on equal footing with their white counterparts: their median home equity had been lower, their incomes and savings smaller, their prospects for a substantial inheritance less likely.

By the end of the Great Recession, in 2009, the share of black American households that were worth zero dollars or less was greater than that of any other population, though Hispanics were close behind. The recovery had been just as uneven, with higher foreclosure rates falling along predictable lines. White and Hispanic households would eventually see a rebound in rates of homeownership, which remains the primary mode of building and rebuilding wealth in this country. But the number of black homeowners would keep plummeting from its 2004 high.

For all the noise that the Justice Department had made while I was in law school, few heads had rolled in the wake of the crisis. Those who had been at the helm of the ship either were still there or had received bonuses for being fired. Government officials had admitted to letting foreclosures go on unabated to soften the hit on the banks' bottom line. The banks had grown even bigger than they were before the financial crisis. This was the American Dream, then: a predatory marketing ploy. In what world, I wondered, was playing along, even with my eyes wide open, worthy of congratulations?

Still, I allowed myself to feel a pinch of contentment. Jacy biked over and spent a Sunday helping me cover the living room walls in *charcoal* and *repose gray*. When the drab eggshell was all painted over, I stepped back and admired our handiwork. Even if this apartment slipped through my fingers, I thought, no one could ever take from me the happiness of having made it truly mine for a moment.

⫯

THE CONDO BUILDING wasn't quite fully occupied at the time of my arrival. Erin, the midwestern redhead on the second floor, had been there longer than most. We usually ran into each other at the mailboxes and chatted while sorting through packages. I liked her. She seemed well-meaning, if a little high-strung, which the crime reports for Petworth didn't help. Our conversations often ended with her dispensing safety tips. Women living alone had to look out for each other. After one of these conversations, she'd forwarded me advice from her friend. Ex-military, she said. The email read: *Find out about the neighborhood watch. Install some security film on the windows. A dead bolt on the bedroom door. A home security system. Bear spray (link attached—"haha!"). Get to know your neighbors. Contact the city if it's dark on the street-facing side. And no bushes covering the windows.*

Dave had mailed me a pepper-spray dispenser while I was in law school. I figured it must've been somewhere in the apartment, congealed in its rigid plastic seal. I kept forgetting to search for it. But did I really need to? Had I missed something fundamental about Petworth? Sure, there was the occasional stabbing, and sure, a handful of houses were known for drug-dealing activity, but none of this called for panic. Our corner was largely serene. On Sundays, the sound of bells emanated from the two churches on Eighth Street and Grant Circle and floated all the way to my windows. Domku, an Eastern European restaurant and a staple of Upshur Street, let me hole up in their window with Norwegian pancakes and magazines for hours. The neighborhood was expanding, too. An upscale restaurant had recently opened across from the small indie bookstore. A yoga studio was on its way.

The condo building filled up soon after I arrived. Newlyweds moved into the unit above mine. A senate staffer and his husband bought on the third floor. My hallway welcomed a thickset brunette named Sheila in the corner unit, a warm Brazilian couple at the other end, and a consultant across from my door. If this place was really so dangerous, would yuppies have descended on Petworth in such droves?

With all my meager savings in the condo, I was too broke to invest in Erin's security measures anyway. A quality roll of the bulletproof film alone cost $300! No, I thought. Better to do what I had always done. No headphones at night. Always walk away from the gunshots. Kindly acknowledge the recurring faces of Petworth: the dazed teen who liked to show off his albino python, the cheerful drunks who idled by the post office, the rowdy teens by the metro station. On my way to work, I waved at the West Indian grandmother who oversaw our street from her porch until nighttime. She and the two or three generations of children who shared her townhouse were our closest neighbors on my side of the building. Like the others, she always waved back.

I thought of her on the day one of the other condo owners in my building emailed the building listserv to celebrate the news that, for what appeared to be the first time in Petworth history, a single-family home in the neighborhood had crossed the million-dollar threshold. It was near enough to us to raise the value of our building. In the short term, our property taxes would go up, but we'd come out ahead. The more yuppies were willing to pay per square foot, the more owners on our block would be able to seek in a later sale. Our condos would be worth more than the year before, without us changing a single lightbulb.

In theory, this dynamic could benefit the West Indian grandmother and her household, too. If she or her heirs ever sold, they were sure to get more for the property than she'd paid. But how this would shake out for them depended on a number of factors, with several opportunities for bad surprises.

If the grandmother left no will behind—an issue more common among black American families than white families—then the property would be passed down to her children in equal parts. The children could sell, assuming the house was paid off or close to it and assuming they could all agree on doing so. After taxes, though, individual shares would be unlikely to afford each heir a home the size of the grandmother's property and certainly not in any location as convenient as Petworth.

Alternatively, they could hold on to the house, but this would mean maintenance costs and property taxes that would gradually rise with the value of surrounding homes. If they fell behind on payments, they'd risk losing the house to the city, just as the Stancils had lost my condo building. The city would auction it off to recoup its taxes, at a fraction of what a standard sale would've given the heirs. A developer would inevitably win the bid, break the house up into two or three condos, and list it on the market at a price none of the heirs could afford. Then, they'd take the proceeds and invest them in the next project. Buy low. Sell high. Repeat.

The ugly truth was that my neighbors and I personally stood to benefit no matter the outcome for the West Indian family next door. As one drafter of the anti-speculation tax had put it, "although renovators and rehabilitators play the same role as the speculator in moving low- and moderate-income families out of their homes and neighborhoods, they do provide some benefits to the District through improvement of the housing stock."[5] This was true only in the narrowest sense. The "district" in that sentence represented a small group of winners: the city's tax-funded budget, the developers, the residents who could afford to stay after the improvements and new amenities, and, last but not least, those of us who owned near the improvements.

My home was a commodity with a life of its own. It operated within DC's cycle of displacement, increasing in value without much input from me, and regardless of my politics or morals. My income, which in my third year at HUD would approach six figures, made me an economic gentrifier. It had allowed me to pay an absurd amount for 610 square feet. And my willingness to do so reinforced the system by validating the real estate industry's gamble that others in my tax bracket, or higher, would happily overpay for comfort. The next round of comparable condos would sell for even more money, fattening my own equity in the process.

In thinking about all this, I tended to dabble in hypotheticals, as if my purchase hadn't already ensured that my predecessor in this apartment, the poor soul who had paid years of rent to the Stancils, could never return. Asch and Musgrove write in their history of DC that by 1790, "the Nacostines were long gone . . . so much so, in fact, that when Thomas Jefferson inquired about the name of the Native Americans who lived along the Eastern Branch, no one could remember." More than any crime alerts, I feared the day someone would describe a Petworth born of a hundred years of gentrification, one where no one could remember its lost black residents.

The system had made accomplices of all who now lived in my building. But still, there was a fundamental difference between Erin or the senate staffer and me. I was reminded of it every time my real estate agent emailed me automated estimates of my condo's resale value. Watching the number creep up, I understood that the reason this was happening—at this speed, without my having to lift a finger—had everything to do with the demographics of the building. Despite institutional efforts to undo Jim Crow, studies consistently showed that the blackness of a neighborhood sank property values. A critical mass of white newcomers had settled in Petworth, and a critical mass of black residents had been priced out. I was part of a tender equilibrium. My neighbors' returns, and my own, depended on there not being too many of me.

As months, then years passed, I began to know my fellow condo owners through the building listserv. I learned that they hated the music that drifted from the West Indian house on the weekends, and were irked by the voices on their porch. The laughter of black children playing late into the humid summer nights bothered them, as did the sight of black men congregating in any number. As of late, some had taken to signing off emails with *Stay safe!* as if our street was war-torn Libya. I thought it possible that, since I rarely chimed in, most of my neighbors had forgotten that a black woman was on the building listserv.

Why did they choose this street, I often wondered, if its liveliness, which preceded our arrival, was anathema to them? I asked myself this again when, in yet another dispatch about the West Indian house, the senate staffer wrote to us, *I've called the police many times over the years and nothing changes . . . I've never tried to talk to them myself as I've found them to be extremely unfriendly.*

Maybe the staffer saw these calls as his last resort. Because the house belonged to the grandmother, there was no boss to complain to, no landlord to rat her out to, no building manager to dispense a stern warning on his behalf. The staffer was too cowardly to address the neighbors in person—rightfully embarrassed, I hope, by the pettiness of his complaints—and so he deployed the state to resolve what was, at worst, a matter of neighborly consideration. But what did he think would happen if he called enough times? Some of the younger adults in the house would be sent to jail? The children would be removed from their family? Or perhaps he hoped the police calls would eventually intimidate the West Indian house into silence. After all, a quieter neighborhood made for higher property values.

Whether the Metropolitan Police Department recognized it or not, protecting these buildings, along with the delicate, fast-growing tax base inside them, was now one of its core duties. The arrival of the moneyed newcomers between 2000 and 2013 coincided with a $157 million increase in MPD's budget. By 2017, the budget had swollen by another $92.6 million, easily gliding past the half-billion mark. That money came with expectations, or at minimum an expectation that the department bring down the district's already declining crime rate even further. DC's history should have foreshadowed that MPD would do this at the expense of some over others. After analyzing police records from 2013 to 2017, the ACLU identified concerning disparities in the force's enforcement. Black people made up less than half the city's population in that period, but 86 percent of all arrests—an imbalance that held even in predominantly white neighborhoods. Of course, the police department was responsible for its own strategy, but calls to 911 were instrumental in directing its attention to particular neighborhoods and particular residents. Given a reason to look, the police could always find crime.

Reading his emails to the listserv, I felt as if the floor between the staffer's condo and mine put us on different planets. In his world, the police were rational problem solvers. They showed up well equipped and willing to defuse tensions. In mine, they were trigger-happy, prone to reacting brashly and later lying in their reports. Even those officers who looked like me—DC boasted one of the most diverse police forces in the country—seemed to think black people were made of different stuff, that they felt less pain than others did. Each routine stop or wellness check, each petty neighbor complaint, had the potential to end a black life. If this had ever been a mystery to the staffer, he should've known better by March 2018. The Black Lives Matter movement was, by then, four years old, and countless news reports had proved me right. Did the staffer simply not care? Was his vision of the ideal home, of the ideal Petworth, so superior that it warranted sacrificing just about anyone?

In a strange way, I understood where he was coming from. The relief at having found an ideal home. The desire to hold on to it. To stake a claim against anyone whose claim might encroach on his. We lived alongside others but each carried our own image of the right community and varying commitments to making that image into reality. In the background were industries and governments that built and razed, opened and shut doors, and redrew the borders of our loyalties along the way. So much of our lives were shaped by the ensuing collisions. Still, we had agency in how we weathered them.

One day, after my neighbors spent the better part of an afternoon speculating about the source of recent gunshots, I reached the end of my rope. In what became a particularly nasty, reply-all type of listserv fight, I asked the staffer to let me know if he wanted tips on how to live his life without harassing our next-door neighbors. Erin piped in to say that *she* didn't think the staffer was being racist. The aftermath was awkward. The newlyweds above my unit either pointedly stopped acknowledging me when we passed each other on the street or simply abandoned any effort to differentiate me from other black faces around the neighborhood. Sheila from the corner unit would later reassure me that, for her part, she didn't see color—an admission I found more chilling than she intended. As for the staffer and me, we never acknowledged each other's presence again. Erin remained pleasant as a sunflower, impervious to the damage caused by her comment.

With the knowledge that some in my building now resented me, I grasped for the first time the strength of my position as an owner with a title equal to my neighbors'. That day, I'd staked a claim on behalf of the West Indian house and other black Petworthians, myself included. There was nothing my neighbors could do to force me out. There was no manager, no landlord, not even a police officer they could call on to punish my bluntness. I was as free as they were. Unless they wanted to suffer another public shaming, it was on them to accommodate my intolerance for their racist speculations. I expected them to try with the same zeal they showed in demanding our block accommodate their preferences. I didn't regret my outburst. If living alongside black people was so antithetical to their vision of the ideal home, they could leave.

And most of them did, in time. I doubt that it was my doing, as flattering as that would be. This is DC; turnover will always be high. The staffer and his husband bought a house north of our building. One of the two churches on Eighth Street relocated to Maryland, where most of its black congregation had already migrated, and sold its building to a developer who tore down the church's dark brick and colorful windows, replacing it with high-end condos. The newlyweds left with a baby. Domku, the popular restaurant, closed after a decade in Petworth—the landlord raised its rent by 66 percent and wouldn't budge. Sheila moved out of the corner unit, to a Maryland suburb with "good schools" for her infant daughter. Brian never made it to the navy and instead relocated to New York City, where he became a prosecutor. Jacy would leave for the Bay Area to be near family. But some stayed. Like Taryn, who moved to DC with the man she would eventually marry. Or my ex-boyfriend Alex, who still lived in the sunny walk-up years later. It had been free of roaches ever since a developer acquired the building, bought out as many tenants as it could, and converted the formerly rent-controlled units into market-priced apartments. (Alex helped organize a tenant association and was one of the few to hold out.)

I still hope the grandmother in the house next door outlasts us all. And maybe she will. Years after my arrival, you could still find her sitting on her porch, watching us come and go.

Don't Know What You've Got 'Til It's . . .

<small>HOME, NOUN. (CONT.)</small>
12 a: a body

MY FRIEND DVORA AND I are sitting at a table at an outdoor restaurant in Brooklyn one summer evening in 2017, when I notice the woman a few feet away. She is slender and tall, with impenetrable black skin. Her hair is cropped, almost to the scalp. I watch her glide into the restaurant with two men trailing her. Dvora slips a crumb to her beagle mix, Lizzie, and carries on chatting. She has not noticed her, but the woman is all I can think about. I cannot put my finger on why, but the sight of her awakens a melancholy, a sense that we have met, or perhaps that I have seen her before. But how? I do not have many friends in New York and cannot place her in my Reno life. Nor is she a law school acquaintance. I would remember.

I excuse myself from the table under the pretense of getting us wine. The woman is at the small bar inside, engaged in a lively conversation with two men. I search my brain while the bartender ignores me.

Finally: an epiphany.

Alek Wek.

This is who the stranger reminds me of.

ONE OF MY favorite music videos of all time, "Got 'Til It's Gone," opens with a pan over black men and women in oversize collars and modest dresses. The beat drops as the camera enters a house party. The year is 1997, but the sign on the wall reads EUROPEANS ONLY / *SLEGS BLANKES*, evoking apartheid South Africa. Janet Jackson snaps her fingers with gusto. She has gathered her hair in pigtails that defy gravity. This is her thick, curly, unapologetically red phase. As Jackson croons onstage, the dance floor comes alive with motion. It is an ode to blackness in sepia, with the full spectrum of undertones represented, midnight blue to albino paleness. The rapper Q-Tip is black, so is the waiter carrying drinks, so are the children holding each other in the dim light. They take each other's portraits and bathe in the open. As if ignited by the notes, they jump and clap and stomp and slow dance. Safe from the white gaze, the people move with abandon and tenderness. This room is made for them; it is free.

As the video draws to an end, Alek Wek appears—her head bald and skin a ripe black. The yellow stereoscope she holds covers most of her face. Inside her lens, a man stands tall, chest puffed with pride. She lowers the stereoscope, recasting herself from observer to observed. A serene smile illuminates her face.

I was nine the first time Jackson's video appeared on a grainy TV screen in our apartment in the Duchère. The anomaly of Wek's presence startled me. French culture of the 1990s rarely showcased black girls, the darkest ones most rarely of all. Despite the thousands of African immigrants who lived in our housing project, and the millions more outside it, media titans had conferred and concluded that black faces were unrelatable to the only audience that mattered, and unrelatability didn't sell. But we featured well as objects of pity. Yellow-eyed and joyless. Bellies distended by hunger. Flies hovering over little buzzed heads. A white man would peer into the camera with an impassioned plea: *For ten francs a month, be a hero and bring clean water to this African child!*

Visibility otherwise demanded a certain exceptionalism. You had to be American, like the cool kid who played Rudy Huxtable on *The Cosby Show*, or be an out-of-this-world athlete, like the figure skater Surya Bonaly. Girls my complexion didn't model in clothing *catalogues* or grow up to present the evening news. Nor were we written into fairy tales. To play princesses as little children, we suspended more reality than our white friends. Brooms morphed into horses and rugs into flying carpets. But our skin also became white, our noses narrow, our hair silky.

Wek was nowhere and suddenly everywhere. A modeling scout had noticed her walking around a street fair in London, five years after she emigrated from South Sudan at fourteen. By the end of 1997, Wek had walked runway shows for Chanel, Jean Paul Gaultier, Donna Karan, Ralph Lauren, Isaac Mizrahi, and Alexander McQueen. She'd also become the first African woman to appear on the cover of *Elle* magazine. Her face graced the pages of glossy magazines in the grocery store and on newspaper stands. I admired the way color vibrated against her skin, the way it declined to blend and self-erase. Her ethereal hue was a worthy canvas.

I found her sudden omnipresence surreal. Here was an Indigenous African woman front-and-center on newsstands. This, even though her ethnicity lacked ambiguity. This, even though there was no soft wave to her hair, no unusual tint to her eyes. Wek was blacker than me at the height of summer. Most of the time, she had no hair! Yet, authorities on the matter of beauty had designated her an icon. Until Wek, the possibility had been inconceivable to me.

*

BACK WHEN MY parents were still married, in Châtellerault, we lived in a rent-controlled building in the Plaine d'Ozon. The neighborhood was young, erected in the '60s to accommodate an influx of migrants from the former French colonies and protectorates. Over time, it had become the most diverse part of town. And the poorest, as its early residents and later their children faced chronic underemployment and discrimination. Our neighbors were asked to assimilate—to abandon their Arabic and African dialects in public spaces, lest they attract the ire of their new compatriots. They were to demand less help yet not be so presumptuous as to expect equal citizenship, and with it, paying work to feed their families. They were to submit to the superior culture without question, as when, in 1994, the minister of education banned what he called "ostentatious" religious symbols from public schools, though his primary target was Muslim girls who wore the headscarf. "The will of our people was to build a united, secular society," the minister had said of the ban. "The national will cannot be ignored."[6] Our neighbors were reminded of this while walking the underpasses spray-painted with *France for the French*. Welcomes had their limits. For people like them, for people like my mom and me, there had to be a *back home*. A safe harbor where no one could claim they didn't belong.

The scope of the segregation was near impossible to measure. The French legislature had ensured that when it prohibited the collection of ethnic demographical information, a "colorblind" law that made it punishable by a five-year prison term and €300,000 fine. But I had a sense, from being gawked at and prodded in public spaces. Outside the Plaine d'Ozon, the looks I drew varied from the curious, when accompanied by my white dad, to the suspicious, as I entered stores holding my mom's black hand.

I was in the checkout line at our local grocery store with her when I saw a girl no older than me, three years old or so, glaring at me from her mother's shopping cart. She sustained eye contact until she had gathered the courage to ask her burning question.

Why are you black?

At a loss for an explanation, I asked: *And you, why are you white?*

The girl didn't have an answer either so it ended there, with her mom pushing her cart onward, seemingly amused, her day undisturbed. But my own mother had seethed all the way back to our little apartment. How audacious, how impolite, of this child to harass strangers. I didn't owe her an explanation for my existence. I didn't owe her anything!

In my mom's retellings of the faceoff, and there would be many over the years, I was a brave and gutsy girl. The administrator of a knockout. I'd stood up for myself and made clear that I belonged. But this was not how I remembered it. Feet dangling from the cart, I wondered in earnest. Why was this girl white and not me? Why did *she* get to be normal?

When our schoolteachers asked where we were from, freckled children with last names like *Dupont* and *Marcel* were allowed to say: Châtellerault. But the rest of us were trained to hear the question within the question. Olive-skinned classmates, almost certainly born within a ten-mile radius, answered with Morocco or Algeria. I'd say that I was from Cameroon despite having left before forming any memories.

No one had instructed us to do it. Or maybe they had, all those times when the question was repeated with gusto—where were we *really* from?—until we kids internalized the echelons of citizenship. Our parents' *back home* was ours, too. We were too young to sense the precise outlines of our otherness, but understood whiteness as the reference against which to measure ourselves. Some bodies were simply more normal than others, born to relate rather than be related with.

*

YET, TO ME, blackness remained an alien feeling. I was four years old on my first vacation to Cameroon, the summer of '92. The night my mom and I touched down, several little cousins materialized at my Mamie Catherine's door in Ngousso, eager to coax me outside. Yaoundé was unfamiliar territory. I felt timid and a bit afraid. This city looked nothing like Châtellerault. A coat of dust tinted its surfaces a ferrous red, from the walls of houses to the overloaded yellow taxis to the children's scrawny legs. Coarse vegetation wrestled out of the concrete and asphalt as if to reclaim its rightful ground.

Darkness blanketed the courtyard. Having read *The Jungle Book* dozens of times, I worried about panthers and snakes lurking in the shadows. Still, I dragged myself outside. My newfound friends and I played for a long time, sharing old games and inventing new ones together, pausing intermittently to giggle at each other's accents. I spoke like the cartoon characters in the French imports; and they like a magnified version of the voice my mom put on during calls to *back home.* Calls to here. After a while, I ran inside and announced: *Maman, they're all black!*

Truth was, I felt white. Châtellerault was mostly white. So were my dad and grandparents. I saw their faces more than I saw mine. We thought alike. The French countryside of their childhood was the countryside of my own. I was more like them and the girl from the checkout line than like my Cameroonian cousins.

Or at least, I felt that I was. I wanted to be. Sometimes, it occurred to me that there was nothing I wouldn't do for the black to wash off me as it had from Michael Jackson.

At night, I bargained with God. If He let me wake up white, I'd never lie again. If He let me wake up white, I'd tidy up my room without being asked. If He let me wake up white, it'd be easier to be good. In the morning, I woke up to find my skin an obstinate brown. Dark as mud; dark as dirt.

More than anything, though, it was my hair that I resented. Maybe because, unlike my skin color, my hair could achieve whiteness without divine intervention. In its virgin state, my wild Afro pushed outward and sprouted knots within seconds of being detangled, prompting a fresh grimace with each pass of the comb. It turned wiry in dry heat and shrunk like cheap cotton if kissed by a single droplet of water. It was voluminous and dense. Dozens of African women had stood over my head and sucked their teeth while roughing up the thickness with their fingers. I wriggled in pain in their halogen-lit kitchens while they yanked and pulled and jerked my hair, as if its nature was a personal affront. The women huffed. *Mmm. Hard hair. Bad hair.* And I believed them. When the day was done, the braids were so tight that it hurt to blink. Individual strands would pop off at my hairline, exposing the root's minuscule white bulb. No use in moaning, however. *Il faut souffrir pour être belle*, the women liked to say. You have to suffer to be beautiful.

I felt prettiest—at my whitest—when my mane was numbed straight. On special occasions, Christmas Eve for instance, my mom would sit me down in the kitchen and place the gold comb on the gas stove before dragging it down the length of hair with a sizzling hiss. I shrugged off nicks to the scalp as a welcome cost. By the time my mom finished with me, long tresses tumbled to my shoulder blades with grace and the faint scent of charred protein. I ran around, inventing reasons to whip my head so my hair would sway like a real French girl's.

I was five when my mom got fed up with it. That morning, she was trying to pacify my Afro into two cornrows, but by the time the first braid was complete, my eyes and nose were running so profusely that my vision blurred. Before I could stop her, my mom stormed off to the bathroom and returned brandishing a pair of scissors. I watched in horror as she snipped off the long braid at the base of my neck. Later that afternoon, she drove me to what must have been one of Châtellerault's only barbershops. I sat in a spinning chair in front of wide mirrors as a large barber carried out my mom's instruction: *buzz it all off.*

I remember the brightness of his shop, clumps of my hair floating to the ground, and the tears choking in my throat, although by then crying wouldn't have mattered. The girl who stared back in the mirror was an object of pity. Hideous, I thought, resenting the cut almost as much as I resented inheriting this unruly hair in the first place.

The haircut taught me that suffering had to be withstood. I absorbed the lesson as a challenge. The next time African women wrangled my hair, I clenched my jaw the way my mom had learned from my grandmother, who herself had learned from my great-grandmother. The women in my family were mountains, impervious to the battering of seasons. And they had to be. No one—no man and no state—was coming to their rescue. All they could do was believe the strife before them could be overcome. Suffering was inevitable but they could build calluses on their own terms. To survive, the women deflected pain as if it were their superpower. I wasn't quite a mountain, but felt I could make them proud by drawing from their towering strength and adopting it like an armor.

BUT THE SOURCE of the stories we told about ourselves could be such a blur. Had my grandmother and great-grandmother believed they could withstand unfathomable pain based on their own experience? Or had the myth seeped in from elsewhere? Perhaps from the white men who bought and stole members of our clans to ship across the seas, and there, to subject them to more pain than they ever would their own people? And so the myth transcends family lore; it is ingrained in ways nefarious and banal, deeply rooted in institutions with material impacts on people's lives, and in their historical foundations. As journalist Linda Villarosa wrote:

> John Brown, an enslaved man on a Baldwin County, Ga., plantation in the 1820s and '30s, was lent to a physician, Dr. Thomas Hamilton, who was obsessed with proving that physiological differences between black and white people existed. Hamilton used Brown to try to determine how deep black skin went, believing it was thicker than white skin . . . In the 1787 manual "A Treatise on Tropical Diseases; and on The Climate of the West-Indies," a British doctor, Benjamin Moseley, claimed that black people could bear surgical operations much more than white people . . . To drive home his point, he added, "I have amputated the legs of many Negroes who have held the upper part of the limb themselves."[7]

More than two hundred years later, a study from the University of Virginia would find that a concerning number of medical professionals still associate the concentration of melanin with an innate, almost supernatural strength. Forty percent of the first-year medical students surveyed believed black skin was thicker than white skin. Thirty-nine percent of the participants who were *not* medical students thought black people's blood coagulated faster than white people's. But these false beliefs were not solely held by white people.[8] An earlier study found that black subjects were themselves susceptible to believing that other black people feel less pain than their white counterparts.[9] I've wondered whether, in answering the study's questions, these black subjects experienced the same warped sense of pride that I saw in so many Cameroonian women, that I still saw in myself sometimes, while imagining a wall of strength in my likeness.

In the sphere of beauty, the myth demands our acceptance of pain as a necessary and even desirable aspect of transformation. Too often, the transformation arced in the direction of the whiteness we coveted while playing princesses. The myth underlay the abrasive products that we applied to our external layers to get there, as if the darkness of our features, hair we called hard, and this skin the color of heat, were themselves indicators of resistibility.

Ironically, Afro-ethnic hair is the most delicate of all hair types. Its scale-like wall of cells, which shields the cortex and medulla, is typically several layers thinner than in straight hair. It's also smaller at points of the strand where the hair curls. African descendants tend to produce less sebum, the body's natural way of delivering moisture to the skin and hair, which makes Afro-ethnic hair prone to dryness. This combination of attributes means that, despite all assumptions to the contrary, my hair is more sensitive to tension than straight hair. In other words, it takes less force to break it. Yet the coarser our hair—which is to say, the more fragile—the harder we yanked, pulled, jerked, and worse.

After my hair grew back, my mom decided we'd get along better if it was straightened permanently. She wasn't wrong. I was seven or eight when she first relaxed my hair chemically. I remember how the boxes were branded with a pledge. *Dark and Lovely. Soft and Beautiful.* And on the sides, little black American girls beaming in sleek ponytails. The longer the relaxer sat in my hair, the more noxious the smell became. The scalp would tingle, then burn. This meant that pliable hair, good hair, white hair, was minutes away. I suffered gladly. The rinse-off left my hair with an unparalleled limpness. Over the next eight to twelve weeks, the compact new growth would clash with the catatonic strands until it was time for a touch-up again. Most African women and girls around the world participate in this ritual at least once in their lives.

Chemical relaxers have been around for more than seventy years. The first generations, commercialized in the early 1970s, were made with lye, a corrosive alkaline liquid present in laundry products, drain cleaners, and disinfecting solutions. Over time, a milder guanidine hydroxide product, also known as no-lye, was introduced. The most common side effects are no secret among users: skin irritation, scalp lesions, hair loss, breakage, and discoloration are all par for the course.

Other potentially serious effects are less understood. But both lye and no-lye relaxers contain phthalates, which are suspected of disrupting estrogen production and other parts of the endocrine system. One study published in the *American Journal of Epidemiology* set out to evaluate the connection between frequent use of chemical hair relaxers and the incidence of uterine fibroids, benign but sometimes painful tumors that can grow on the uterus.[10] Black women are the largest consumers of chemical relaxers; they are also much more likely than white women to suffer from uterine fibroids.

I've evaded them so far, but fibroids are such a common feature of black womanhood that they've always been part of my vocabulary. My mom and aunts had them, as did my stepmom, and many of the African women who once braided my hair. Fibroids were a mere inconvenience until the bloating turned excruciating, the heavy periods nailed you to bed, and the aching made vaginal sex a nonstarter. The tumors could be removed surgically but often mushroomed again, at times obstructing the viability of embryos and fetuses. One sure way to be rid of them was to excise the uterus altogether.

That the study in the *American Journal of Epidemiology* was the first of its kind was surprising and not. Questions particular to black women's health garner less attention from the scientific community. The researchers reported a positive trend between the use of chemical hair relaxers and uterine fibroids.

Despite this, the Food and Drug Administration has continued to let manufacturers of chemical relaxers run their multibillion-dollar industry without requiring warning labels for even the mildest, most well-documented side effects.

I am still not sure which type of relaxer caused me to develop a sustained soreness in the middle of my scalp for half a decade. But nothing about this struck me as odd at the time. We had to suffer to be beautiful.

*

I STOPPED RELAXING my hair in middle school, three years after Wek appeared in Janet Jackson's video, the year that my mom and I settled in Harlesden. The timing was no coincidence. Our new neighborhood was incredibly diverse. In 1999, Harlesden was nearly 40 percent black—evenly split between West Indians and continental Africans—and 30 percent white, with a significant East and South Asian population.

The public, all-girls Catholic secondary school that I attended for Years Seven and Eight reflected the neighborhood's makeup. Never before had I been taught by a black woman. As for my classmates, they were self-possessed, smart, hardworking, and outspoken black girls—deeply British, to be sure, but also proud of their parents' heritage. The sheer quantity of blackness represented at the school shaped its culture, from what music trended and what clothes were fashionable out of our uniforms, to what hairstyles became popular.

In Harlesden, blackness was a ticket of admission rather than the burden that it felt like in France. Despite my thick French accent and tenuous grasp of British idioms, there was underneath a common experience on which to found new friendships. When my friends took me to the London Carnival I picked up the dance moves easily, recognizing the drumbeats of soca as distant cousins of the Bikutsi rhythms from *back home*. There, some white girls *wanted* to subject themselves to the pain of cornrows. The point of reference looked like me. And while my newfound comfort didn't quite rise to assimilation, those three short years in England were indispensable in transforming my relationship to this body. For the first time, I felt proud of being black-skinned.

I've wondered, though, whether I'd have had less to unlearn if I'd been raised *back home*. As elsewhere on the African continent, it was common for little Cameroonian girls to wear their hair cropped to the scalp. This was not coded with gender or beauty. Rather, heads were routinely buzzed for convenience, to avoid lice and big tears until a girl had the maturity to get through braiding day. Among Ewondos, my mom's clan, shearing one's hair also bore spiritual significance. It could be a last sacrifice and tribute to a loved one.

When headmen still ruled over tribes and great families, widows used to be forced to shave their heads. Now, the custom was voluntary—a true act of sacrifice. Soon after my dramatic haircut, Mamie Catherine had chosen baldness for a year to honor my grandfather who had just passed. How little then, and how much more, hair could mean. I envied my grandmother's clarity. It wasn't that she didn't care for her looks. Far from it—my grandmother had a penchant for smart dresses, preferably cinched at the waist, which she paired with cornrows braided in bold patterns when her hair was long. She was deeply feminine and loved to feel beautiful. But a lifetime in her homeland had inoculated her against the standard that shaped my childhood. Neither the advent of chemical relaxers nor the spread of European faces on the African continent had caused her to measure her beauty in white terms, to question her worth.

Not that the African continent has been immune to Eurocentric standards of beauty. Proximity to whiteness continues to be revered in Cameroonian culture. Being light or appearing *métissée*, as having any amount of non-black ancestry, is considered fortunate. A mark of beauty and superiority. For those of us raised in the West by Gen X and baby boomer mothers, whiteness often became a point of reference at home, despite our mothers' childhoods on the continent.

We heard our mothers on the phone, speculating about whether long-lost acquaintances were stricken with illness given the depth of their blackness these days. And we noticed aunties growing yellower everywhere but their joints, an improvement they credited to good health and good genes without once mentioning the pink tubes of Fashion Fair Cream on their vanities. For whatever reason, the bleaching lotions struggled to penetrate the skin at the knuckles, elbows, and knees.

Creams in this family typically lighten the skin using one active ingredient, or a combination of three: mercury salts, hydroquinone, and steroids. Misuse can lead to a range of health issues, from bacterial infections to blood poisoning, damage to the neurological system and kidneys, and even comas. The market is poorly regulated, so the ingredients' incidence varies between brands and sometimes from batch to batch. Several African nations—Ghana, the Ivory Coast, and Rwanda included—have banned their use, but the overall market remains robust.

In late 2018, the African American model Blac Chyna partnered with the Cameroonian Nigerian pop star Dencia to launch a bleaching line together: Whitenicious x Blac Chyna Diamond Illuminating & Lightening Cream (priced at $250 per 100 grams). Dencia had previously told a British news channel that the *white* in *Whitenicious* means pure.[11] The comment ignited an uproar, but Dencia had simply admitted what each of my aunties assumed when they doused themselves in Fashion Fair, what each of us read into our mothers' urgings to cover up our arms and legs before playing outside in the summer.

Instructions on the Fashion Fair tubes recommended applying the cream on areas marked with permanent discoloration, skin made darker by scarring and sunspots. But what if you were praying to be pure all over?

*

EVEN IN THE midst of the resurging natural hair movement, when odes to body positivity and black self-love are one click away, the power of white supremacy persists in beauty standards. Embracing my own skin was a process, a state arrived at. Getting there had taken seeing the confidence in other teenage black girls, over and over. It had taken attending Pastor Ilunga's congregation and being around unapologetically African women every Sunday, for the three years that we called London home. It had taken living in Tata Balbine's deeply Cameroonian household for most of my freshman year. And then reminding myself of my worth, on days that my subconscious saw fit to unleash torrents of self-hatred. If there is a permanent cure, I have not found it. My ego still feels vulnerable to relapse. Like a person in recovery, I must monitor my relationship to the things that activate my insecurities, stop myself from resenting my skin and hair, from coveting lightness. It's harder when the trigger is in the body.

Nor do I have the luxury of opting out of this preoccupation altogether: racial implicit bias is a core feature of American life. What certain people feel about black women's hair, its texture and what we do with it, bears material effects. It's the difference between getting a job offer and getting passed over, getting an apartment and getting denied. I can accept the body that I get to call home all I want—and I do, it is mine, and most days I am grateful for it—but until everyone's outer layer is equal, and whiteness is no longer the point of reference, I must continue to balance the degree of attention I pay to my appearance with the self-awareness to occasionally pause and ask myself: what feelings am I trying to elicit in other people by wearing my hair in styles coded as white? And is it worth it? An exhausting exercise, but I've been conditioned to suffer worse.

I had been at HUD for five months, in January 2013, and things were going well at work. My assignments were engaging and my supervisors generous with me. I was working hard because I wanted to be perceived as sharp and industrious, but also because being the only black hire in the entering class of junior lawyers made me doubt whether I deserved my job and wonder whether my colleagues agreed. The fear of being a token fed my imposter syndrome. If I was found to be excellent, I wanted it to be based entirely on my own merit and not some impression of the kind of black person my supervisors thought I was—the kind who adhered to certain norms of respectability, to white-approved standards of hair that seemed "clean" and "professional," the kind of person I'd led them to think I was when I'd taken out my nose ring and styled my hair in a straight bob before my in-person interview. I had done it to project conventionality and, I think, make my bosses feel comfortable around me. I had wanted to be relatable. I was keeping up the jig months later, still running my hair through a searing flat iron even though the intense heat was thinning my hair and frying the ends into oblivion. Nevertheless, I continued until the tresses drooped to my neck and swayed when I turned. But the more time I spent in this routine, the more I felt the little girl who whipped her hair like a real French girl come creeping back. A little girl who would do anything to be white.

One Friday morning that January, I packed a knitted hat for the cold and left for the day. After work, I took the metro to a hair salon in northwest DC, and spun in my hairdresser's chair. Nicole was finishing another head. I waited for her in front of the wide mirror, remembering my mom's voice at the barbershop. That day, my body had been a shell I didn't like and had no control over. A little thing futilely reaching for whiteness. But not today.

Nicole passed her hands across my scalp. I liked going to her because she never treated hair as insurmountable. In her shop, hair was simply protein; a blank canvas for play. There was no hard hair or bad hair. Only people without the know-how to appreciate its vulnerability and care for it accordingly.

So, what are we doing? Nicole asked.

I looked at my hair one last time. *Buzz it all off.*

♪

THOUGH THE WOMAN at the bar in Brooklyn reminds me intensely of Alek Wek, the math does not add up. If Wek was already successful when I was in fourth grade, then she would be nearing forty years old. But this woman was my age. I wonder if she might be a doppelgänger or possibly a relative. Loose threads of a stale news story flash back to me. Something about another fashion model's mysterious disappearance from New York, a couple of years back. As the story gained traction, the missing model's face had circulated around social media. I'd again been struck by her resemblance to Wek. (Ataui Deng was, in fact, Wek's niece and was eventually found safe.)

I wait for the bartender's attention, pondering whether to interrupt the woman's conversation. I am guessing that she's received this comparison a thousand times but cannot help myself. At the first lull in their conversation, I approach and ask if the woman is Alek Wek's niece.

She smiles but shakes her head. I feel like an idiot. Is it worthwhile to explain now, without boring her two friends, who Wek was, and who she was to me, how her streak through the fashion world had changed my warped conceptions of beauty, how she had made me feel seen as a small erased person? Instead, I apologize to the woman for the strange question, eager to extract myself from the disastrous interaction.

It's just that you look so similar.

I'm not her niece, the woman says. *But I am Alek.*

A rush of shyness and awe imbued with sadness overcomes me at once. No words seem enough to articulate what I owe her. All I tell her is how important her work was to me as a kid, that it'd meant the world to see someone who looked like her in magazines. Wek thanks me gracefully.

Back at our table outside, I try to put what had just happened into words. I think I have reached my limit for surprises when Dvora responds, *Oh, Alek is in there?*

My eyes brighten before I can conceal my astonishment. Dvora is a sportswriter raised in Orthodox Judaism. Of all the models who could have left their mark on her in the '90s, Wek wouldn't have been my first guess. Then again, I was living across the Atlantic at the peak of her career. What do I know?

Dvora chuckles. *Our dogs are friendly!*

Wek waves goodbye to us on her way out and I wave back casually, despite the boundless gush shaking my insides.

Hours later, I am curled up in my Amtrak train back to DC, still reeling, when my phone vibrates. Dvora's name pops up.

FYI Alek Wek is texting me about you.

Was I weird?

No, Dvora writes.

I wait for the follow-up.

Silence.

I recall the little girl who'd first encountered Wek on a grainy television, who didn't yet understand that power—economic, political, or cultural, or a combination thereof—was a function of control. I know better now. It isn't enough to be present and observed, to be represented. Power requires holding the levers that produce capital, steer institutions, control the creation of art. But representation is not meaningless either. As French media erased little black girls from the public eye and African women erased their own pigmentation all around me, seeing my blackness elevated had mattered to me.

The million-years-long minute passes. Dvora finishes copying and pasting Wek's message to me.

Finally:

She is what makes me not give up creating meaningful images in fashion.

Tonight, We Scream

HOME, NOUN. (CONT.)
13 a: a safe space

THE WORKSHOP IS CALLED *SELF-DEFENSE for Yogis.* My neighborhood studio has offered it a few times since I arrived in Petworth but it takes me until November 2015 to sign up. I dread it from the moment I hit the purchase button. Taking the class feels like an admission of my inability to navigate the world without help, of how often I feel afraid when I step out of my apartment, of how tired I am of my own body.

The men who have sexually harassed me have come in all stripes. Young, old, black, white, tall, short, rich, poor. Heterosexual and gay. Educated and not. They've been strangers, friends, and friends of friends.

My outer layer has long been an invitation for men to smack their lips lewdly, grab my calves, pinch my hips, follow me home, call me names for lovers, and yell obscenities at me on the street. I've learned some things; others are unlearnable. Summer is worse than winter and spring worse than fall, but the nuisance is year-round. The amount of skin I expose is an unhelpful metric. My face could be masked up and cars would still slow down so men could crane their necks out of open windows. The unwanted attention does not make me feel beautiful, nor is it meant to. I realize that it isn't about whether I'm pretty or about wooing me. My shell is an afterthought. A canvas for splattering insecurity and dissatisfaction.

Exiting the interactions intact requires caution. At times, I project obliviousness convincingly—blessed be the headphones, for they shall deliver me elsewhere. When the men insist despite this soft rejection, I take the careful approach and give them an ear. It's hard telling which of them are carrying knives. The pepper spray Dave sent me is buried somewhere in my apartment, unopened. It had been a kind gesture from him, but a part of me suspects that escalating these forced interactions with a chemical assault would not end well for me. I opt for a reserved smile and pray the men have somewhere else to be, so they can feel in control of ending our conversation. If we must keep talking, then the letdown must be gentle and always, always impersonal. These are fragile men.

While the world conditioned me for public humiliation, it taught them that they deserved access to me. Or, at the very least, the pretense of access. And so, the list of valid reasons to deny them excludes a lack of desire on my part. If I walk away, it must be due to an exhausting workday, or because I've mysteriously lost my command of English, or better yet, because I already belong to another—preferably cisgender—man. Nor am I permitted to seem afraid. I've been called a bitch enough times to appreciate that the pace at which I extract myself from these forced exchanges must be tolerable to the men.

There are often plenty of eyes around. Sexual harassment has tainted each street I've ever strolled, every bus stop I've stood at, every campus I've crossed, every bar I've sat in, and every cab I've ridden in—regardless of whether I was the intended recipient. It's happened in deserted alleys, but also in plain view, in places that should feel safe, if only for the sheer number of bodies around.

Sometimes, I think people who have been on the receiving end must be better equipped to notice. Then again, having eyes isn't the same as seeing. The people alongside me are eager to get home; they're busy talking to lovers, instructing waitstaff, smoking cigarettes, waiting for the light to turn, reenacting that last work meeting in their heads.

I never cease to be surprised by the number of my male friends, sensitive feminists, who believe street harassment exists, as any sensitive feminist would, but claim to have never seen it with their own eyes. I doubt they are lying to me. It's easy to miss what's in front of us without a reason to look. But to be routinely harassed in a sea of people, without so much as a blink, without anyone asking if I'm all right, if this man is bothering me, it makes me doubt my sanity. Did the exchange happen as I experienced it? Did it happen at all?

Without eyewitnesses, only two records exist. The version of the harasser, long gone, but who would maintain the remark was innocent, a playful flirtation between adults—that is, if he were to admit to anything at all. Then there's the harassed, who has only her recollection and her word to convince others, and perhaps herself. If she's anything like me, fiercely protective of her reputation as a reliable narrator, she might sanitize emotion out of the facts. Loath to be called unfair, hysterical, an attention whore, or simply a whore, she downplays the magnitude of the incident—edits out details, expunges recurrences, omits names.

In recounting what happened, I editorialize with gratuitous detail to elicit a smile from my audience. The man who sexually harassed me in a dark alley becomes the man who sexually harassed me *at the crack of dawn, before either of us had caffeine*; the man who sexually harassed me *while hovering on one of those absurd motorized scooters*; the man who sexually harassed me *with bits of cheeseburger dribbling out of his mouth*. If we're all joking about it now, how bad could it have really been?

On the rare occasions that the lewd comments are lobbed at me in front of my sensitive feminist friends, though, and they notice, none of us laugh. Rather, my friends react as many of us would upon seeing something we weren't supposed to: look away, keep silent, hope it ends without disturbing our day. We speed away briskly and, until the next intersection, avoid eye contact with each other. A close friend of mine would later describe his embarrassment at witnessing my sexual harassment as not unlike "when someone starts masturbating on the subway."

I feel a perverted sense of vindication when it happens. For a brief moment, men had experienced the sidewalk as I did, seen it for the menacing, crass place it could be. The feeling passes, and when it does, I am left wondering whether my friends think any less of me for letting these strangers dress me down with their words. Do *I* think less of them for seeing misogyny in action and doing nothing? Did I want them to fight my battles—just this once?

Was it even fair to expect?

*

THE SELF-DEFENSE CLASS lasts an hour. The instructor is a karate black belt. Through a dance of footsteps and elbowing, he teaches us to get away in one piece. I will forget the precise sequence as soon as I leave the studio, but the basics stick. Eyes, throat, balls. Don't be afraid to use your teeth. This is the easy part.

An endless trove of security footage shows women and young girls being kidnapped in open air, as people they've never met shove their alarmed but eerily silent faces into vehicles. People are often around at the time, putting carts away in the parking lots and filling their trunks with groceries, blindfolded by the immediacy of the small tasks before them.

How well my gender is trained, from a tender age, to take up as little space as feasible. We pride ourselves on not interrupting. We hesitate to cause a scene. A reliable narrator must never overreact. The self-defense instructor tells us that aggressors count on this socialized instinct. Screaming just might stun them long enough to save our lives.

So tonight, we scream.

There are born screamers—and then there's everyone else. I think the better test of which category one fits into isn't shock or sex but anger. I watch the naturals with envy as their voices escalate steadily and without effort, unchained by proportion or the median range of decibels in the room. The rest of us seethe discreetly.

We are trying to scream.

The problem is that the hotter my rage runs, the harder my throat works to stamp out the betraying notes. Instead of rising, my voice lowers into a trembling growl, then a loud whisper, and finally, silence. Useless in the face of danger. A few women in the self-defense class soar to an almost convincing pitch but I can tell they're still holding back.

We are learning to try to scream.

My first attempt is meek, wouldn't grab a toddler's attention. It's been years since the last time I screamed, and I mean *really* screamed—the kind that empties your lungs, drains your strength, won't let anyone look away. I was a teenager in my parents' home. Even then, I wasn't awake enough to deserve credit. The bloodcurdling sound had pierced through my nightmare. Only once my mom and Dave appeared in my doorway, their faces aghast, did I understand that the scream had emerged from my chest.

My second effort is better but not great. Still, walking home from the studio that night, I feel a little bolder. The studio is two and a half blocks from my apartment in Petworth. Knowing my parents would check the city crime alerts, I'd hesitated to give them my precise address until the apartment was mine and it was too late to reverse course on moving. The alerts emphasize carjackings and armed robberies, but I don't have a car to jack and don't look much worth robbing. The street offenses that cause me anxiety are rarely reported. Harassment that falls short of rape doesn't warrant the note. Nor am I convinced that men are worse within the city limits than elsewhere. All sexual harassment being equal, I choose proximity to the people and amenities I love. And though my parents still fret about Petworth, they of all people understand that total safety is an illusion.

My mom and Dave had worked as hard as anyone to make our home in Reno danger-proof, defending it with ramparts built of tight curfews and prayer. I attended church two to three times a week, and prayed with my parents nightly. Our daily life was infused with God and evangelical theology through practices intended to sanctify the walls of our home. This was true in a literal sense, as when my mom dabbed holy oil on the windowsills (to keep demons away), and figuratively, in the type of media that we absorbed (also to keep demons away). Throughout high school, I was to be back under their roof by nine P.M. on Fridays and Saturdays, and certainly couldn't go out both nights. Sleepovers were mostly forbidden. And still, this had not sufficed.

*

ON AN AFTERNOON in March 2004, Pastor Ilunga had phoned from London to inform us that he was coming to see us in Reno. Our duplex would be a tight fit, and the self-invitation was short on notice, but we were thrilled to receive him. Dave could finally meet my mom's spiritual father. Just two weeks later, the man of God stood in our doorway. I was fifteen years old, more of a teenager than when we left London two years earlier. Pastor Ilunga, on the other hand, had not changed much. There was his same timbre, booming with authority, and his same playful eyes, perhaps in a pudgier body. Had his cologne always been this strong?

Dave carried his luggage up to my bedroom. I was to take the sofa downstairs for the length of his stay. While our guest settled down, I tried to shake off the shyness that stiffened my limbs whenever I felt intimidated. At dinner, I ate without speaking unless spoken to first.

The hugs began on his second or third day. They were sporadic at first. I was emerging from the kitchen when he rose to his feet and asked me to embrace him. When it happened again, I was reading a textbook on the sofa. The time after that, I was working on the desktop downstairs. Pastor Ilunga was a man of God, an elder and a guest in our home. It was my duty to go to him when he called, though I felt a tendril of guilt. Clearly, I'd not missed him as much as he missed me.

By the fourth day, the squeezes felt like an eternity. He'd just demanded another one when I searched the room for my mom's eyes so she'd take note of my exasperation. Minutes earlier, she was humming in the kitchen. Where was she now? I considered the previous hugs. Each time, my parents had been close but out of sight. Doing laundry upstairs. Picking up the mail. Searching for a fresh set of batteries. This was creepy. But what could I do besides obey him? This time, the pastor clutched me so tight that I feared it might crush my ribs. He buried his nose in my neck and inhaled long as if to empty me. Hours later, I could still smell his fragrance on me.

"Ness, can you take him to the indoor pool?" my mom said from the kitchen one evening. She was stirring a pot on the stove. Our neighbors in the complex rarely swam around dinnertime. It was sure to be just the two of us. I pictured myself standing on the edge of the water, barefoot, reluctantly in a swimsuit. And Pastor Ilunga, watching. What if he asked me to get in? What if he insisted on touching me?

"I have homework. And don't feel like swimming."

"I don't want him to get lost on the way there," my mom said. I begged her with my eyes. *Please don't make me go. For once, don't make me.* Pastor Ilunga sat nearby, pretending not to listen. My mom looked up with mild irritation but missed my telepathic plea.

"It won't take long," she said. "You don't have to get in the pool."

Having made sure to leave my bikini and towel behind, I waited tensely on a lounge chair while Pastor Ilunga swam some laps. He was agile, stronger than he looked. I braced myself for another embrace but when he was done, he simply put his clothes back on and signaled that he was ready. On the walk back, we talked about God and faith. I tried to seem relaxed, to play normal.

He veered on a tangent. There were things a man of God was permitted, he explained, things that could seem immoral if anyone *other* than a man of God did them. He didn't list examples. I told him that theory didn't sound right to me.

On the fifth day, after another insistent hug, I snuck my phone into the half bath and dialed my friend Christina. We had met this school year, our sophomore, and though our friendship was young, I trusted her instincts. I told her that I was at a loss with what was happening. Here was a spiritual leader who seemed to *really* care for me. His attention should have felt flattering. Maybe Pastor Ilunga was seeing something in me that I didn't. Yet, his touch repulsed me. I asked Christina what she thought, whether all this seemed right to her. Was I overreacting?

"Oh my god, Vanessa. This is not normal. You *have* to tell an adult," she said. "Promise me."

The alarm in her tone surprised me. I told her that I would. But after we hung up, I sat on the toilet and sounded out the words in my head. *Pastor Ilunga won't stop hugging me.* My parents would look at me as if I'd lost my mind. The hugs had to be innocent. This was our home. No man would be so brazen as to be improper toward me in my parents' vicinity. I felt ashamed of doubting Pastor Ilunga's intentions. How conceited of me to believe a man in his sixties, a grandfather, might desire me like men on the street sometimes did. But even if I was right, and I wasn't, his visit was nearly over. I could get through these last days without a fuss.

On his second-to-last night in town, the pastor called my name in a raspy whisper. I was in the hallway upstairs, getting linens out of a closet, after just having wished my parents goodnight. The voice came from my bedroom. A sliver of light passed through the ajar door.

"Come here," he said.

My mom was talking at Dave while brushing her teeth. I reasoned that if I could hear them, they could hear me, too. I advanced toward my room but stopped in the doorframe. Pastor Ilunga was flattening my comforter with great focus. He refused to look up.

"Yes?" I asked. He shuffled something on the nightstand. Maybe his Bible. I couldn't see well. "Did you need something? A toothbrush or a towel?" Another minute passed or perhaps seconds. Too long for silence. Then, finally.

"Come here." My stomach clenched but I crossed the room's threshold. "Close the door." I obeyed but stayed within reach of the doorknob. This was safe. I was safe. "Come here," he said again.

Without asking this time, Pastor Ilunga wrapped me in his arms so forcefully that it pressed out my breath. He loosened his grip twice: the first time to smell me rabidly, and the second time, to lean into my ear and say, "Do you want me to come visit you?"

I paused to digest each word, in that order, in that moment. "You're always welcome to come back . . . and visit us in America." I felt my mouth warp into an involuntary smile and the rest of my body rigidify, as if the blood in my veins was congealing all at once.

Pastor Ilunga leaned back, without letting go, and took a good look at me. He cocked his head to the side and smiled. "No. Tonight."

"I can't . . . I have homework . . . and need to go to sleep." The absurdity of my response jolted me. I shoved him off, hard. As I released myself from his grip, his large hand fell sloppily down my breasts and across my stomach. I hadn't noticed it crawl up my shirt, and over my bra. I ran out.

Downstairs on the sofa, alone, I replayed his words in my head. How dense of me. I hadn't actually said "no." What if he came for what he wanted anyway? In a matter of minutes, the duplex would be dark. My parents would fall asleep. The possibility of waking up in the middle of the night with his heaviness on me made me nauseous. If he covered my mouth, no one would hear me scream.

I knew just what to do. Asking to sleep in my parents' bedroom would raise alerts. But neither would flinch at the notion of keeping their door open. That'd make the pastor think twice about executing his plan. My mom was a light sleeper. A "win-win" as Americans liked to say. I bolted upstairs and asked for this small favor, in French so as to not inconvenience Dave.

My mom's face twisted immediately. "Why? Did someone touch you? Did someone do something to you?"

Sitting on the edge of her bed, I tried to recount what Ilunga had asked of me but couldn't process enough air to finish my sentences. My first panic attack. After I calmed down, my mom informed Dave that I would be sleeping on a cot at the foot of their bed.

I slept through the soft tap on their bedroom door at four A.M., and my mom's steps as she accepted Ilunga's offer to go on a walk for a conversation that she would not describe to me until he was gone. They circled the grounds of the complex. My mom says that she let him talk first. Whatever I'd reported—she wouldn't reveal what, so he guessed—it was all a figment of my vivid imagination, the antics of a teenage girl starved for attention. My mom looked him in the eye and warned him if he ever laid a finger on me again, she'd kill him.

On Saturday morning, we delivered Ilunga back to the San Francisco airport, his body too close to mine in the back seat, and Dave at the wheel, unaware of the secrets crowding the car.

Summer came and went.

Some days, I returned from school to find my mom in a troubled mood. Another long letter mailed from London. Ilunga addressed them to her but meant them for me. He wrote that I was possessed. That I was a liar. That I wasn't the little girl he knew in London. He proposed to perform my exorcism himself. Said he'd pray for us. Left voice mails, undeterred by my mom's silence. Once, he returned to Reno and stayed with a friend of my parents, a Congolese woman who spoke his dialect. She was aware of what he'd done—her daughter was a few years younger than me, so my mom thought it important to warn her—but the friend was still honored to host him. I was hurt to hear it. Though this auntie knew me better than him, no one was more reliable than God's servant. Or perhaps she did believe me, and considered the hugs innocuous—ill-conceived but harmless. Ilunga hadn't raped me. I was lucky.

The letters stopped coming but I still caught waves of his cologne, despite having aired my bedroom, vacuumed the carpet, and changed my sheets with near compulsion for a year. It was as though he'd sprayed it into my mattress. The scent triggered palpitations. I resented him for haunting my bedroom and waking me out of my nightmares. As unsafe as this room now felt, it was in this same cage that I holed up for hours, too nervous to venture downstairs so long as Dave was alone with me (despite the fact that he was a stellar father to me, and never ever inappropriate with me). I hated when the youth pastor offered to drive me home after the Tuesday service. Whatever lust I once felt for whiteness became subsumed by a desire to become altogether invisible to older men.

I wondered when Ilunga had first spotted my inclination for silence. Was it after the first hug? At our front door in Reno? In the car on that rainy night?

Or perhaps he'd picked up another scent altogether, whatever lingered on me from that evening, when I was nine and sleeping over at the home of family friends, the year my chest began to morph, and the husband waited until his wife and child were doing bath time—I could hear the happy splashing from the living room—so he could hoist me onto his lap and fondle my incoming breasts, slowly and deliberately, before releasing me like a tagged doe. Had the husband also sensed my propensity for editing out details, expunging recurrences, omitting names?

I PASS THE self-defense studio again one chilly evening in March 2017 as I head to the Petworth metro station, down New Hampshire Avenue, past the signs that ornate front yards with *Black Lives Matter* and Pride rainbows. A band I've been itching to see, Adult Mom, is playing at the Black Cat tonight. It's warm enough for leggings and a loose sweatshirt. I could've walked or biked, but it's a little past eight and Taryn is already waiting for me at the venue.

The train platform is scattered with people, but much more tranquil than during rush hour. Along its length are coffee-brown pillars painted with the yellow-green line itinerary, and double-sided benches made of concrete. I slouch on one, a foot on the seat and the other on the ground. A young white couple sits on the backside. To kill the wait, I scroll down my Facebook feed aimlessly. A man takes the spot on my right. He's around my age, late twenties or maybe early thirties, with shoulder-length dreadlocks. His complexion is as dark as mine. I register his face as handsome.

He taps my arm but I'm not in the mood to indulge men tonight. Undeterred, he motions toward the iPhone in his hand. I look at the screen. It's a note, just for me: PLEASE SIT LIKE A WOMAN. The man joins his hands in prayer with a pleading face.

I scoff at him and get back to minding my own business.

He taps my shoulder once more. Another note for me, longer this time. I refuse to acknowledge him so he taps me again, and again, and again, like a petulant child. With my headphones still in and gaze fixed on my own phone, I inform him coolly that I'm not planning to look so he might as well give it up.

Train lights beam out of the tunnel. I stand up, thinking the exchange is over. The rails grind so loud that I almost miss the shouting. I pull an earbud out. It's the tapper, calling me a ho from fifteen feet away. When did he get that far back? I yell back that I like sitting like a ho, that it's *very* comfortable to me. He continues to hurl insults at me, his voice dripping with disdain. I am so vile to him. The feeling is mutual. I can't explain why I refuse to cede the space as I have dozens of times before. Instead, I tell him what I think: "You are garbage and you can go fuck yourself."

The train doors open. Rather than enter the car closest to him, he doubles back toward me. He's moving quickly. I stumble toward the door closest to me. My instinct won't let me turn my back to him. I don't know what he's holding anymore. I can't see his hands. Only his face, zeroed in on mine. I accept that he's going to hurt me and that I'm not going to get away before he does it. I decide that it will be a fist. No one has ever punched me but I know this will hurt. Tata Hélène's face had stayed bruised for days. The time my ex slapped me, that time at his place, and afterward, he went to sleep while I lay in his bed, wondering why I was still there and not on an Amtrak train home, my cheek had burned for a half hour. He hadn't even put much effort into it.

I am firmly inside the car when the tapper rushes in. He pushes aside a young brown woman in a green sweater to get to me. A black teenage boy watches the scene placidly from our corner of the train. We are all characters in his video game. The white couple that shared our bench hesitates to enter the train. They look through me with neutral faces, I think, calculating the personal cost of skipping this train and getting to their dinner reservation seven minutes late. Are they assuming this is a quarrel between lovers because the tapper and I are both black? The couple stays on the platform.

The tapper stares me down. He wants to do it so bad, I can tell. It'd be easy with me frozen there, big stupefied eyes, practically begging for it. But he catches himself. He's a better man than that. A woman probably raised him. He has sisters or a daughter. So he tilts his head back, slurps up a thick wad of saliva, and spits it all in my face. It's on my chin and in my eyes and in my hair. He runs out before the doors close. The train drags south. My fellow passengers stare out the black windows; the teenage boy reabsorbs into his phone. But the brown woman in the green sweater is talking to me while furiously digging through her purse. She says that she saw the whole thing, that I didn't deserve it, that I didn't do anything wrong. I let her dab my face with a tissue.

This is the last time that I take the metro until summer. I don't report the tapper to the police. Even if I wanted to—and what good would that do me now?—my brain had erased his features as soon as the doors closed. Only broad details remain. Around six foot two. Athletic build. My skin tone. For months, I recoil at the sight of dreadlocks—every other block in Petworth—in fear that it might be him, prepared to finish what he started while my neighborhood watches passively.

Would I be reaping what I sowed?

Compliance and complicity share a root in the Latin word for *together*. Both intimate an agreement of wills and participation, however reluctant. Both are essential to letting men assert dominance over our homes and bodies. I'd complied and been complicit more times than I cared to admit. I'd let catcalls go, minimized them, and surrendered rather than speak up. I'd told my parents about the pastor and, in time, about the family friend, but reported neither man to their families or communities. My silence had allowed the pastor to return to his church unscathed. As for the family friend, his punishment was the mild discomfort of pretending not to notice my extensive maneuvers to avoid being left alone with him more than twenty years later. The men counted on my silence and I performed as expected. We all did.

How many people stood idly by while twenty-two-year-old Tiarah Poyau was having fun at a Caribbean music festival in Brooklyn, and a stranger insisted on dancing with her, then, upon being denied, gunned her down? How many looked away when another catcalled nineteen-year-old Ruth George, who was walking to her car in a Chicago parking garage, and convinced themselves that she must've known him, this man who would choke her to death minutes later? And who saw twenty-nine-year-old Janese Talton Jackson's killer follow her out of a Pittsburgh bar, after she rejected him, and shoot her in the chest? Were the Harlem streets empty when yet another man killed twenty-one-year-old Islan Nettles, the woman he was catcalling moments before realizing that she was transgender?

A little spit never killed anyone. I'm supposed to feel lucky.

*

THE SELF-DEFENSE INSTRUCTOR was onto something when he encouraged us to use surprise to our advantage. My off-script reaction had stunned the tapper, just as it had allowed me to get away from the pastor all those years ago. I could've gotten away that day, screamed my piece and run out of the metro station. But I wanted to stand my ground. I, too, deserved to feel safe in this public space, in my own neighborhood. I assumed that I'd be safe because of my neighbors. He bet on the same, in spite of them.

In the end, the tapper was right. Most wouldn't bother to see if everything was all right with me. No one would force him to back off or demand that he apologize for harassing, then assaulting me. The platform would pray for a swift end to the disturbance. This is what we have inherited and built upon: a culture of nonintervention, where individual comfort trumps the collective good. Screaming embarrasses us. So, we look away.

The cost of this group apathy has never been borne evenly. In their 2019 study of sexual harassment in the workplace, academic researchers Dan Cassino and Yasemin Besen-Cassino found that, between 1996 and 2016, complaints to the Equal Employment Opportunity Commission dropped by 70 percent for white women compared to 38 percent for black women. I suspect that sexual harassment follows a similar pattern in the street and, perhaps, in the home. And why wouldn't it? "The shift . . . indicates that harassers are conscious of power relationships, and choose to target more vulnerable women," wrote the researchers.[12]

Nothing about this vulnerability is innate. Rather, it is the byproduct of a history that was never interested in distributing oppression evenly when it assessed blackness, in all its gradients, in order to price and put to service and sexualize and inflict violence on bodies like mine—sometimes for profit, often at no consequence, and in certain instances, with the blessing of the state. This same history informs men's perceptions of my standing within our stratified society. It influences their calculus, consciously or not, of whether their sexual harassment will be noticed, of the likelihood anyone will take me at my word, or intervene if the interaction sours.

Reimagining the events of that night, this time in the shell of a white woman, I doubt the train platform observes the incident with such cool detachment. I wager that the tapper doesn't set his target on me to begin with. Instead, he taps the shoulder of the darkest woman around. She might be wearing a green sweater. Wisely, this one gets up to wait elsewhere on the platform. Perhaps, in this white shell still, I notice metro police officers riding down the escalator. An enlightened citizen, I look out for the tapper's safety instead, conscious that public spaces are far more hazardous for black men than me. The train pulls in. The white couple gets to dinner on time.

It isn't that sexual violence doesn't reach white women. It does, with disturbing frequency. But a woman's screams never land in a societal vacuum. Collective passiveness means that my lone scream might save me one day and kill me the next. The ultimate outcome rests on luck, but the odds are a cumulation of history.

Still I refuse to believe in the impossibility of reclaiming our homes, our neighborhoods, our right to enjoy public spaces. It will be difficult. It will demand more than well-intentioned signage or symbolic marching. Reclamation cannot be entrusted to a state that responds to trauma by inflicting trauma. Nor can it be outsourced.

On the contrary, the impulse to undo this apathy must come from within the whole. And with it, a new ethos. A rejection of complacency. Compliance with braver rules of solidarity. Complicity with the intent to defend one another. If I refuse to believe that it's impossible, it is because the alternative—a world in which certain bodies are sacrificed to harassment, in which certain bodies are forbidden the comfort of a safe space—is too unfair to accept. This must be a group exercise. Our homework is to scream together.

Of Iron and Soil

Home, noun. (cont.)
14 a: a family property

I PACED THE LOBBY OF the shotgun house to the soundtrack of the dial tone. Warmth radiated against my right cheek. A sliver of light settled on a layer of our friends' shoes and umbrellas. It was December 2018, and my boyfriend, Sam, and I were in New Orleans for a few days. We had just returned from Sunday brunch with our hosts, Lydia and William.

Everyone headed back to the kitchen while I tried my dad on the phone. We took turns calling each other every other weekend, though we sometimes went three weeks if one of us got busy, but never longer than that since our decade of estrangement. As much as he complained that his mother kept the rudimentary flip phone he bought her for emergencies under a pile of newspaper ads on top of her fridge, my dad refused to get one for himself. It was the way the flashing icons held an almost mystical grip over people, the way buzzes aborted their thoughts and sent their eyes darting mid-sentence. It irked him. At the risk of being missed, my dad preferred to be present.

"*Allô*? Vanessa? *Bonjour*, it's you!" Even when it was my turn to call, a tinge of culpability lingered in his throat. "So how are you, eh?"

"Fine, fine. We got to New Orleans on Thursday. It's in the south of the country, you know. Louisiana?"

"Oh yeah. *La Louisiane*. I've heard of it. Wasn't that ours at some point?"

"Ha, yeah. Long time ago. That's why a ton of streets here have French names, but you have to pronounce them in this bastardized accent or people will look at you like you have two heads."

"That's funny. So you are on vacation with your boyfriend?"

"Sort of. Sam has a big argument in an appellate court tomorrow—his first ever. He's really been working and preparing all week."

I had met Sam in DC a little over a year earlier, first at a happy hour for Harvard Law graduates doing public interest work, in October 2017, and again a couple of months later, at the apartment of our mutual friend Sana. By then I had transitioned to a different job, in the enforcement division of the Consumer Financial Protection Bureau, where I felt I could do more to protect people from the finance industry's traps. Though I barely remembered seeing him at the happy hour, Sam had made an impression on me at Sana's. He was funny and seemed kind, humble, down-to-earth. I liked, too, how his mass of dark curly hair framed his thin, handsome face like a halo. He had finished law school two years after me, which meant we had overlapped for a year, his first and my last in Cambridge, but had never crossed paths. (Sana was in the class between us.)

I learned, over the course of our first dates, that Sam could have probably cashed in at any white-shoe law firm after graduation—not because he would ever admit something so uncouth, but because his stellar grades spoke for themselves. Instead, here was this sweet white, Jewish boy from the Midwest, determined to represent clients suffering in some of the country's most horrid prisons. To say that I was intrigued was an understatement. He and my dad had not met yet, but I hoped they would before long. Sam was the person I had been looking for when I left my husband. I could not see myself with someone else.

Our friends' cat, Gumbo, grazed me with an indolent tail as I offered my dad a clumsy explanation of the circumstances. The case that had brought us south was being heard in the Fifth Circuit Court of Appeals on Monday. Sam's client was held in Angola, a Louisiana state penitentiary originally built on a cotton plantation by a Confederate veteran and sometimes nicknamed "The Farm." Despite the client's legal blindness, the prison had forced him into strenuous manual labor in the fields and on machinery. The resulting injuries—torn pectorals from catching a bale of hay and the partial loss of a finger on a machine—had been entirely avoidable and, as Sam would argue tomorrow, a blatant violation of federal disability law.

William had tried the case in district court but lost to an unfriendly jury. He had then tapped Sam for the appeal. Two of the three judges on tomorrow's appellate panel were Democratic appointees, but Sam still thought the case could go either way. Courts were notoriously deferential to law enforcement and hostile to incarcerated plaintiffs. All week, Sam had been preparing for the least sympathetic audience: headphones in, flashcards in hands, pacing the length of the narrow house while muttering the parts of judges and counsel. His client wouldn't be there to witness the argument but William, Lydia, and I planned to go watch.

I remembered catching a snippet of life in French prison on a news segment, while watching television with my dad after dinner, a couple of years earlier. Each cell had a bed, a TV, a desk, and a sink. Luxury accommodations compared to Angola.

"The justice system is really different here, you know," I said to him now. "Harsher. But this is my first time down here this time of year. It's beautiful for early December. We actually just walked back from brunch in T-shirts. Crazy. How is it where you are?"

My dad said that Châtellerault was misty and gray. Or rather: it was *merde* weather. Too wet to ride his bike to the pond. I pictured his silhouette in the window, eyes scanning the overcast cul-de-sac, a boyish pout on his lips. Behind him: my stepmom Lisette, ironing a basket of laundry in the middle of the rust-colored living room. And on the sofa across from her: two teenage daughters, my half sisters, watching *Buffy the Vampire Slayer* between glances at their phones.

Lately, he fantasized about retiring in the sun. There was Lisette's hometown on paradisiacal Mauritius or, closer to home, Morocco and Portugal, where clusters of Francophone retirees were already stretching their pensions. I found the reminder that my principal foothold in the Poitou-Charentes might someday vanish distressing but more than anything, wished to see him happy, tan and well-rested on a beach of his fancy. The odds of this coming to pass was another story. My dad had never visited me in my sixteen years in the US. Nor was he fluent in any language other than French. Anyhow, retirement was

distant still. Between his teenage daughters and aging parents, my dad was wed-
ded to French soil for another while. Besides, I reminded myself, the dreaming
was free.

"How are Mamie and Papi?" I asked next. A customary question always
accompanied by a customary answer. *Your grandmother has bottomless energy.
Your grandfather is neither worse nor better. You know how it goes.*

But my dad hesitated. An ominous grunt.

Delivering bad news had never been his forte. The week that Mamie's Briard
dog passed away, when I was nine or so, he had called me at our usual time and
spent our twenty minutes chatting about everything and nothing. Only once
it was time to say goodbye had my dad revealed that, "by the way," Vishnu had
died. "Of what!" I exclaimed in a fountain of tears. "Well, pet, he was fourteen."
The dog had died of living too long. I remembered the deliberate faith it
had required in that moment for me to accept the truth of this news. What had
befuddled me the most was the possibility that our beloved companion could
have ceased to exist when I had last seen him alive. More than that, his being
had depended on my knowledge: all things were alive so long as I believed them
to be. Had my dad postponed his delivery, the dog would still be present in my
world. Now I was to immediately accept that he would be gone for a length of
time so massive, so uncontainable, that not even the greatest mathematicians
could measure it to its end. Strangling one finger with the rubbery purple
phone cord in the hallway of the Internat Adolphe Favre, I had wondered how
the farm would ever feel right again without his golden mass of fur trailing my
grandmother's every step. How could any place go on with an integral piece of
itself missing? And yet, it had.

"There has been an accident," my dad said quietly.

"What do you mean, an accident? What happened?"

Papi was opening the fridge door, he explained, right there in the little
kitchen on the farm, when he lost his balance and crumbled to the ground. In
the fall, my grandfather had shattered his femoral neck. Or, as the surgeon on
call had suggested, perhaps the shattering had preceded the fall—it was hard
to tell. A fire truck from a neighboring town had shuttled him to Châtellerault
for emergency hip surgery. All in all, the ordeal had gone well. The surgery had
worked and more importantly, Papi had woken up—a cause to celebrate given
his eighty-eight years of age. He had since been transferred to a rehabilitation

center in the small town of Loudun. The trouble now was that in the three days since the accident, my otherwise sharp grandfather had been forgetting faces and refusing to eat.

"But why didn't you call me, daddy? I would have wanted to know. This sounds really serious. I mean, what if he had—"

"No, you're right. I should have said something."

"How is Papi now? Is he awake?"

"He's doing all right. Lisette and I went to see him this morning. He was talking and recognizing Mamie. Oh yeah, much better. If you had seen him the day right after it happened . . . It's hard to see my father like this. Weak and without color. This morning, though, I'm telling you, he looked stronger." My dad pauses as if to convince himself. "You'll see, Vanessa. He's tough, your *papi*. It's going to be all right."

"For sure. Listen, are you saying that he was recognizing each face when you saw him last? And that he was eating again? That he ate in front of you?"

I wanted for him to be right, but an enormous number of days—three!—had passed since the fall. My father's grief-stricken optimism could neither change how much time remained for Papi, nor shorten the 4,767 miles between this shotgun house and his hospital bed.

"Well, I would say he was still a little confused this morning," my dad admitted.

"Daddy, should I come home?"

"*Non, non.* Your Papi's a fighter." My dad paused here. "It's going to be all right, darling. Look, I'll call you again soon with news."

"No news too small, okay?"

"I promise."

As we hung up, I felt the weight of that night in the Lyon housing project, watching my mom churn an impossible math in her head: meager savings in her bank account against the long hours to Yaoundé, where her own mother was at once going, went, gone. Never, I had decided, sitting on her bed, did I want to feel that helplessness again.

My measure of success had emerged from that grief. I would not garner wealth for the sake of wealth or academic achievement for the sake of academic achievement. It would not be to make my mother proud. Rather, success would be this: the financial security to bid farewell to my loved ones in person and at a moment's notice. By that standard, I had made it. A simple series of taps on my phone would book me on the earliest flight home. My greatest need now was sober data. I dialed Mamie next. A deftly practical woman herself, she would understand.

"I don't want to be too late, Mamie," I said. "Should I come home?"

She paused a moment.

"What I can tell you is that yesterday I went shopping for a black coat."

FOUR DAYS LATER, Mamie and I were riding through the countryside in her little Clio to see Papi at the rehab facility. A man called in to RTL radio to express his dismay at the French police's latest excess of force. I had arrived at a tumultuous time. Since mid-November 2018, protesters had been blocking highways in Paris and across the regions. They called themselves the *gilets jaunes* in honor of their signature neon-yellow vests. My dad and I had passed one of their works on the drive home from the Châtellerault train station: tires stacked alongside the road that bordered the Auchan department store. A warning of sorts, though my sleep-deprived brain could not discern what kind. This was not, however, the protest that the listener was calling about. While the *gilets jaunes* were growing in strength, a round of high schooler strikes had begun after the announcement of purported improvements to the BAC, a monumental end-of-high-school exam requirement for all French students. Teens around the country were walking out of their lycées over concerns that the changes would favor wealthier peers.

Then, shocking footage had emerged out of Mantes-La-Jolie, a poor suburb of Paris with a large black and Arab population. Youths kneeling on the ground. Hands resting on the back of their necks. Around them, police decked in defensive gear. A passerby might have assumed the kids had been caught planning the next Bataclan massacre. The image had turned the spotlight on police brutality. Tasked with damage control, the minister of education had been insisting that the police had ordered the teens into this awkward position for the teens' own safety, so that the police could search them for evidence relating to a nearby act of vandalism without anyone getting hurt. It was all precautionary, he assured the public. But the window for saving face had already shut.

The man on the RTL radio line said he was in his seventies, old enough to remember the country's flirtations with fascism. And though she remained quiet, I figured that Mamie did, too. In one of the earliest childhood memories she had recounted to me, a Nazi soldier fond of her blonde curls repeatedly bounced her on his lap whenever she and her mother ran into him at the market. The next caller was certain that kids in Paris's affluent sixth arrondissement would never dream of being subjected to such treatment. It was unconscionable.

I sat in the passenger seat astonished by these reactions, shocked that the brutalization of black and Arab kids would register as unjust and disproportionate to these callers, who I presumed to be white. And if I was right, had mentalities really changed this much since my emigration from France?

No sooner did I wonder this than the next caller got on the radio, adamant that these teens were savages. A smile escaped my lips. Ah, there was the France I knew. I pictured the production team scrambling to drown the caller in elevator music before the woman's inevitable graduation from dog whistles to more explicit opinions. The show abruptly cut to commercial. Eyes trained on the narrow road, Mamie's face remained impassable.

In the sterile room painted in dandelion yellow, Papi appeared lost and exhausted. A little embarrassed, too, to be caught in the silk shirt and pants that Mamie had brought to spare him from the center's ass-baring gowns. I caressed his papery hand. Gazing through me, my grandfather reached for the invisible shapes floating in his mind.

It was strange to think my half sisters had only ever known him as a shadow of himself, frailer than a leaf in the wind, his life condensed into a number of chores for Mamie: being helped out of bed, being showered, being slipped pills to fog the pain, having his hearing aid checked, wiped, and reinserted, having his meat sliced into small bites and his fish picked apart for choking hazards, being lifted out of his special dining chair and later, being tucked into bed.

The grandfather of my childhood had been industrious and austere, a colossus to me. I had never seen him in pajamas until this day. On weekends when I slept over as a kid, Papi had dirt and soot under his nails long before the first rooster call. I would pop out of my dad's childhood bedroom and hunt for Mamie, in the kitchen first, then in the chicken coop, despite knowing that she would likely be in the loafing shed, squeezing buttery milk from a goat for the greatest breakfast in the world. I preferred mine lukewarm with a blurry film of cream still floating on top.

Back in the kitchen, I would scoot into the nook across from the shelf of vintage tins of cocoa powder and wait for Mamie to heap a spoonful of the dark stuff into my bowl. The tins always struck me as pretty. One featured the famous Poulain horse and another the Banania man, the only other black face in the village on those mornings. I would stare at the Banania man and he would stare at me, his deep complexion in stark contrast to his iconic fez and thick lips, each the color of fresh blood. I would dip my buttered tartine into the chocolate milk like a little *paysanne*, as my mom always said with a smidge of disgust. But it was the way my grandfather ate his toast and the way my dad ate his, and so it was the way I liked to eat mine.

Sensing my grandfather's disinterest in children, I learned to make myself scarce unless explicitly invited to tag along to pick up snails for grilling or to watch him tie floppy lumps of flesh onto a high line and unzip their furry skin with decisive hands. Too young then to connect his signature pot-au-vin to the rabbits' periodic vanishing, I observed in awe. I saw him as a man afraid of nothing—not of climbing high up to store grain, not of fetching wine and potatoes in the black cellar, and not even of fire. The street on which the farm sat, rue de la Forge, had been named for his blacksmith shop. I would stand at its entrance and speculate as to what creation might emerge from his glowing anvil: horseshoes for a neighbor, a fence to enclose a coop, an iron gate like the one abutting the farm or, my grandfather's words, "scissors to cut stone."

He was not the kind of patriarch who told grand stories and played silly games, unless one counted his weekly round of *pétanque* with other grandfathers from the hamlet after Sunday lunch. He was nothing like his wife, whose biting wit and bottomless well of opinions made her an entertaining date. As a matter of fact, it was a wonder my dad had turned out to be such a goofy, affectionate, and sensitive man when his own father was a wall of stone, issued from a generation of men who construed masculinity rigidly, and who struggled to relate to women or traits otherwise perceived as feminine. If Papi had ever been different, before circumstance forced him to become the head of his household as a teenager, holding the family together for his mother and sister, with little money, we would never know.

I strained to recall a single instance of him laughing until tears streamed down his cheeks, and could not begin to imagine what would bring him to such a state now. But I had once seen unbridled joy on his face. It was on the night of a small family reunion at the farm. My grandparents had filled a banquet table with two dozen guests, hours past mine and Vishnu the dog's bedtime. As the night wound down, Papi had pulled out an accordion and sang, to everyone's delight. He could be surprising in that way.

My mom hadn't been sure of what kind of grandparents her in-laws would be to me when she joined the family in 1987. Her mother-in-law had been protective of her only child. Her father-in-law, she was told, was as conservative as he was country. Her first chance to spend extended time with them had come in early 1988, the year she and my dad moved onto the farm. They had wanted to save money for a nest, a future baby, and their first trip to Cameroon together the following summer. If Châtellerault was provincial compared to Yaoundé, the hamlet of Nueil-sous-Faye was a time capsule frozen in the 1950s in ways that went beyond its lack of indoor plumbing. Neighbors routinely slammed their shutters dramatically as my mom rode her bike past their windows. One or two had even muttered vile things at her under their breath.

She had worried about how Papi would receive her, but it was Mamie who waited until my mom was out running errands to rifle through her suitcases—baffled, my mom concluded, that a black woman from a different world could sincerely love her son. My dad often returned from the factory to find each woman sulking on opposite ends of the farm.

As for Papi, he had stunned them with his openness. I suspected that he was impressed by my mom's good work ethic and her willingness to help out on the farm. And that, for better or worse, she refused to let his wife push her around. Soon after my adoption, Papi had quietly renounced his lifetime membership to the xenophobic National Front party. Word had only gotten out because Mamie would tell anyone with ears. My grandmother's animosity toward my mom had eased after my arrival and never extended to me.

From the moment we met, Mamie and Papi had been my grandparents, and I, their first granddaughter.

ʃ

MAMIE'S GOOD HEALTH had spoiled us. She still rose early to tend to her wiry hens and meticulous garden with a grace that made caring for the farm seem easy if not downright pleasant. It was a simpler operation to manage now that most of her posse had been sold or unreplaced: her mare, Carioline, re-homed at another stable, the goats and rabbits gone for good, along with the geese that shot me venomous looks as I learned to bike on their dust. But as modest as the farm was, its upkeep was tiresome. Hard as she tried, Mamie could not entirely conceal the extent to which the work wore her out. We had all noticed how the five-course lunches that made Sundays a highlight of my childhood had grown humbler—her glorious *îles flottantes*, typically whipped with family eggs and crowned in spun sugar, replaced with fruit pies from the local supermarket.

Of course, none of us minded. We wanted her to slow down if it meant more time together, though communicating this was a delicate matter. My grandmother was happiest when her hands were productive and she fiercely cherished her independence. She also enjoyed, I could tell, the aghast looks on our faces each time she reminded us that the vines neatly dripping down the house had not trimmed themselves. "Oh, don't you worry," she would go on with a wicked smile. "I have your Papi hold the ladder."

Time had been less merciful toward him. A form of Parkinson's shook Papi's calloused hands and Paget's disease glitched his cells, causing them to rebuild bone too fast and brittle, while bending his back and legs into painful bows. Decades of blacksmithing without protection had blitzed out the delicate cilia in his ears, locking him in an increasingly silent chamber. While he could distinguish Mamie's voice most of the time, he could no longer register mine. To get his attention, I tapped his pant leg gently before mouthing my words slow and clear. But on my last trip home, two months earlier, Papi had seemed desensitized to my touch.

The sheer effort it took to communicate with the outside world exhausted him. At Sunday lunch, my grandfather would pour the aperitif for all of us, then complain about lunch being sour or salty—it wasn't—before retreating into sparse nods for the rest of the meal. On more than one occasion, when the two of us were alone in the kitchen, he had confessed to me his wish to leave this world.

By the time he had given in to a cane, he had become too slow to accompany Mamie to the grocery store. In practical terms, this meant leaving him alone for an hour or two each week, in a home built for a man who did not foresee the day that the tiled steps separating the kitchen from the restroom, dining room, and bedrooms would transform into perilous obstacles. So much could go awry in a single hour. Which is to say, only one of my grandparents could now realistically survive without the other.

I hoped Papi's fall would be a wake-up call but there was little I could do from the other side of the world but worry. Even the hypothetical suggestion of long-term care would ravage me with dread over the costs. My dad was often astonished when I told him the extent to which Americans were expected to handle sickness and death without support from their government. France was far from perfect, but at least the end of the road for my Papi would not be marked with mountains of bills, fights with insurers, and debt collector calls.

Between coverage from the French state and their supplementary insurance, my grandparents were almost definitely entitled to an aide of sorts. But for years, Mamie had insisted that her husband was vehemently opposed to the idea. The way she always changed the subject left me unconvinced. Since when was she a pushover? If my grandparents had gone on this long without help, it was undoubtedly a product of her own resistance. While their stubbornness frustrated us, we took comfort in knowing that once they finally asked for help, the state would simply hand it to them. Until then, though, my dad had committed to doing the forty-five-minute drive from Châtellerault to Nueil-sous-Faye more frequently than Sundays.

Certain people and lands held such power over us that being back in their midst rewired us, transformed our voices, uncovered hidden faces, and to know someone, really know them, demanded that context. A week or two in Châtellerault always dusted the American right off me, but the fragrance of my grandparents' farm had a particular way of reviving the little girl that I was on that soil—shy, unskilled, intrigued by its every nook. I had imagined the farm watching over me as divorce and economic security pulled us apart, watching and refusing to give up on my return, continuing to believe even in that prodigal decade away.

I wanted badly for Sam to meet them all and see the farm while the option remained. I remembered pinning my phone screen to the car window on my trip home earlier that year, in an attempt to capture for Sam a trepidation that was difficult to put into words—the sudden quiet as the bustle of town ceded to rolling hills, idle tractors, and lonely houses built of stone and terracotta tiles. Broods of cows and horses. Fields crisping in the canicular heat. And as far as the eye could see: stillness.

Behind us on the road, on the placid Vienne river, Châtellerault was cratering into itself. Year after year, its cobblestoned center bled tenants. Shops were shuttered and cafés fought to survive. It was easy to blame the youth and their dreams of flocking to anywhere-but-home, their disdain for tradition. But maybe it was the dearth of good jobs. That, and the impossibility of matching Amazon's power to deliver anything anywhere, including the bowels of the countryside. (My grandparents and their neighbors had taken to calling a local manor Château Amazon after an American transplant purchased it, instantly spiking the presence of smiley-faced trucks on the roads surrounding the village.) Others yet thought the Poitou-Charentes' woes preceded all that, starting with manufacturers like Renault exporting their operations to Eastern Europe where labor was cheaper than my dad and his unionized colleagues. But there was also the obvious: the skies above frying the regional harvests with vengeance. No, the weather hadn't been right in years.

I had deleted the footage almost immediately, finding that I could no more bottle up the countryside on camera than do the full moon justice with eight megapixels. One shot had survived the day and made it to Sam via text: Mamie standing in the summer light, grinning over the cherry red gingham tablecloth as she cut into a tarte, and Papi at her side, eyes on her motions and mind halfway to nowhere. Not pictured: the scents imbued in their skin, hers of sandalwood and black soap, and his of iron and soil.

*

THOUGH THERE WAS no upside in dwelling on the past, I could not help regretting the ten years we had missed from each other's lives. The cutoff between my dad and me had been swift, unexpected, and for me, deeply painful. I had spent the transatlantic flight that my mom and Dave offered me, back in May 2012, torn over whether to announce my arrival to my dad. What had he done to deserve any grace from me? Had he even asked when I would be graduating? Or what those three years of school had been like? No and no. I was twenty-three and my dad, my *daddy*, knew nothing about me. I wanted him to suffer for breaking my heart and yet missed him more than I ever had missed anyone—enough in the end to hand him a final chance to hurt me. As the train crept into Saint-Pierre-des-Corps, I dialed his phone number. I still remembered it by heart.

Back in my hometown, I found the dad who had waved me goodbye from the two-track train platform a decade earlier—charming and warm and funny, so effortless in his rightful role that I wondered if the magnitude of our rift might be escaping him. I would not pretend that we were the same. He was a stranger to me and I was a stranger to him. Perhaps someday we would know each other again, but not without answers first. I waited until we were driving out to the farm alone to ask the question that had stumped me since ninth grade. Why had he abandoned me?

The way he remembered it, my mom had informed him of our imminent departure for America. Not to seek his opinion or approval or input, but as a mere formality. The first time, to London, had pained him, but the distance seemed surmountable. England was but a train ride away. The second time, to Nevada, was different. My dad had felt like a bystander being erased from his own family. Hurt and discarded, he had decided to extricate himself from our lives, as seemed to be my mom's wish.

"But it wasn't fair to me," I said. "No one had sought my opinion in any of this. I was a child who went where she was told. I had no money to buy myself a ride home and no money to call."

I didn't know why he had suddenly stopped caring about my birthday. Was I supposed to read his mind? I stopped there, sensing the distinct pinch of incoming tears rouse my nostrils. This man would not see me cry today.

"I know, I know," he said.

In my daydreams of this confrontation, my dad assumed full responsibility for his actions; begged me to let him back in. He did more than tell me that he knew, he knew, with an apologetic squeeze to my left thigh. But the ensuing silence confirmed that this was all I would get today.

The iron gate of the farm appeared like a vision, awash in colorful blooms, and behind its dark green bars, my grandmother, milky-faced and vigorous. A curly-haired dog yapped at her side. As she held my face between her hands and soaked me in, I thought briefly of where she and my grandfather had been in that lost decade. Had they missed me? Had they tried to convince my dad to do the right thing?

But the cane on which Papi was leaning and the bright white of Mamie's hair told me we were no longer in the beginning of the story. I had a decision to make: to demand answers that might only disappoint me or to live in deliberate ignorance and forgive them. Conditioning the future of our relationship on arbitrary benchmarks would serve neither side well. What the Jucquois clan did or did not do from this point forward was not within my control. It had never been. What was in my own hands was the choice to love them in spite of our mutual history. Doing so would have to be a unilateral act, unmoored to reciprocity. I felt the options were this or to wash my hands of this family forever.

As we parted ways that afternoon, I promised to return once a year, no matter the circumstances. In the six years since, I had made good on my word. As for my dad, he had taken our biweekly phone dates seriously. I might have even liked the onerousness of our arrangement. It reminded me of those two years at the municipal boarding school during fourth and fifth grades, back when reaching me required my dad to make an effort—to thread between dinnertime and peak landline traffic. It made me feel wanted. We rarely had anything of consequence to talk about but tried to be faithful to our schedule. Missing our call still felt to me like a referendum on the state of our relationship.

*

AFTER WE HAD left the rehabilitation center in Loudun, I asked to stay at the farm for the night. Mamie and I killed time gossiping and chastising her possessed little terrier. Intermittently we found ourselves returning to the inescapable coverage of the *gilets jaunes*. Holiday sales were down from the last year, the newscasters and pundits insisted, though it was not clear to me that the protests were more to blame than the lagging economy. Storekeepers were afraid of the next marches on December 8. A collective presumption had formed that the violence would be worse. Some merchants were preemptively boarding their storefronts and hiring private security—safeguards that seemed to fuel the rumors of impending chaos. The government reassured the public that it would not deploy the army, though it had mobilized 89,000 law enforcement officers around the country and was rounding up purported troublemakers as a precaution.

Mamie seemed most annoyed with the looting. Where my dad stood was more of a mystery. His support seemed to vacillate from day to day, dependent on whatever position he thought would get a rise out of Lisette. He was a centrist and like thousands of French people, he felt disappointed in Macron's performance thus far. To him, the previous president and socialist leader, François Hollande, had been a champion for the poor. Macron seemed bent on catering to the rich. Who, then, was fighting for the working and middle classes? On this point, at least, my dad sympathized with the *gilets jaunes*.

I thought it could have been him out there, were he not so close to quitting the factory, which was once again on the brink of failure. The situation was so dire that a judicial administrator had been put in charge of it. They had but a few weeks to find a buyer. My dad's boss had recently called him to put retirement on the table. It would depend on whether the government's asbestos fund approved his application for an early release from work.

I doubted his younger colleagues, millennials, would fare so well. Most had been brought in under CDDs, the temporary contracts that had made my mom's income so unpredictable in the 1990s. Counting on CDDs to build the solid middle-class life offered to my dad with a GED was like pouring a foundation on sand, but people took the jobs they could. With national unemployment at 9 percent and Châtellerault's at 8.2 percent, options were limited. I bet that any number of them would swarm the foundries for my dad's backbreaking job with its guarantee of a pension, asbestos exposure and all.

WHILE MAMIE SEASONED slabs of salmon for dinner, I decided to roam the property in the dimming light. I loved this place. The dining room where we gathered on Sundays and holidays remained herself, her *paysan* flair elegant in its simplicity and kitsch. Decades ago, Mamie had draped its walls in red paisley florals that crawled from ceiling to doors. It was my favorite wallpaper in the world and, I imagined, the first thing any American realtor with sense would strip while preparing the home for sale. Perhaps they would replace it with a fashionable white paint—Dover SW 6385 or Snowbound SW 7004 or Marshmallow SW 7001—no longer a symbol of half-assed effort and sterility, before mounting the walls with inoffensive abstract art. The humble furnishings carved from heavy wood would make way for a glass table and modern clear chairs, transforming the room into a neutral ground, liberated from nostalgia, culminating in what American orthodoxy deemed "true potential."

Mamie would probably scoff at the thought. In more than half a century on rue de la Forge, I do not believe she and her husband had ever considered building this home for anyone's consumption but their own. The farm was their livelihood and, in that way, an extension of themselves. They ate, and fed their loved ones, from what they grew, milked, raised, and forged on this soil. For a woman with an elementary school education, the farm was even more than that. It was a guarantee of survival. Crises could come and go, but my grandmother could always count on this soil to sustain her.

Above the fireplace mantle hung a demoded hunting rifle and delicately painted ceramic plates. In one corner: decommissioned oil lamps projecting playful beams as the sun shone on the cylindered glass. And by the door: a portrait of Mamie immortalized at the age of six next to a white plaster bust of another striking young girl in a headscarf. Sometime before the age of five, I had decided the bust had to be of my dad's sister, Juanita.

On my visits as a kid, Mamie would sometimes announce that she was going to see her. "Coming with?" she would ask, and I would say yes because I would rather be walking among the dead than waiting alone with the insects. I am not sure where Papi was, but we went without him. We passed headstones made of marble and granite, some demure and plain, others grandly decorated with celestial beings. The engraved date ranges always made me feel funny inside. How unsettling that a whole world had preceded me but remained a vivid part of my loved ones' present. Mamie would dust off her eldest's headstone with a handkerchief and set down fresh flowers from her garden. "It's been a long time," she would sometimes say with a trace of disbelief.

I knew little about this prodigal daughter other than what my dad had mentioned: that she had been ten years his elder; that she had been a curious girl, hungry for new experiences; and that she had deemed Nueil-sous-Faye and her father bucolic to a fault. They had fought in the kitchen loudly and often. Juanita had left home as soon as possible.

An accident had claimed her life in 1977—not in the big city as Mamie and Papi had feared, but on the web of country roads that they had driven a thousand times. She had been on a trip home with her boyfriend. The theory was that something must have startled them. Either way, they had overcompensated and veered into an oncoming truck. The boyfriend had lived but Juanita had passed away a few days later. Though my grandparents were not Catholic beyond obligatory baptisms and first Communions, they had opted to hold a wake. My dad remembered his sister lying in the formal dining room for hours.

After her death, my grandparents buried their sadness in work, looking up at the world every once in a while by taking turns peering at the newspaper— Mamie holding the thing at arm's length and my grandfather to the tip of his long nose. Nations heaved. Globalization crept closer. Looming in the cities: waves of Africans pursuing their dreams in the lands of their former colonizers. I imagined my grandparents reading these reports and arriving at the realization that there was not much either could do, they put one foot in front of the other. Life had to go on.

At sixteen, my dad's future was altered forever. He and Juanita would never experience the complicity of being siblings in adulthood. Any ambitions he might have harbored of leaving the Poitou-Charentes had vanished with her. It was not that my grandparents had demanded that he stay. But my dad grasped the burden of becoming an only child. Mamie would not survive his disappearance. And so he had settled for an adventureless life in a simple apartment and a decently paying job in a one-hour radius of the farm.

I still wondered how much this single tragic death explained other choices my dad had made—his marriages to women from below the equator and by extension, my presence here, now.

AS NIGHTFALL COATED the air in a frosty blackness, I meandered back toward the house, past the blacksmith shop where Papi's rusting equipment slept in a tangle of iridescent threads, and away from the coop where Mamie's last hens were balled up into feathered loaves. The opaque sky reminded me of glassy waters. Devoid of ambulance sirens, circling helicopters, thumping basses. What a luxury it would be, I thought, to live and work in such peace.

It was this most idyllic site of my childhood that my brain had conjured as my eleventh-grade English class read Flaubert's *Madame Bovary*, during passages where the miserable Emma Bovary "would gaze out over the solitude of her life with desperate eyes, seeking some white sail in the mists of the far-off horizon."[13] I recalled how her haughtiness toward the countryside and her insatiable boredom had exasperated me. Emma's inability to adapt to her circumstances had struck me as a moral failing. There was a tension, I realized, between the coldness I felt toward her and the compassion that came to me naturally for Juanita. Both of their spirits had been incompatible with the smallness of village life, a smallness of both spirit and space, for in a literal way, it was this smallness—roads better suited for horses than two-way traffic—that had eventually taken my aunt prematurely.

But as an adult, I saw the peaceful atmosphere of the countryside, which had tormented the young Emma, differently. The stillness concealed leagues of grief: from the hundreds of agricultural workers who committed suicide annually—372 in 2015 alone[14]—to the thousands more expiring slowly from decades of handling pesticides, their hands trembling like my own grandfather's. A few acres over, neighbors might be trying, furiously and invisibly, to pay off massive debts, but in spite of their best efforts, losing to a relentless future—mergers between conglomerates, an obstinate economy, a fickle climate increasingly hostile to harvests.

Survival here had always been buoyed by violence. The precise degree and scale depended on one's primary way of making a living. My own grandparents, for instance, had supplemented their income with a small orchard, the blacksmith shop, and for a short time in the '70s, a little gas pump that Papi ran. The farm had required them to separate kids from their mama goats and slaughter male chicks. The homemade pâté and rillettes that delighted me had been ground from the rabbits Papi shot in the junkyard, the very lumps that I had once watched him skin with admiration. Death was inextricable from this place.

*

LATER THAT NIGHT, lying in my dad's childhood bed, I struggled to fall asleep without my nightly dose of bottomless scrolling. The tiny "loading" wheels teased me with each refresh of the apps, spinning into oblivion before freezing totally. Years ago, the village's mayor had pledged to install public Wi-Fi at the town hall, which happened to be directly across the street from the farm's iron gates. Nothing had materialized, though, and the nearest spot of service remained, according to my teenage half sisters, on the lawn where Papi and his mates used to play *pétanque*. It was cold out now and a desperate walk to the lawn seemed even more pathetic than my lamenting the dearth of stimulus to occupy me in the wee hours.

A wave of anxiety blanketed the void with an urge to figure out, right then and there, what would become of the farm without my grandparents. Did my dad have the know-how to care for the flowers and vines as well as Mamie? Was there any point, if the farm was empty? And would it be fair to hold on to it, if we could not care for it as my grandparents had? What did my dad, or I, owe this home in return for the thick layer of history it had granted each of us?

No more farm sleepovers for me, I swore to myself in the light of day.

Now if only there was a trick to not missing this place the minute we drove off.

*

ON OUR NEXT VISIT, a day or two later, Papi's eyes were glossy and restless but more alert. He seemed to recognize me or understood enough to pretend that he did. I hoped the unusualness of my presence, my second visit in a year, had not sunk in. The last thing Papi needed in his feeble state was more reason to be alarmed.

Our eyes kept drifting to the television mounted between his bed and that of his suitemate, a purple-nosed man with an abnormally distended belly. The December 8 marches had been mostly peaceful so far, with the Champs Élysées and Place de la Bastille emptier than anticipated. In one anticlimactic standoff, a group of *gilets jaunes* kneeled before ranks of police in aggressive gear, restaging the dramatic image of the high schoolers from the banlieue. Cameras seemed to be in search of rating-spikers, riot units nabbing protesters and tear gas grenades volleying between the two sides. Soon enough, their wish would be granted. Armed with that footage and dozens of interviews with denouncers of window-breaking, the studios would have enough to cycle through one more week of news.

While we were distracted, Papi had slumped in his mechanized bed. We swarmed him. Whatever the nurses were feeding him was not sticking to his bones. My grandfather was a rag doll in a pool of silk. I fidgeted with his food tray while someone else tried to straighten him out using the bed remote. Afraid that by overhandling him, I might dislocate something in his tender frame, I stepped aside to let the grownups take over.

"Could you imagine," my dad began with a naughty smile, "if we pressed the wrong thing and he just folded up like that? *Paf!*" He clapped his hands as if snapping shut an alligator mouth. He giggled tensely, hands back in his pockets.

Ah yes, I thought: *The stern Mr. Jucquois of rue de la Forge. Sent to an untimely death by an accidental pancake-like flattening of the body. May his humorless soul rest in peace.*

Lisette and I shook our heads in mock disgust. Mamie straightened the bed to a comfortable position, to my grandfather's obliviousness.

I would miss him. Though Papi had been short on words and even shorter on displays of affection, his care for us had never been in question. I considered briefly verbalizing my love for the first time, but the end had arrived too quickly and I feared now that a sincere goodbye would bring him too much sorrow. Mamie and Lisette were gathering their purses and my dad was practically through the sliding glass doors. It was better to leave him this way, unaware of the gravity, his watery eyes staring vacantly through us.

"*À bientôt*, Papi," I said and left.

ʃ

MY DAD APPEARED in the parking lot where we were set to meet looking supremely French in a white-and-navy striped shirt. I gave a goodbye kiss to my godmother, with whom we had stayed for the last few days, and introduced my dad and boyfriend in French and English. It was September 2019, and my first return home since Papi died. My dad addressed Sam and paused for my translation.

"He wants to know if you're enjoying the trip so far," I said quickly.

"*Oh oui, oui. Très bien*," Sam answered in his thick Anglo-Michigan accent.

Which was mostly true. Sam and I had flown together from DC to Spain in late August and spent a week biking around Valencia with his childhood friend and his partner. Then, we had come up to the Poitou-Charentes and spent the last few days with my godmother, who was a formidable host but did not speak a lick of English, which made it difficult for her and Sam to get to know each other. (Her husband, my godfather, was an avid hot-air balloon pilot and was away at a competition.) I had warned Sam that the silence around these parts could be unsettling, but had forgotten to mention other details, like the three-hour lunches and general lack of cell phone service. The French leg of our trip had been fun but also isolating for him.

Perhaps sensing how much Sam meant to me, my dad appeared determined not to let the language barrier get in the way of communicating with him. We were on the sunny side of the patio of his home, later that afternoon, when he turned to my boyfriend with a passing thought.

"He says that my grandfather never bounced him on his lap," I relayed with an apologetic smile. Grief had a way of sneaking up on people.

My dad continued. "Never in his life. Strange, huh?"

"Yes, that is quite strange," Sam said.

"Stranger still," my dad went on with a chuckle, "the casket was hardly in the ground" when his mother removed his father's photos from public view and disposed of his coats.

I laughed.

Three weeks had passed since the funeral. Incredibly, Papi had held on for months after I left in December of the previous year. So long that I had assumed that he would be there to meet Sam at the iron gate on this long-anticipated visit. The center had sent him home, mid-January of 2019, in a wheelchair and motorized bed, which were installed for him in the dining room. For the next seven months, two aides had taken turns driving to Nueil-sous-Faye, six days a week, to help lift him out of bed, bathe him, and administer his medications. Papi's condition had stabilized enough for him to lucidly berate both the aides and his wife while they helped him out. But five weeks before Sam and I made it home, I woke up to missed calls and a written Facebook message from Lisette. Papi had passed away in his sleep.

I had searched for composure as my grandmother's landline rang. Mamie was tough, as if forged of iron herself, but this was her husband of almost seven decades. I was reminded of something Sam had told me long ago. There were people you should only grieve *in* with, which was to say, to set aside your own feelings in order to be a comforting shoulder to those who were more intimate with the deceased person. Only with others, people more removed from the deceased, and in the position to support you, could you allow yourself to grieve *out*. With this concept in mind, I had called my mom first and cried on the phone to her. Then, I had gathered my emotions to offer my condolences to my grandmother.

"How are you holding up?" I asked her. A silly question but what else was there to say.

"I couldn't do it anymore," she said, her voice almost confessional. "It was like living in a prison. All year, I could not go anywhere. And he could be mean, your grandfather. So very mean. The things he said to me."

There was no other way to describe it. At eighty-five, my grandmother was free.

We agreed as a family that it did not make sense for me to return for the funeral with a planned trip so close. I sent a card and wreath for Papi's headstone in the little cemetery a block from the farm.

For days after my call with Mamie, I found myself pondering both her reaction and my own. Why had her transparent relief shocked me? Papi had many redeeming qualities, but it was no secret that he could be an asshole, and most so toward her, in the way hurting those closest to us came so easy. It might have been that in the years that I had seen him sick, Mamie never once com-plained about the effort. She had said nothing of the twilight years that his illness and ensuing disability had stolen from her, years she had wanted to spend traveling abroad with her sisters and groups of likeminded seniors.

I understood, deep down, what those last months must have been like for her—the bittersweet irony of surviving the violence of the countryside, of being freed from labor from necessity, only for duty to confine her again. For as much as the land beneath the farm had provided for her, it had also determined her trajectory from teenagerhood. Her father, a butcher, had shown no inter-est in sending her to school despite her obvious wit. She had been pragmatic in choosing marriage and this particular life. Because how else could a woman of her class raise two children and avoid burdening them in her old age?

In order to protect the purest moments of my childhood, I had shielded myself from her reality. I had wanted to believe my grandparents were happy enough despite their perpetual jabs at each other. I had wanted to believe that they never longed to be elsewhere, despite the restraints that staying imposed on them. I had wanted Mamie to perform the part of the bereft, saintly widow, because that was what people were supposed to do, and because simple people and simple places are easier to love. I had wanted this, despite having made the conscious choice, years ago, to love my grandparents regard-less of their imperfections.

*

MAMIE WAS IN a jolly mood on the morning that we picked her up, the four of us—my dad, Lisette, Sam, and me—for her appointment at the notary. We parked on the plaza of Richelieu, where a smattering of seniors were going about their business. It was a weekday, but my dad was freer than ever now that the government's asbestos fund had approved his application, allowing him to semi-retire at the age of fifty-eight. The timing had coincided with Papi's release from the rehab facility earlier in the year. As a result, my dad had been able to spend more time on the farm in the last year. A good son until the end.

Rather than translate dull jargon for the next two hours as the grownups sorted through Papi's finances, I took Sam to the parc de Richelieu. The morning was bright and crisp, and the town largely tourist-free. As we crossed the gates, I pointed to the empty green expanse before us and explained to Sam that my dad and I used to ride our bikes from the farm to these beautiful grounds when I was a little girl. That the real-life cardinal from the *Three Musketeers* novel once had a castle right here. It had been taken down in his lifetime and never rebuilt. Or something like that. I could not say for sure without more internet bars, but it was nice not to have them, to be present.

We paused to watch a family of white swans float down the glistening waters and dreamed out loud about leaving our day jobs to write here, away from the distractions that made DC such a tempting place to live. My dad and Lisette could watch our prospective children or we would send them to my Normandy cousins by train, with identifying lanyards around their necks. In this alternate life, we would start each morning with a long bike ride before taking the winding roads back to the farm. Around noon, I would help Mamie with lunch. And at dusk, we would share a coffee with her on the chairs near the blacksmith shop while combing through old photo albums. The smallness of the village would be comforting and the silence a salve for our overstimulated minds. The vines would trim themselves. My grandmother would live forever and it would all be so nice.

Parting with this place felt impossible, even as I saw clearly that sustaining it would require more than love, so we left untouched the Outline in which the farm welcomes a new family, resuscitating the sounds of animals and children discovering wonder in every cranny. I shunned the thought, abruptly jealous of them, saddened that my own children, and someday my half sisters' children, figments of my mind still, might never have a chance to forge their own memories here. Perhaps someday my own memories would fade. Yet, holding on to the farm in idleness, for sentimentality's sake, would be a waste of land—a denigration of my grandparents' decades of labor.

My dad seemed to agree but like me, could think of no ready-made solution to give the farm the love and usage it would deserve after the end of the story.

"What are we to do then?" I asked him, as if our home was not already in the process of being lost.

Home Bound

REASONS FOR POSTPONING A TRIP back to Cameroon always abounded. Flights were priced too high at peak season. I was too fresh a hire to take time off. Then, the vacation days were there but cases at the Consumer Financial Protection Bureau were keeping me busy. I was also freelancing on the side, podcasting and publishing pieces about politics in a handful of magazines, projects that created their own set of deadlines.

Then, the mother of all delays hit—a global pandemic. I had flown out to Los Angeles for an investigation during the last week of February 2020, and on the way back a few days later, made a pit stop in Nevada to celebrate my mom's birthday with our Reno family. COVID-19 was getting increasing news coverage, but airports were still operating, restaurants were still serving, and schools were still teaching. My family and I followed developments with incredulity, unsure of how worried we should be. I made my way back to DC on March 8, boarding two separate full flights, which were split by a three-hour layover at a crowded gate at the Phoenix airport.

I remember feeling silly as I emailed my supervisor the next morning to ask for permission to quarantine at home for the next fourteen days, despite having no symptoms. But this virus seemed to be making people really ill and I was afraid of infecting anyone if I had contracted it on my travels. On March 11, the National Basketball League announced the immediate suspension of the 2019–2020 season. The rest of America, my office included, quickly followed suit and shut down.

Until then, I had been happy to date Sam from the comfort of my perfect condo in Petworth while he lived in neighboring Park View, then in a three-bedroom rowhouse in northeast DC that he shared with his younger brother Jacob. But the unclarity around how exposure to this new virus worked made it difficult to quarantine apart. I was more of a lone wolf than Sam, but even I was not immune to cabin fever. Besides, his new place was bigger. I brought a suitcase over containing enough clothes to last me a month.

We worried, at first, that the quarantine would hurt our relationship. For the last two years, we had seen each other several times a week, a pace that had worked well for us. Now we would be spending every waking hour together. But June 2020 rolled around, and things were still going smoothly between us. We began talking about the logistical steps of permanently moving in together, and debated the merits of entering into a domestic partnership versus getting married. Sam had just turned thirty-three years old. My thirty-second birthday was coming up that October. Did we want to commit to having children? And if so, when? Did it make sense, given the mountain of evidence we had about climate change? Given how frightening this pandemic was?

Meanwhile, my mom and Dave were floating a move across the country. They had left Reno soon after I graduated law school and had since lived in Texas and Virginia, before settling in Dave's native Washington State. But they missed the DMV. I offered them my empty condo. It was small for two people, but free, and a ten-minute drive from our house. They could take their time looking for a new home. I was excited for them to live close enough that we could at least meet up outdoors. My parents arrived in DC the fall of 2020.

Cameroon remained on my mind. I missed Maman Florence, Tata Nicole, and the rest of my sprawling family. I guessed the half siblings on my biological mother's side—Laetitia, Willy, and Reece—were different people than the children I had seen on my 2008 trip. In my thirties, I had matured, too. And I was interested in seeing Ésaïe's children again—my half brother Charlie, with whom had I spent a lovely afternoon, my half-sisters Elisa, Maggie, and Ange, and any other half siblings who might be in Yaoundé. I had the time and money to go *back home*, and had for some years, but the barriers between us now exceeded these concerns. I struggled to keep track of which borders were closed, to whom, and under what conditions. It appeared the coronavirus was not devastating sub-Saharan Africa with the zeal that the West predicted, but whether I could trust the case numbers that Cameroon reported was another story. The prospect of an effective vaccine still felt remote. Historically, their development took time—a year and a half, two years, perhaps longer. First, the science had to prove safe. Then the Federal Drug Administration and Centers for Disease Control had to act fast and in concert. Short of a miracle, quarantines and closed borders could be our new normal for ages. I regretted not returning to Cameroon when it was all simpler. But as 2020 drew to an end, two signs made it clear to me that, pandemic or not, it was time to come home.

First: a call to my cellphone, on New Year's Eve, from a phone number in Québec. I picked up hesitantly. On the other end of the line was a voice I'd not heard in five, possibly six years. My half-brother Franz, Ésaïe's third-oldest son. I remembered him fondly. He spoke in protective undertones, with a veneer of authority to which I did not mind submitting. On the phone with him, I felt deferential, eager to cede to my elder. In this way, he reminded me of Charlie. Both half brothers had shown me nothing but kindness. I had been their little sister, a full member of their clan, from the moment they met me in the maternity ward.

Franz invited me to a group text. All our siblings would be on it, he explained, save for the eldest of the Assae children, Cyriaque, who had an impossibly difficult personality. The goal was to evaluate Ésaïe's estate, which comprised a compound and, among other effects, an old truck, a rifle and handgun, farming equipment, things of that nature, all of which had been left behind without a will or administrator when Ésaïe died in 2006. I had been offered the chance to see the compound in person during my 2008 trip. Tonton François, our father's first cousin, had said he could take me to our ancestral village. I had wanted to accept but my mom had put her foot down from Nevada, kiboshing his plans to take me south. She trusted no one, not even this ex of hers and relative of mine. In the end, I had been too influenceable, too afraid to accompany my uncle to the village. Regret still haunted me when I received my half brother's call.

I agreed to join the group but warned Franz in clear terms that I would choose to walk away empty-handed at the first sign of real conflict over the estate. I had seen land disputes cause my maternal family strife for decades after my grandfather's passing. The trouble hardly ever seemed worth it. Besides, preserving and caring for a property in a rural area seemed awfully challenging. Of course, this was easy for me to say after thirty-two years outside the Assae family. As much as our father's absence had pained me, it had also spared me from the expectation that an inheritance would rescue me. I felt a sort of pride, a freedom in knowing that I owed him little other than half my genes.

It became evident, upon joining the group thread, that this was not his children's first attempt to resolve the estate question, though it was the first time both out-of-wedlockers—myself and a younger boy, Philip—were included. The initial exchanges started on a positive note, we even did a couple of group video chats. But the honeymoon ended soon. Demands mounted relating to what was still at the compound and what had been stolen or sold, or remained unaccounted for. Ancient fights, to which I was not privy, resurfaced between the older siblings, tainting demands with accusation and responses with defensiveness. Within a matter of weeks, the group text died with huffy departures.

Before the ensuing silence, though, the thread had offered glimpses of the compound. Furtive shots and angled videos taken by Ange, the youngest of us ten. Equipment to make palm oil and parts of pumps were gone, stolen. Villagers had stolen mattresses from the guest houses on the property. Ange had arrived to find children picking fruit from the trees. But she could confirm that our father's rifle and handgun were still there. And here were documents bearing his face in monochrome: youthful, alive, hungry. I flipped through the photos and videos eagerly. Elsewhere, an appraisal of the property conducted in the fall of 1996, a few months before my mom and I moved into the sterile one-bedroom apartment in the Duchère. The valuation numbers were so massive that I took out a calculator to make sure I understood their meaning; that it was not just a matter of inflation. Our father had been as wealthy as my maternal family had hinted over the years. Wealthy enough to buy luxurious accommodations in Lyon, London, Reno, and even DC.

I was surprised to find that this information left me neither bitter nor angry. On the contrary, I felt content discovering traces of my father in these children and artifacts. At most, I wished to have been there with Ange. Or better yet, to see it through our brother Charlie's eyes, Charlie who had been so welcoming to me in 2008, and who since had moved closer to the ancestral village to better protect the patrimony our father had poured so much of himself into. I had hoped, in pondering this new trip, that the uncle we shared was still willing to take me.

The second sign that it was time came in late March 2021, when Maggie, the daughter born right after me, texted me in the middle of the night. She wanted to see if I had time to talk; there was something she wanted to discuss. I sensed that the matter was important to her but wondered what it could be about. The group thread had dissolved weeks earlier. Even while it had been active, I had made myself disposable, shared few biographical details beyond my location at the time—*New Orleans, down south*; what I was up to—*working*; and my health—*nothing newsworthy*. I could be shy amid strangers, and these siblings, though they shared my face, were strangers. But there was more to it. A part of me wanted to remain unknowable to them. I felt safest on the fringes—being one of them, but not so much as to give any of them the power to hurt me.

I called Maggie the next day. My sister sounded nervous, she talked fast. It was about our father. Papa, as she called him. They had been terribly close, as close as I had been to my daddy. When life was uphill and relentless, she said, as it was for her this last year, she could not help but remember how our father would have made things right for her, how he would have intervened to protect her. She had been with him until the very end, she said, sleeping in his room and tending to his sores.

I asked her what he was sick with. My maternal family thought sorcery had killed him but Franz had offered a more benign, if equally vague, answer: respiratory issues. Maggie knew more. Our father had suffered from asthma and diabetes, she said, but there was more, conditions that physicians never fully ascertained. He had been poisoned, too. More than once. Maggie delivered this news almost as if it were the most natural outcome in the world, and perhaps it was. Our father was arrogant and fiercely driven. A man who would have done anything, even betray others, to be appointed as a minister and head a presidential cabinet. This, Maggie admitted, was the only flaw she reproached him for: "That his noes were not always noes, and his yesses were not always yesses."

She had only ever known him sick, in and out of hospitals and healers' tents. But he had fought to live. This will had helped him rebound time after time, and made her all the more unprepared for his death. Which brought us to the purpose of her contact. On his deathbed, he had made her promise to give me a message. She had not been certain of when or how to convey it. But then Franz had added me to the thread and she had found me approachable, nice even.

Maggie sniffled loudly. She wanted me to know that our father had spoken about me to her and our other siblings, that he was aware of my academic success, and that he was immensely proud. She swore that he had tried to contact me. Many times. Of this, she was absolutely certain. But from what she'd heard, the aunt who raised me had rejected his calls multiple times. She did not wish to excuse her father, but it was important context that the mother of his other out-of-wedlock child, our half-brother Philip, had shut him out, too, refusing to answer the door when our father tried to establish contact with the boy. Maggie ventured that the double dose of rejection had caused him to abandon efforts to reach me. But she knew her father. He regretted the way he had handled things with his children.

I wondered, while my sister went on: could my adoptive mom have deliberately kept Ésaïe at bay? She had always been protective of me. He had a litany of children and Maman Florence had birthed three more after me, with other partners, but I was my adoptive mom's one and only. It would have been hard enough for her to deal with the distinct feeling that Maman Florence had seemed, at times, to rethink her decision to give me up, disappointed by the lack of proximity and emotional connection between us as I grew up. But that complicated family dynamic was something my mom could navigate with the support of other siblings, and of Mamie Catherine, when she was alive, who still saw the wisdom in the arrangement, and the opportunities that it would open for me. Our family remembered the pain behind the sacrifices that led to my departure from Cameroon, in the summer of 1989. Our family understood, too, the tough shell one had to cultivate fast and early to survive in a country like ours and, while they were not so naive as to presume that a childhood in the West would shield me from struggle, they saw that it would not be the same, that life would be softer.

I wondered, too—if Ésaïe ever got it in his head to steal me back, could my mom count on him to consider all these things: the fact that I had only ever known one set of parents, one standard of living; that taking me away would mean not only that my cousin Nadège's chances at a different future had been spoiled, but that mine would be as well? I understood now that the summer of 1989 was, to him, a fog of betrayal. While out on a recent walk together, the two of us, my mom had revealed to me that after Ésaïe discovered my adoption and disappearance, he had gone to Mamie Catherine and reminded her who he was, what he had the power to do with just a few phone calls. She had talked him down from acting impulsively that day, but my mom had received the long-distance message. She could not, for one second, forget the threat he posed to her motherhood.

Perhaps my mom had intervened more than she let on. But what of it? I could not bear to ask her now and yet still be left to wonder, afterward, whether she had told me the whole truth. Perhaps I would have asked, in a different time, during those teenage years when the urge to know my father and be known by him felt vital. But the chance for that had vanished with his death. All that was left now were the parents who remained and a few puzzle pieces to make sense of, with completion as the sole reward. For what it was worth, I would not resent my mom today if indeed she had ignored my biological father's calls. Protecting me had been her first and foremost duty. She was my mom. I understood her burden.

My sister continued, unfazed by my silence. Here was what she had reached out to tell me: our father's last message to me was that he loved me and that he wanted the Assae children united.

Maggie was sobbing.

I tried to console her. I wanted her to know that she was brave for baring her heart to me, a person she did not know, to fulfill her father's last wishes. And that the gesture meant more to me than she could ever imagine. She had given me a gift: another side of our father. I knew that Ésaïe was a lot of things—imperfect, sometimes contemptible. But through her, I also saw his capability of being a good and loving father. That he had raised her, such a kind and considerate daughter, that he had become worthy of her affection, could not entirely undo the effects of his absence on my life, but it redeemed him in some sense, made him human.

Before we hung up, I told Maggie that I understood the rawness of her feelings half a lifetime later. That I, too, was once a daddy's girl. And that I looked forward to seeing her again in person soon.

I FLEW OUT to Yaoundé on one of the hottest afternoons of the summer, in late June 2021, with my mom and Dave. Sam accompanied me to Dulles Airport in a rideshare. We found my parents standing in the check-in line, which was long and distinctly West African in both the sheer number of languages spoken and the stacks of luggage per family. A perfect introduction for Dave, who had never set foot in Africa, let alone Cameroon. I kissed Sam goodbye and promised to take good care of myself. Three weeks. By far the longest we'd be apart since the onset of the pandemic our living room elopement, just a month earlier. (Jacob had officiated.)

I would miss him, but Sam was proud to see me off. He understood, I knew, that returning to Yaoundé was an imperative, that going so long without visiting our maternal family was a gamble—people died unexpectedly—and that I had important unfinished business to attend to, concerning my biological father, who was proof, for whoever still needed it, that death marched on the beat of its own drum, unmoored to any of our timelines.

We had reached the Brussels Airlines ticketing counter when it occurred to me that my yellow fever immunization card was sitting at home, in a clear pouch at the bottom of a drawer. My mom said I would not be able to enter the country without it. This had not exactly been an oversight on my part. In the last month, I had sent a color copy of my yellow card to the Cameroonian embassy via certified mail. Twice. No visas could be granted without this proof. The issuance of a visa implied vaccination. A thirty-day visa currently graced my passport. Flashing a physical copy of the card at the Yaoundé airport seemed redundant, but I was beginning to doubt that Cameroonian customs would see my ironclad logic. Here was a country that had not updated its entry requirements since the earliest days of the pandemic, and that had denied our initial visa applications for failing to provide proof of a family medical emergency.

I had vacillated between indignation and acceptance of the visa denial. Cameroon did not recognize dual citizenships, and so my place of birth was in a way no longer my own. To cross its borders demanded a justification, payment of a steep fee, a pledge not to overstay my welcome. But of course, this was a small price for people like me—a privileged holder of two of the most powerful passports in the world. The European Union and United States had denied my maternal family visas for lesser reasons, more times than I could count on my hands. Was this reciprocity not deserved?

Besides, if I was honest with myself, the decision to cancel the trip being made for me would come as bittersweet relief. I needed to go, without a doubt. But I had been sick with heartburn, inconvenient bouts of nausea, and uncharacteristic fatigue. One of my work cases was marching stubbornly toward trial. And a column of cardboard boxes required pick up from Petworth so my new real estate agent could transform my condo into a marketable blank slate—a minor task I had put off for weeks, even though this had done nothing to stave off the anxiety of parting with the first 610 square feet that had ever felt truly mine. I was too exhausted to accommodate the whims of a dysfunctional bureaucracy. If Cameroon wanted to shut me out now, so be it.

But my family wouldn't hear it. Without my lifting a finger, visa-appropriate emergencies had been conjured, memorialized on formal letterheads, and expedited to the relevant authorities. The embassy had finally relented, ten days before departure. Too many people had toiled for me to now chance a rejection at the border for missing my yellow fever card.

The more zen my mom displayed in the face of my conundrum, the more I felt the blood rise and swell in my arteries. We were already here, she said. Sam could text me a picture of the immunization record so I could present the screenshot at the border. But I worried about her plan. We had absolutely no idea that it would work. What if we caught someone on the wrong day, or worse, happened upon one of the country's few honest agents? I sent my husband an alarmed text. He would have to race to the airport again and bring me my immunization record within the hour.

Sam made it back quickly, thankfully, but in my frazzled rush to the international gate, I then forgot my laptop at security. By the time I noticed, it was too late to do anything about it. The laptop would have to await my return somewhere in the underbelly of the airport. I tried to remind myself of what mattered. I was happily creased into a narrow seat, the card now safely tucked into my backpack. I could finally allow joy to sink in. Only a few hours separated me from Maman Florence, from Tata Nicole, my uncles Essomba and Engo, and their children. I was excited to spend time with Charlie again, to give Maggie the warmest hug and, at last, to see our father's village and tomb.

The plane pushed back from the gate with gentle ease, and rolled onto the runway. I shut my eyes. In the recurring dream that had haunted me since 2008, this was the part where the floor split in two and the fuselage vanished, where our seats hung in midair and I woke up torn with self-reproach. Instead, my eyes opened to a serene cloudscape. A map of our trajectory flashed across the overhead screens.

I was home bound.

I FOUGHT TO stay awake, not having slept in twenty-two hours, as our car tumbled toward the heart of Yaoundé. It was after nine P.M. but the road teemed with yellow taxis in various stages of decay. Bodies ambulated on its edges, undeterred by the absence of sidewalks. Some were carrying bags in their hands, others buckets on their heads. We tumbled past bar terraces, neon-lit shacks where soccer fans swilled beer and half-watched reruns of the European Football Championship. I cracked open my window. A permanent layer of diesel fuel competed against wafts of smoked meat, grilled corn, fried beignet dough. Few traffic lights and even fewer rules of engagement applied. Signaling turns seemed optional. Road panels decorative. Functioning tail-lights, a rare extravagance.

More motorbikes, most functioning as uninsured taxis, cluttered the streets than I remembered—the product of worsening traffic and sky-high unemployment. The young men who drove them were fearless, reckless. At times loaded with three, four, even five passengers—not all of them adults—the motorbikes razored between cars and semis with impudence. No helmets, of course.

One of these motorbikes had plowed into my little cousin Synthia, Tata Nicole's daughter, around five years ago. She had suffered a concussion and shattered her lower leg bone. Then, the resulting wound became infected. At thirteen, she had almost lost her leg. My mom and I had sent money to cover bills at a private hospital.

Then, a few days before Thanksgiving of 2020, two of these taxi-motorbikes were racing each other, this time with my half-brother Willy, twenty-six years old, sitting on one of their backseats, when one of them crashed, propelling Willy across the asphalt, knocking his skull against a car. It was a miracle that anyone had bothered to bring him to the hospital, that he had lived at all. For a frightening week, he had been unable to speak or move. His ear needed to be reattached and carefully tended to stop it from rotting. We had worried about the long-term effects of his traumatic head injury. It was the kind of accident that could short-circuit someone's persona. But on the phone, he had remained the sweet, cheeky boy I met in 2008, insistent on calling my mom and me to personally thank us for covering his hospital stay, even though speaking that soon after the accident took so much out of him. I gently rebuffed him, embarrassed. Sending money felt like the absolute least I could do. More than anything, I had longed to spend the night by his side, taking my turn to watch over him, as any good sister should. I was grateful that he and Synthia had made a full recovery, but hated that we could have lost them both. It was also for them, for these children born after me, that I needed to return.

Before our arrival in Yaoundé, my mom had sworn up and down that she could still drive around this place, but the gasps she emitted after each close call—and there were so many—told another story. Thankfully, she would not have to. Tonton Engo, who was without question the best driver and most unflappable member of our enormous brood, had recently lost his job as a car mechanic but loved driving, and had volunteered to be our chauffeur during our stay. Still, I thought, now would be a good time for her God to watch over us.

"Essomba, I don't recognize anything. Where are we now?" my mom asked again.

"Mvog Belinga. Our grandmother's village. She was born somewhere around here. See, up there?"

My uncle was pointing toward the driver's-side window, but nothing about the scene outside looked like a village to me. The imposing cement bones of unfinished buildings and second homes overlooked slum housing, which was splattered haphazardly across lower terrain.

"This all used to be bush," my mom said.

If this was the after, then I missed the before.

We turned off the main street and onto a steep hill, at the bottom of which a yellow apartment building emerged. A guard in a black knit hat pushed the metal gate open. We had hardly stepped out when a flurry of hands dragged our heavy suitcases toward the stairs.

I embraced Tonton Engo and greeted his son Yanis, a shy boy of seventeen. I took in the other young men surrounding them. Time had blurred most of their nicknames but their faces felt familiar even with all the baby fat melted away. I kissed them, wondering which was Eyenga, which was Bambino, which was Emerick. But the one who was a head taller than them all, I could never forget. Maman Florence's youngest. He approached timidly.

"Reece," I whispered, cupping his face in my hands.

"Sis," my little brother said.

The seven-year-old who used to nick my toothbrush had morphed into a six-foot-four man with a cool haircut. I was glad his naughty dimples had not gone away.

A dozen more family members awaited us upstairs. I marveled at the young adult faces around the living room. Katrina, Tonton Essomba's eldest of five and only daughter, was twenty-one. Tata Nicole's little one, Synthia, had turned eighteen last year and walked without the slightest limp.

Laetitia and I locked eyes. She had almost reached her full six feet by the age of fourteen, when I saw her last, but a little sister is a little sister. We hugged for a long time.

Willy's job had transferred him to an office in Douala, the country's largest city, out on the coast. But he had promised to take a bus down to see us soon.

I took in the faces new to our family. Two reserved girls, barely out of their teens, had come. Daughters of Tonton Essomba's girlfriend, someone informed me. Standing with my brother Reece was a warm boy in his mid-twenties whom everyone called Messi. A half brother of Pat, on his mother's side, no blood relation to me. But such distinctions rarely survived in our clan. We were all family now.

An array of dishes adorned the dining table. Grilled beef on skewers and braised fish. Sweet plantains, fried and steamed. Steamed cassava and, in another bowl, cassava in fufu form, made from flour. The women must have started cooking at dawn. As I admired the pots of *ndolé* bitter leaf and my favorite dish, the milder *tégué* leaf stewed with fresh ground nuts, Tata Nicole directed my attention to two smaller pots. These batches had been made without onions and garlic, which I had struggled to keep down in my first trimester. I thanked Tata Nicole profusely, the muscles in my face working double-time to conceal my mortification at being an imposition from day one.

"For the baby," she said with a light pat to my belly, which remained flat sixteen weeks into my pregnancy.

Here were my grandmother's descendants summarized in one gesture— never ones to have much, yet always copious in their generosity.

I had missed them.

Tonton Essomba joined me on the balcony. This far up, the air was clear of fumes and motorized growls. We had hoped for a pied-à-terre in a safe and quiet area, not too far from the familial property in Ngousso, with running water and air-conditioning to ease my stepdad's transition here. Tata Nicole had found this luxurious rental in the Santa Barbara quarter, near two massive water towers. For a monthly fee of one million Central African francs (CFAs)—at the time, 10,0000 CFAs were worth eighteen dollars—we were guaranteed a washing machine, a short fridge, modern plumbing, a third bedroom for company, and cable TV.

The breeze made my ponytail shudder.

"You chilly? This is cold for us," my uncle said, rubbing his upper arms with vigor. He was short and slim, a problematic knee trapping him in the posture of a gawky teenager. Somehow, his face remained frozen with youth well into his fifties.

"Oh no, this is really nice." DC had been flirting with the nineties on our last day. I was only wearing long sleeves now to protect myself from the most dangerous mosquitoes, which I heard preferred to hunt at night. Tonton Essomba laughed at my answer.

"See that building out there?" he asked.

I synced my gaze to his. Night had painted the city in charcoal but I could still make out the cornstalks separating our two nearest neighbors, and in the far distance, the half ring of sparsely populated hills enclosing the city. A lone compound, imposing in its brightness, overlooked the leftmost peak.

"That's the Presidential Palace."

"Where my father worked?"

Tonton Essomba nodded.

"Even gave me a tour once."

*

THOUGH IT WAS the "little rain season," it had not yet rained in Yaoundé since our arrival, compounding hot days with little reprieve. We convinced Tonton Engo and Dave to drop us off at the bottom of the Fougerolles open-air market and take refuge from the sun at the Ngousso house. Our walk home would be short enough.

I followed Tata Nicole and my mom across the median, then up a rust-stained alley. With great care, we stepped between arrays of palm nuts the tint of flames, stalks full of mature plantains, finely chopped green legumes in basins, spices ground into fragrant powders. Market was a business left mostly to women and girls, the chicken coop no exception. Tata Nicole saluted the mother who ran it and approached the cages to examine the flapping hens. She emerged holding a white bird by the feet. A teenage girl in rubber slippers trailed her with a second one.

"And you defeather them good this time, okay?" my aunt told her, handing her the second pick. "Not the nonsense you left me with last time. I had to finish your work at home."

"Yes, *la mère*," the girl said with a sheepish smile.

The trend had arisen during my absence—younger people calling strangers *the mother* or *the father*, usually while trying to endear themselves to an elder in the midst of a transaction. I found the nakedness of it charming.

"She used to be my student," my aunt said.

My mom and I picked a spot to stare at, away from the beheadings.

Back at the family property in Ngousso, we found Maman Florence in good spirits and eager to help with dinner, despite a bout of what she suspected to be either malaria or typhoid. To cover all her bases, she had picked up medication for both. The grounds had not changed much. My grandparents' house, on the raised part of the land, had gone to Tonton Essomba—by virtue of him, I surmised, being the first and last living son. Its interior was still laid out as they had it, with the furniture they had left behind. Whether from photos or from memories, I always felt an odd sense of intimate recognition on the rare occasions that I ventured inside. Perhaps it was because this was where I had come home from the maternity ward and lived for the first eight months of my life, and also where we had stayed the summer of 1992, and where, right there in that courtyard, I had met a toddler-aged Joyce for the first time.

Maman Florence, Tata Nicole, and Tonton Engo lived in three adjoining bungalows on the lowest end of the property. I had not entered Tonton Engo's house, but the sofa and small television in Tata Nicole's bungalow had not been upgraded. She had a shower and a modern toilet but without running water, so each bathroom trip required filling and dumping a bucket of water to flush. The shower served no purpose. Maman Florence's bungalow was meagerly furnished but enjoyed a second veranda with a view of our large lawn, which was bordered with banana trees and hibiscus bushes, and protected by a gate to stop trespassers. She also now had air-conditioning in her bedroom, running water, and a backup generator for when the electricity went out.

While my mom checked on Dave inside the house, Tata Nicole started on the *morue*, soaking the two large cod that we had purchased dried and salted from the Mfoundi market. I watched her pull a bundle of lemongrass from the garden and dump it in the same water, to temper the fish's pungency. The large pot boiled over the wood fire dug into the ground outside her bungalow, next to the very spot where I had learned for the first time, years ago, the meaning of my last name. Floating feather, tree. After an hour, Maman Florence brought the pot inside and resumed washing the fish inside her bungalow.

"Oooh this girl is lazy," Tata Nicole was saying as she plucked stray chicken feathers, wearing a pair of disposable nitrile exam gloves from America. She rinsed the chickens and withdrew their entrails before browning the flesh on the wood fire. Sporting the same type of gloves across the yard, her daughter Synthia prepped the makeshift barbecue—a tire rim welded to iron legs and topped with a circular grille—on which the meat would later be braised.

The gloves had arrived at the bottom of two belly-high barrels that my mom had sent months ahead of us, by sea. Trustworthy and affordable shipping was virtually nonexistent for this country, but a friend of hers swore by a little Cameroonian-owned company based in Maryland. My mom had spent the last months putting great care into choosing goods for each branch of the family, with some to spare. Only a few items—wet wipes, bottled water, a roll of paper towels—were intended for our own use during the trip.

Despite the owner's assurances that he had been doing this for a long time, our barrels had languished in the wrong city, Douala, where the largest port was, for two days before my mom discovered the error. When they finally arrived, she had opened the late barrels to find that every single pair of jeans and the nicest shirts she had picked out for the boys had vanished, as had the bath towels, paper towels, wet wipes, and gallons of American water for me, in case local brands were not trustworthy. (There is no safe typhoid vaccine for pregnant women.)

I had covered the shipping costs but my mom had shouldered the work of acquiring the goods on her modest teacher's-assistant salary. It infuriated me that paying a fair price had not been enough, that nothing ever seemed to be enough. The company's owner was quick to blame customs, though I distrusted his people just as much. We could stew and swear that we would never use him again, but had no recourse. This was how things were here. Decrying the country as corrupt was like calling the sky blue. Cameroon had been broken for almost as long as President Biya had held power, since 1982. I felt stupid for having any faith that everything would make it in the first place.

"Can I help with something?" I asked Tata Nicole.

My aunt looked around, searching for an easy task. I could practically read her mind. She was right. My palms were softer than theirs, tangible evidence of the vast difference in comfort between our lives. But my mom had raised me, expecting that I understand kitchen basics. I was more skilled than my demeanor suggested. And while it was sweet of them to treat me like a porcelain doll with a condition, I was growing dreadfully bored on this veranda.

"What are you doing with that okra?" I asked.

"Cutting off the ends like this. Then scooping out the grains."

"I can do that," I said, slipping a pair of blue gloves on my own hands.

"Hmm. That would free me to work on the peanuts."

"Perfect."

My brother Reece and my new cousin Messi returned from the fields after dark, after our cousin Pat had come home from his job at Afriland Bank. One of our great-aunts had asked them to install a chain-link fence around one of her fields. The boys extended their palms proudly to let me admire the cuts and calluses. The day before, the great-aunt had sent them home with as much fresh *tégué* and *pouem* leaves as they could carry. Two basins of it had rested on the veranda overnight. But they had no complaints. This time, the great-aunt had paid them in cash.

I thought of my paternal uncle as the family ate together. Tonton François had announced that he would swing by Ngousso this afternoon, but there was no sign of him yet. We had gotten up early and I was running on fumes. Had he changed his mind?

After the plates were cleared, I sat with Reece while he scrubbed and chopped the great-aunt's legumes on the veranda. Messi's shadow flickered in and out of the black. One minute he was gathering stems from the front garden, and the next, ferrying a basket across the courtyard—making a traditional remedy for Maman Florence. Her afternoon burst of energy had faded and she was resting inside, somewhat ill again. The concoction would be bitter, very bitter, I was told, from the quinine in its ingredients.

Reece was fifteen minutes deep in a description of an elaborate get-rich scheme that involved seducing an imagined finance minister's daughter and finessing his way into her father's business deals. He seemed to be making it up as he went along, each twist more ridiculous than the previous one, but somehow the plotline held. Once he stole your attention, it became his mission to hold it. A natural class clown and people-pleaser, his youthful boastfulness only made his antics funnier.

"Do you know who else wears this?" he would ask, waving his number ten jersey at us. "Messi! Zidane! Only the best! If you see this number step on the field? Nah. You know it's gonna be fire."

A soccer goal shot from three feet away gradually morphed, as the day went on, into a thirty-foot goal, shot barefoot, on the most slippery ground imaginable.

I nicknamed him The Peacock.

The metal gate opened around eight P.M. A silver SUV parked short of the lawn. The driver walked around to let the front-seat passenger out before returning to the vehicle. My uncle made his way to us. He wore thin glasses and a suit without a tie. His forehead was pearled with sweat and he had a rich man's gut. Asked how he made money, Tonton François always kept it cryptic. He was in "business." Deals were involved. Some international travel. I did not know more, nor did I endeavor to.

"I am sorry," he said. "This traffic here is terrible. I came straight from church. It was for this minister's widow, for the ceremonial removal of her black attire."

I nodded in understanding. Like Mamie Catherine after my grandfather's passing, the woman must have worn black for a year to publicly mourn her husband.

Tonton François grabbed ahold of my hand. Maman Florence led us to the back veranda and slipped away, but my mom and Dave stayed, their backs leaning against the rail, watching, listening, protecting. My uncle sunk into one of the two armchairs, beckoned me to sit by him. He turned to face me more squarely.

"Goodness, you resemble him. My mother was his father's sister, you know," he said. "But it's my father who raised him as a son in our village. After his mother left home. Do you understand?"

He went on.

"His father was from a village fifteen miles away. Uh-huh. And that's where your father chose to build, in Ayéné. He was stubborn like that. When it was time to build, he said no, I am going to claim what is mine."

Ayéné was five hours from the capital. If I wanted, Tonton François said, we could spend the night in the spacious home that he owned a few miles from the compound. The castle, he called it—jokingly, I think. And of course, my parents and Tonton Engo would come along. He suggested that we go toward the tail end of my trip. After many years, the road was finally paved most of the way south. The issue now was that the state was dragging its feet on paying the workers. Last he heard, men were blocking entire stretches in rebellion; go too early and we would get shaken down for cash. But Tonton François had it on good word that the situation would be taken care of in three days, four at the most.

"Better head out when the money has been distributed and the men have eaten well with it," he said, laughing.

We settled on my last week in town.

"Well, my girl," he said while hoisting himself up with some effort. "I would stay, but I have another ceremony to make. The son of a general I am friends with is being decorated by the military tonight. It started at eight but you see? I came to you first!"

*

MY FATHER'S THREE youngest daughters met me at the rental apartment one early afternoon, a few days later. I apologized for not being able to do something more fun than sit on the balcony. We were almost done with our market errand, two days earlier, when I had sprained my ankle. A sharp pain had shot through my right foot, sending a cold rush up the joint, but I had underestimated the injury, walked on it for an hour more at the market, and failed to ice my swollen ankle until it was practically midnight. I was paying for my carelessness with a bad limp.

I brought out sodas for them and a water bottle for myself. We sat in shy silence, unsure of where to start. Ange, the most gregarious of us four, filled the silence with small talk. She had a beautiful symmetrical face, a raspy voice that seemed too deep for her petite frame, and a general air that conveyed she was always down for a good time.

I had met Elisa on the 2008 trip and we had even spent New Year's Eve together at a nightclub, with her then-boyfriend who, in his whiskey-induced stupor kept staring at me and mumbling, *Wow. The exact same eyes.*

Elisa and I were distant Facebook friends. She had written to me a handful of times after that visit, mostly, it seemed, to gauge my relationship with Jesus Christ, which remained fraught post-divorce. I had politely but firmly explained that religion was not for me. She had insisted that it could be. I had snapped at her and stopped responding. But that was many years ago now.

As for Maggie and Ange, they had been teenagers in high school on the day that they found me standing in their living room, talking to our older brother Charlie, while their mother cleaned fish for dinner outside. We had exchanged hellos and nothing more.

But here they were now, all three of them, happy to accommodate me and my bandaged foot with a boring catch-up on the rental's balcony.

I asked Elisa if she was still with the guy that I met on New Year's Eve.

"Absolutely not," she said. "That man . . . whew."

Her sisters' giggles said the unsaid. But she had met someone else, married, divorced. Her children were twelve and four. I squinted at the math.

"I was pregnant during your last visit," she said.

Maggie and Ange were also mothers. Ange with her ex, at twenty. And Maggie, with a husband she was still completely smitten with. Their mother was watching all these children during their visit with me. I asked about our other nieces and nephews, their names, their ages. Were there many?

"So many," Ange said.

"You have a thirty-year-old niece," Elisa said.

I gasped. My own child would be the eldest of his generation on my maternal side, my grandmother's first great-grandchild, just as I had been her first grandchild. But on my paternal side, they would be the twenty-fourth. Some lived here, in the capital, but others were scattered between France, Belgium, Canada. Children for whom *back home* would be an elusive concept. A picture their parents could paint in words and show in photos that fell short of making it real. Would these children ever meet mine, I wondered? Or feel the sisterly bond my cousin Joyce and I had shared as little girls?

I was aware of the age gap between my biological parents, fifteen years, but realized that I could only guess at my siblings' ages. The girls tried to fill in the blanks.

"Well, okay, Cyriaque is fifty-four . . . Charlie is fifty-two . . ."

"What? Charlie is twenty years older than me?" I asked in disbelief.

"Oh yeah, he's old. Christelle, the one who looks just like you? She's forty-seven. And her son—"

"The boy who has my exact face? I've seen him on Facebook. I mean he looks like he could belong to me . . . or be my brother. It's uncanny."

The girls laughed.

"I always thought that," Maggie said. "But yes, that one is twenty-four. Franz is forty-four. Marlène is thirty-nine. Philip and I are thirty."

"Wait a minute—"

"Yep. These men!" Elisa said. "I'm thirty-five."

"And I'm almost twenty-nine," Ange said.

Elisa was some kind of virtual pastor—her description, at which the other two girls snickered, imitating her taking selfies left and right—and she also sang gospel music. She would send me a link to her music later, if I wanted. Maggie was home with her children but looking for work.

When the girls asked what I did, I explained that I was a lawyer for the federal government, and that sometimes my job involved going to court, but that most days, I was investigating corporations or people that fleeced consumers in the financial industry, which was common in America where credit was a much bigger part of life than here. Maggie smiled. "Papa would have been proud. You're ambitious, like him."

As for Ange, she had been splitting her time between the capital and Djoum, the closest town to the village where the compound was located. Charlie lived down there, too, with his family. The two of them were cultivating ponds for fishing and developing fields. She had studied agriculture and liked the independence of running a business.

The conclusion of the group text made better sense to me now. Things had really heated up with demands that Charlie account for the state of the compound. He was more or less in charge of it, for lack of a formal estate administrator, and by virtue of being the eldest sibling still in the country. Charlie had blown up at the request, posted an irate voice message to the thread. To appease the group with photos and videos, Ange had quickly taken a bus south. Maggie was supposed to join her, but a last-minute bout of malaria nailed her to bed. I was impressed at the time that the youngest was willing to make the long trip to the village alone. It was brave. But I also understood now that the route was familiar to her; she knew the grounds from working nearby.

The smell of spiced ground beef floated over the balcony. I checked my phone. Six in the evening. We had been on the balcony for almost four hours. I was getting hungry, but hesitated to extend a dinner invitation. I was thinking of their mother. Had they been instructed not to eat here, as I had been instructed by my own family on the day I visited their home? Was it preposterous to expect them to eat with the family of their father's former mistress? Would I make them uncomfortable by asking?

I recalled a story Tonton Essomba had recently shared about the time my father had invited him and Tonton Engo over to dinner at his home. This was ages ago. My two uncles had been in technical college, barely out of their teens. The crux of the story, which was otherwise devoid of details in Tonton Essomba's retelling, was that the girls' mother had deliberately tried to scald my uncles with boiling water. My father had ushered the boys out and taken them to a restaurant instead. Very mean lady, Tonton Essomba maintained to this day. But of course, the mother had been nothing but polite with me.

I was pondering whether bygones were just that, bygones, when my mom poked her head out of the kitchen.

"Would you girls like to stay over for dinner?"

Elisa practically leaped off her chair. "Oh yes, Auntie! It smells delicious!"

*

IN THE TWENTY-SEVEN years she had lived in Cameroon, my adoptive mom had never been to the coast. This was her chance to play tourist. We left for the beach town of Kribi before sunrise, in the middle of our second week home. I sat in the back seat with Synthia and my mom while Dave took the front passenger side. Tonton Engo was at the wheel. As we exited the city, the scenery changed from brown shacks and wires dangling out of unfinished structures, to dense layers of bush, interspersed with spindly trunks and short palms, and a horizon carved by black hills. The narrow road overflowed with loggers transporting gargantuan trunks, Ayous and Sapellis, to the ports. I closed my eyes and hoped for the best each time Tonton Engo passed a truck.

My uncle knew the route to Kribi well. He liked it out there, went at least once a month. There was a cousin in town who worked at a resort, but I doubted that Tonton Engo crashed with him every time. He was too handsome for that.

He was slim with a serious face the color of honey and the finest features. An oddball among Maman Catherine's troop of collected children. Our family used to speculate that he might be half-German or French. His mother, my great-aunt Josephine, could be mysterious. But the clean truth had emerged eventually: his father was a wealthy Muslim from the north, where the Sahara and its nomads bled into Cameroon.

My suspicion was more or less confirmed during the first downpour of our stay, a few days earlier. Tonton Engo had complimented my fancy rain boots on more than one occasion. I could leave them behind, he finally suggested.

"For Tata?" I asked, surprised that his girlfriend might want something like that. I doubted the boots would fit her, and anyhow, they seemed a bit childish for a woman her age. But if he thought she might like them, then I supposed—

"No, no," my uncle said with a rare smile. "For a little girl I like."

"Oh . . . for a daughter? Wait. But since when do you have a daughter?"

"Ha! Not a daughter."

The Department of Transportation had set up a checkpoint outside the Kribi prefecture. At the sight of our car and, we suspected, Dave's glaring white skin, the men in salmon-pink vests raised a thick rope from the ground. Two of them approached the driver's side. My uncle rolled down the window.

"License, registration, and everyone's IDs, please."

We handed over identification cards and American passports. Through the rear windshield, I watched the men point at our backpacks and suitcases while mouthing questions at my uncle. Extinguisher? Tonton Engo shook his head. Triangles? No. Medical kit? No.

My mom stepped out of the car. This was a joke, she yelled. While they fussed over our trunk, half a dozen overloaded motorcycles and cars practically held together by a shoestring had flown by. Where was their immense concern for safety then?

The men shrugged as if to say, just doing their job.

The four of them negotiated a while longer, then crossed the road to a makeshift stand. My mom and uncle returned to the car after fifteen minutes. She tossed her wallet back in her purse.

"So how much did they want?" I asked her.

"Twenty-five thousand CFAs."

"And of course, no receipt," my uncle said with a bitter chuckle.

"Because they know it isn't right," my mom said. "But we are not going to let them ruin our trip. We are not. In the name of Jesus."

The resort was on a private beach. Quiet, well-maintained, and equipped with all the amenities to welcome those accustomed to certain luxuries. Upon hearing where we were staying, Maman Florence had laughed. "Your father made me discover that place."

While my parents and Synthia waited for our continental breakfast on the restaurant terrace, I ventured out with my novel to sit on nearby wooden steps that fed onto a strip of sand. A scattering of green coconuts lay amid the lounge chairs and orange-dipped lizards. Before he disappeared with the cousin, who worked maintenance on the grounds, Tonton Engo had warned me to watch my head out there. The coconuts sometimes tumbled before they were ripe. How exactly one could be "careful" about these things, my uncle had not specified.

I had been looking forward to the coastal smell. Briny algae and saltiness—a harsh air that quenched the skin. The tide was too high to swim. Curiously, though, the air was odorless. I wondered how this could be. The ocean waves were no less real on this side of the Atlantic. They swelled and crashed against the steps, splashing my knees, tendering shells, branches, plastic bottle caps, and sweeping off the gifts with sporadic ferocity. Fishermen crossed the water in long pirogues. Afar, a stationary oil tanker incised the horizon line.

The paperback sat unopened on my lap. I was distracted by the voice memo Maggie had sent me the night before. She wanted me to know that one of Ésaïe's older daughters, our sister Marlène, lived in Kribi. Somewhere above a grocery store named Tangi. Or was it Tandi. The audio was garbled in places. I found it odd that none of the Assae siblings had a working number or firm address for this sister. Nevertheless, Maggie seemed convinced that Marlène would be thrilled to see me. She hoped that I would try to find her. I had thanked her for the information without prying into the state of their relationship or committing to a visit.

The town was a sort of second home for Tonton Engo. For the next two days, we were at the grateful mercy of his tastes, free from the burden of deciding where to eat and what to see. Being relieved of planning was nice. I was loath to put a wrench in the schedule by insisting on visiting my paternal half sister. Who knew how long it would take us to find the apartment? And even if we did, Marlène had no clue that I was in the country, let alone coming to see her. What if Maggie was wrong and our sister resented the intrusion?

In the evenings, we convened on the patio of a small but popular bar across the resort. In the short alley bordering the bar, a woman was seasoning and braising freshly caught fish. I nursed a malta while my uncle outlined tomorrow's plans. We would begin at the industrial port being built a few miles away, see art at a small museum in his friend's village, and finally, visit the waterfalls where the Lobe River converged with the ocean.

I asked if we might start with a pit stop.

MY COUSIN SYNTHIA and I left my parents and Tonton Engo in the car, parked at a gas station. It was ten in the morning but already, the heat was blistering. A man in uniform was guarding Tandi. I looked up at the two floors of windows above the grocery store, hoping one belonged to my sister's apartment. I had, from Maggie, her married name. Mailboxes would help us figure out the rest.

We had not gone two steps into the side alley when a brown mastiff mix leaped out of a wooden shed. Synthia yelped. I thought the chain around the dog's neck might be too short to reach the rightmost side of the alley, but my cousin seemed too shaken to risk going farther. We returned out front and pressed the guard to help us get inside by handling the dog. The young man hesitated.

"Please, sir," I said, widening my eyes for effect. I hoped the combination of our youthful faces and colorful dresses made us look harmless enough. "My big sister lives inside."

He let us in but my plan beyond that point was poorly thought out. Cameroon had not enjoyed a functional postal service in decades. Its address system, if one could call it a system at all, was chaotic. Of course there were no mailboxes. The doors were unlabeled and unnumbered.

The inside of the building was pristine, painted in bright white and scrubbed clean. Well-off people lived here. We decided, without discussion, to climb to the top. It was possible that all three floors would be identical and that we would learn nothing by taking stock of the whole building, but there was also a small chance that a full lay of the land might help us decide where to knock first. The second floor turned out to be as anonymous as the first, but at the top, we found the glass doors of a commercial agency.

A woman in a tailored suit approached. I asked her if a couple bearing my sister's last name lived up here. To my surprise, the woman pointed to the door on her immediate right. Synthia and I looked at each other, struck by our dumb luck.

I knocked on the neighboring apartment.

"Who is it?" a male voice asked from behind the door.

"Marlène's sister. I am looking for Marlène?"

"What sister?"

"Vanessa. Vanessa Assae Billé. From America."

"Oh?" the voice said in a distinctly friendlier tone.

The door opened a crack, and a middle-aged man in a polo shirt and slacks eyed us suspiciously. I took a step back to allow him a better look at me. If only he could just take stock of those Assae eyes, he would know that I was not an impostor standing at his door.

"I recognize you. When you said sister, I thought . . . well, I would have not opened the door if—" He paused again. "I am Marlène's husband."

"Hi, I am so sorry to show up unannounced. I'm in town for the day and did not have a number or address. I really am her sister."

"Yes, yes. From the photos, of course. Come on in."

"This is my little cousin. On my mother's side."

"*Bonjour*," Synthia said.

We found my sister sitting in a floral silk robe. A newborn slept peacefully in her arms. A rosy little creature, born six weeks early. My cousin and I sat on the sofa across from her. I said that it was so nice to see her again. But this was our first time ever meeting in person, my sister corrected gently. She had been out of the country during my last trip. I realized what had happened. Someone, most likely our brother Charlie, had shown me a photo of her. From there my mind had built a memory of her walking toward us, holding a little girl's hand, a radiant smile on her face. But the Marlène in my freeze-frame never spoke. She was right: we'd never met. I apologized, a little self-conscious of my mistake—would she remember me as a strange girl?

If this was the case, Marlène did not let on. We talked about her pregnancy and mine, about my trip so far, their lives in Kribi, away from the capital, and about the sweet nine-year-old daughter who joined us in the living room.

My phone buzzed. Our brief time was up. I excused myself again for the surprise drop-in and for being unable to stay longer. But Marlène was gushing with joy. This was a good surprise. No one could say if or when we would ever see each other again. But in this moment we were here, reunited.

She turned to the little girl in the school uniform. "This is Maman's sister. Your auntie, just like Tata Elisa and Tata Maggie and Tata Ange. Maman's sister. Do you understand?"

My niece nodded dutifully.

WE REACHED THE art museum early that afternoon, on the road back from the partially constructed port. The hamlet, Luma, bordered the ocean. A university professor native to this place owned the collection. Our guide, his cousin, showed us around.

I marveled at the geographical breadth represented. Masks from the Tikars hung behind warrior statues from the Maï-Maï. Voodoo statues from Benin and Liberia. Whale bones and the preserved skin of a python caught in nearby bush.

We paused before two thick, square bases made of iron, resting in opposing corners of a room. Each was painted in deep red and was welded to a small, vertical post. The commode on the floor between them was topped with an antique globe and the replica of a ship.

"These were weighing scales, for slaves," the guide said. "This one belonged to the Portuguese."

"And this one?" I asked, pointing to the more ornate instrument.

"The British."

I leaned closer to examine the carvings on its post, the British crown and its emblematic lions.

We walked out onto the sand. The hamlet was sleepy today. A few pirogues idled in the shade. No one seemed to be home in the villas that the professor and his late brother had each built. The ocean grazed the beach, retreated again.

"So slave ships passed through Kribi?" I asked.

"Slave ships came to where we are standing today, miss. Unfortunately for us, Brazil is on the other side of this water. Men and women were held separately. Some ships arrived from the Cape already carrying slaves. But many of the people also came from around here. The surrounding villages would sound the drums to alert their neighbors of the ships, so they could bring anyone they wished to sell."

"We sold our own?"

"Yes, miss."

*

TIME WAS GETTING away from us quickly. We had returned from Kribi the evening before, on a Friday. This meant Dave and I would be flying back to the States in five days, while my mom stayed behind for ten more days. We made very few plans for my last weekend home. Willy was taking a night bus to see us off. And my sister Laetitia would try, workload permitting. My cousins Nadège and Rose were planning to drop by the Ngousso house. There was the remainder of the barrel goods to distribute. And, importantly, we had to prepare for the trip to Ésaïe's village, which was coming up on Monday morning.

Tonton Engo was concerned about our safety. It was true that the roads south were better than in the '90s, but some stretches were still under construction, if not altogether unpaved. Depending on the time of day, loggers steering unwieldy lorries might be heading in the opposite direction.

To shield ourselves, we decided to rent our own SUV and hire a driver. A seven-seater with room for my paternal uncle, who was planning to leave with us from Yaoundé, and for my sister Ange, who we were picking up from Djoum, the town closest to the village. We were deep into our search when Tonton François called to say that a business deal that had fallen through required his attention, and that he would not be able to join us. But not to worry—of all the Assae siblings, Charlie had the best handle on our patrimony and happened to be in Yaoundé, staying at his mother's. We would be in good hands. My brother would show us around the compound and even take us, if we wanted, to the plot where the grandmother whose first name I bore was buried. Tonton François had already made arrangements with him. All we had to do was tell Charlie where to meet us.

We were set. Yet, my mom's mood seemed to sour as the day went on. By late afternoon, she was issuing ominous warnings while Tonton Engo studied our itinerary on his phone.

It was no secret to me that she was a reluctant participant in this part of the adventure, that if it were up to her, we would never set foot in my father's ancestral village. I knew my mom was not being malicious. The problem was always fear. In 2008 it was the conviction that someone on the paternal side of my family would hurt me if she was not present. And now it was the conviction that some tragic accident would befall us on the route to the village.

I could not begrudge her, as a mother and grandmother-to-be, for impressing her fears on me. Nor were her fears entirely irrational. The trip would be risky. But I had not come this far, thirteen years after missing my first chance, to renegotiate my decision with forty hours to go.

I told my mom that if she or anyone else preferred to wait for me here, I would certainly understand. This pilgrimage was not their burden. But I was entitled to see what my father had built, and to stand where he was buried. No amount of arguing would change my mind. I was going to Ayéné.

꜅

NADÈGE AND ROSE arrived the next afternoon in their Sunday best. Synthia, Reece, and I greeted them on the veranda. They asked where the others were— my mom, her siblings, Tonton Engo. Praying in one of the bungalows, Synthia told them. I had my suspicions as to the main topic—a miraculous changing of my mind on the matter of Ayéné—but held my tongue. We sat down.

Rose was watching me with wonder. I knew of Nadège, whose fate had intertwined with mine in childhood, but did not remember Rose. She remembered me, though.

"They used to beat me for you, you know," she said, amused by the memory. "Oh yes. When they came home and found you crying. And whew, did you love to cry!"

I pieced together that she had been one of the many children under my grandmother's care. We had overlapped in the little house behind us, thirty-two years ago. She swore that my face, which she had memorized over many hours of babysitting, had not changed. Her own children were grown now.

My mom emerged from the bungalow. She hugged Rose and held Nadège even longer, with a tenderness that made my presence feel like an intrusion. It was strange to see them together in person, connected by a history that preceded me.

I wondered what Nadège thought of me; if she saw in me the alternate self that I saw in her. Nadège had six children. The last ones were twins of toddler age. She seemed happy enough but this city was hard, the government maddeningly corrupt, the classrooms crowded. She had not stumbled into a prestigious graduate school, or ended up in the kind of job that paid enough to absorb the costs of bad surprises. It was one thing to guess how one's life might have turned out under different circumstances. But rarely was the answer so readily available. I had taken another fatherless girl's place, claimed her adoptive parents and grandparents for myself, inherited her passports, her childhood in the West, her diplomas, her lucky breaks. Would I have been her? A mother of five or six, in this unforgiving land?

Nadège smiled at me sweetly. I sensed her taking in my demeanor as I moved around the veranda, as I settled onto a small bench, and tried to simulate ease among these intimate strangers. The curiosity was mutual.

I answered her and Rose's questions about my current life vaguely, careful to minimize the extent to which my life in DC was comfortable, almost unfairly so. I wanted to spare her.

*

I CALLED MY brother Charlie that night from the balcony of the rental, where I could see the Presidential Palace, bright as a lighthouse. I thanked him profusely for agreeing to ride with us to the village, and told him that I was looking forward to seeing him again after so many years. Charlie said that he was, too, that it was his pleasure to join us. He would wait for us in the Kondengui quarter, around the corner from the family home where he had met me last trip—did I remember? he asked. But the years had hazed my recollection.

Our plan was to leave at four in the morning and return to the city on the same night. An ungodly hour, for this I was terribly sorry. But Charlie said it was no trouble. He was not sleeping much these days anyway. I wondered why but thought there would be plenty of time to ask him on the ride south.

I woke up at one A.M., almost on the dot, again at two, and then at three. I went to the bathroom, and upon my return, lay flat on the mattress. I placed a hand over my uterus, tapped it. Other than waning food aversions, no outward signs revealed that a fetus had been growing in me for eighteen weeks. But in this position, a curve the size of a large orange pushed my hardened belly out. I had not felt this child move yet, although Gabi and Taryn swore it would happen any day now. Both were due to give birth this year, a few weeks before me. I could not fall back asleep. My spine was wired with anticipation, my head preoccupied with the task I had postponed for thirteen years, that I had come all this way to complete. It seemed improbable now that I had managed to perform the requisite motions in the necessary sequence—from purchasing my ticket to standing my ground with my mom—to end up here, in the place of my birth, with less than a half-day drive separating me from my father. The stamina that had fueled me now seemed foreign. It was as if another person had acted in my place.

That detachment had crept up on me before. It typically appeared in the aftermath of a grueling journey between point A and point B—getting through college and law school, arriving at divorce, purchasing the apartment, starting a family. While my body ran on autopilot, my mind refused to fully invest in the final destination until every possible threat to the plan was neutralized. Only once this happened could the two safely converge.

My restlessness was, ironically, a product of the peace reached between body and mind. Some unknowns remained about the road to Ayéné, but my fear of the worst had dissipated. We had driven that long a distance to Kribi, in a smaller car, and survived the loggers' trucks' traffic, the afternoon heat, and the onerous stops. The odds of completing my mission were more than favorable—they were close to certain.

An hour later, I was down by the gate, dialing my brother's phone number as my parents and Tonton Engo loaded the trunk with provisions. Charlie answered promptly. We would be there in less than a half hour. My brother said that he would see us soon. We hung up.

Tonton Engo settled up front, to keep a close eye on the driver and on the route. My parents sat with me. The driver was going a bit fast for my liking but the city was largely asleep. I felt tired and irritable. And, though I was careful to hide it, I also felt resentful of my parents and uncle for coming. We were still within Yaoundé's borders, but already, I felt protective of this long-awaited reunion with my father. I did not want them to wonder what I thought, or to comment on the estate, or to stand with me at his grave. It was ungrateful and unfair of me, I knew it, but the feelings had appeared without first asking for permission. I hoped to sleep them off on the road.

We reached the meeting spot in no time. My uncle hit the redial button and handed me his phone. The line went straight to voicemail. I copied the number on my own phone and tried Charlie that way. Voicemail, again.

Had I imagined our whole conversation twenty minutes earlier? Would my brother really blow me off out of the blue? The driver was getting nervous. It was not good, he said, to sit idle in the dark at this hour. Law enforcement might come around to ask questions. I texted my brother.

My mom gasped in the backseat. She had realized that she had forgotten her and Dave's passports at home, and had no proof of ID for the inevitable road stops. We would have to grab them from the rental and come back to the meeting spot. The driver turned the car around. I stared at my phone during the detour, relieved for the purchase of time.

The dashboard flipped to 4:58 A.M. Charlie had neither called nor texted. Now back from our detour, we watched the surroundings in silence, craning our necks each time a silhouette appeared out of the shadows. A motorbike accidentally dropped its load, stopped in the middle of the street to pick it up. I tensed up as it swerved away just in time to narrowly escape a garbage truck. Men in long robes were ambling to Fajr prayer. It was 5:07 A.M.

"He's not coming. People here. Instead of telling you, they do stuff like this." Tonton Engo spoke these words with typical measure, though the anger beneath was palpable.

"Do you want to go, Ness? It's getting late," my mom said.

My uncle turned to face me. "She's right. We can still make good time if we leave now."

I pleaded for another three minutes.

None of this made sense. Charlie had been so kind during our first and only encounter in person. Our shared paternal uncle and sisters described him as dutiful and trustworthy. I could not fathom what had changed in the last hour. A sudden fit of illness? A pulverized phone? But even if this were the case, others were home with him—his mother, to be sure. Charlie could have dragged himself outside, or sent someone, anyone, to apprise us of the situation. It pained me to pull away without him. But barring the most tragic explanation, it was clear. My brother had chosen to abandon me.

*

TONTON FRANÇOIS HAD not exaggerated. The road south was relatively well paved. Traffic was scant that morning and the loggers few. The side of the road was layered with underbrush, banana trees and palms, and taller species of trees that I could not name. We passed clusters of yellow houses and little goats sniffing the dirt. Field hands, given away by their machetes, walked along the side of the road. Small children waved at us and Dave waved back cheerfully, unaware that the children were begging for a ride rather than greeting us.

At around eight, we made a restroom break at a gas station in Sangmelima, where Tonton Engo and Tonton Essomba had attended technical college. The driver stretched his short legs. I offered him cookies that he declined politely.

We had almost reached Djoum when the dreaded road rope appeared and floated midair, bifurcating our line of sight. Three gendarmes approached in military police uniforms. I watched them leaf through our passports, then peer at the faces in the back seat. "Let me see your COVID tests and yellow fever cards," one of them said.

Once more, I did not have my yellow card with me. We showed the gendarme our COVID vaccination cards and tried to reason with him. With all due respect, I told the gendarme, his request was pointless—any test result we showed him would be outdated. But our visas, which he could find inside each passport, were proof that we had met the public health requirements to enter the country. And anyhow, since when was it the business of the military police to enforce vaccine mandates?

The men pocketed our passports for further examination. We followed them back to their shack across the road. Dave and the driver waited in the car. The gendarme who had been leading the charge thus far noted that our last names were local. Nevertheless, he launched into a rant. It was a shame that people like us came to their home, to their land, and acted like we owed them nothing.

His young colleague spoke up softly. "But they are Cameroonian, they only live in the United States."

Though taken aback, I quickly seized onto his sympathy.

"That's true," I said. "See my last name? My father was from here. From Ayéné, after Djoum. That's where we are going, so that I may see his tomb for the first time. But all this, respectfully—it is wasting our time, *messieurs*."

The young colleague smiled; his senior, too. A sign that we could stop the charade and get down to the true purpose of their stop. My mom warned they would not get more than 5,000 CFAs. Plenty to buy themselves a round of beer. The gendarme in charge nodded, his hostility shed immediately.

"Ayéné . . . that's in the direction of General Assos, I believe," he said.

"We thought so," Tonton Engo said, graciously leaving out the fact that he was well aware of the route, that the General Assos after whom the area was named had been a friend of my father.

"You'll want to drive carefully. The road is narrow and unfinished that way, and there are massive logging trucks."

"Is Djoum close?"

"Fifteen minutes maximum," the gendarme said.

I felt a pang of dread as I called Ange. I had no backup plan, no address for the compound, if she, too, pulled out at the last minute. Had she and Charlie spoken? Had they coordinated this in any way? But my sister answered her phone. I told her that we were right outside of Djoum but that Charlie had not made it. Ange's surprise sounded genuine. It was too early for grilled meats to perfume the street but the town was awakening. A lively little market was set up across from the gas station where Ange was meeting us. My mom and I stretched our legs nearby while the driver went off in search of coffee.

Ange surfaced a few minutes later, in freshly buzzed hair that she had dyed platinum blond. The style suited her. She hopped in the back of the SUV and projected a set of simple directions at the driver. Ayéné was a mile or two away, off the main road. The sun was high but clouds were moving in. I thought of the red dirt we had bumped and trampled over after Sangmelima. Ange must have, too. She hoped out loud, for our sake, that it would not rain later.

I asked if she had heard from Charlie since my morning call with him. She had not, she said, but pulled out her phone and called him right then. The line again went to voice mail. A part of me felt relieved to see that mine were not the only calls he was not answering. Perhaps Ange was right that something had gone wrong, that perhaps their mother had fallen sick. Whatever was going on, this was unlike her big brother. Charlie was a stand-up guy, he would never. Really, he would never, she said.

The trouble now was that Ange had no key to the main house. There was also no phone service in the village. If we did not hear from Charlie, he would not be able to help us get in. But maybe there was another way, Ange added. Thieves had broken in and damaged the doors before. She had heard that one could still be pushed in or unlocked from the outside.

"Do you see this palm grove, these trees? This is all Papa's property. Two hectares wide. The palms are actually from a couple of species. Papa was into trying different techniques to breed them. He really liked his little experiments." My sister chuckled. "But the maintenance to produce good nuts is very involved, and there was no one here to do it after his death. Before this year, I hadn't been down here in three years. I can live in Djoum but not the village. I don't know what he was thinking. It's too isolated for us. There's nothing. No phone service. No people. No restaurant. So we have not dealt with the palm grove for a while."

The driver proceeded slowly, honking before each turn to signal our presence. I had no idea where we would seek refuge if a logging truck suddenly materialized and pushed us off the slim path.

After the grove was a small village of five or six homes. I glimpsed the outline of a few adults and their children playing on the dusty soil.

"Our cousins," Ange said. "My mother would rather I just be in and out, and have nothing to do with them, so we won't stop here. But *this* is actually Papa's village. He only built in Ayéné because there was more land available to buy."

"Does your mother ever come here?" I asked.

"Never."

The road ended at the compound. We parked on the grass outside two metal gates, one of which was dented and permanently pushed open. Inside the courtyard, our father had planted palms, but also guava trees, mango trees, banana trees, and other species of fruit trees. Grass infringed on the pebble footpath and the white lampposts had seen their share of weather, but I could see the remnants of an ambitious landscaping plan.

The property was anchored by a two-story villa hemmed with a wide veranda out front. On its left were two bungalows for visiting guests. A brick pavilion hosted a kind of outdoor oven or pit. And directly behind the villa was another house, which my sister said was initially a large kitchen. Another family lived there now.

We found the family's young mother sitting on the ground in a *kaba*. I waved hello. Ange asked her if the man who had the spare key was home. I wondered if this was the woman's husband, a cousin, some kind of groundskeeper, or some combination of these roles. The woman said that the man had left for the peanut fields hours ago. Before I could ask, my sister turned to me and shook her head. The fields were miles away. Even if by some miracle we landed on the right one, finding the man could take hours. We were better off circling the villa for an opening.

My parents, uncle, and our driver waited out front while Ange and I split the perimeter of the house. I wrangled my left arm through the grills protecting the French double doors, where the door was ajar or where the glass had been broken in. I found that I could jiggle the handles but not unlock them without a key. I arrived at the front veranda before Ange had completed her round.

The center door on that facade was among those missing a glass panel. I leaned in again, inserted my arm, and this time twisted my wrist to shift aside the panel of red-and-gold curtain. I realized, once I could peer inside, that this was the primary entrance to the house, what my father's guests would have seen upon being urged to make themselves comfortable while someone brought them an aperitif. I could not tell what the thieves had stolen. Through the bars and void left by the glass, the floor tiles seemed in impeccable shape. Several European-style paintings hung on white walls. White Hellenic busts posed next to lean statuettes carved out of ebony. The dining set, undoubtedly a foreign import, was old-fashioned but refined.

But what one saw first was the portrait of my father. The photo hung beneath the balustrade, above a cased opening that divided living room from dining room. A subtle smile marked his lips. Smugness? No, more like self-satisfaction. He looked youthful despite his receding hairline. I wondered how far into his career and marriage the photo had been taken.

My maternal family had taught me that my father's wife was a village woman. By this, they did not mean that she had come from his village. Rather, it was a commentary on her curiosity about the world. What they meant was that she had a small vision of life's worth and possibilities. A lack of exposure, academic and worldly, that made her uninteresting to them and, perhaps, explained my father's affairs. I had accepted this as absolute truth because no contradictory information was available. But while reminiscing about our father's ambition on the balcony of the rental apartment, my sisters had told me a different story.

Their mother had come from a well-off family, her own father having been a diplomat of some kind. He had balked when presented with Ésaïe as a suitor. Our father had less than nothing in those days. Their mother had been given an ultimatum—either abandon her marriage plans or be cut off from the family. She had placed her faith in our father. And he had delivered. The plot reminded me of the elaborate, comedic fantasy my brother Reece recounted on the Ngousso property as he chopped legumes. Somehow, my father had pulled it off. He had made himself somebody.

Ange joined me on the veranda. I gathered from the look on her face that she was giving up on finding the weak door.

"I'm sorry. I thought I could show you photo albums and some of Papa's effects but—" she said.

"Everything would have been different if we had a key."

"But at least you saw the village, right? Even if we couldn't get inside?"

I shrugged despondently. None of this was her fault. She had kept her word. Yet, I could not pretend that seeing the grounds was enough. I did not want to perform good gamesmanship. I felt entitled to be unhappy under the circumstances.

We rejoined the larger group, who were standing beneath a tree too slight to protect them from the sun.

"No luck?" my stepdad asked.

I shook my head. None of them complained but I sensed their growing discomfort. It was almost lunchtime. They were sweating. The ride home would be long and bumpy, more so if we got caught in the rain. And my growing despair was unmistakable. I was annoyed with them for coming at all, for putting me in the position of having to cater to their feelings while I grappled with my own disappointment.

"Should we go?" my mom asked hopefully.

"I would still like to see my father's grave. It's the least I can do while we're here."

"Sometimes things happen for a reason," she said. I refused to look at her.

"It would be good for her to see the grave," the driver said.

I tried to hide my surprise at this unexpected show of allyship.

"Ange, would you show me?" I asked.

My mom and I followed my sister around the side of the house. Ange pointed to a white shed in the near distance.

"It's far. Behind this boxed thing," she said, though she didn't know where exactly. Only that it was far. I asked how far. A hundred meters or so, she guessed. I stopped myself from laughing—a hundred meters was one city block. Our father's body was resting three hundred feet away and I was supposed to just give up? No, I was going.

My sister cautioned me against it. Her deep, raspy voice sounded hesitant. We were not dressed for the occasion, she said. After the shed, the grass was even taller, the land reclaimed by the bush. If Charlie were here, he would have cleared a path with a machete to make sure we could safely pass. But without him, we would be vulnerable to snakes and whatever else lurked in the underbrush.

My mom jumped in. She agreed, it was too dangerous, and what about the baby? I shot her a vicious glare.

Ange said there was another problem.

"Even if we could cross, I don't actually know where the tomb is. Before he died, Papa gave very precise instructions about the funeral rites. For example, he did not want to be buried in special clothes, only his own."

I nodded. Maggie had mentioned this to me.

"But he also did not want a headstone. His grave had to be unmarked. He wanted to be buried under a mango tree, so that's what they did."

I looked longingly toward the shed. The mango tree narrowed the spots. How many could there be back there?

"On top of that," she continued, "Papa did not want his girls to see where he was buried. He said so in his instructions. So while we were present for the funeral rites, when it came time to put his body under, the men went and we stayed behind. Charlie knows where the mango tree is but I don't."

The reminder only made me angrier at our brother.

"I wish he had given us directions. Anything but this."

"I have only been to the grave once since 2006. I don't believe I could find it and frankly, sister, I really don't want to." She paused to compose herself. "I don't want to cry today."

"I'd like to walk around a bit more. Alone."

"Are you all right?" she asked me.

"No. I'm not."

*

I WAITED UNTIL their pitying gazes had disappeared around the corner to contend with Charlie's betrayal. Tears welled in my eyes. For years the distance between the Assae siblings and me had shielded me from the possibility of this moment. I had known where to find each of them but maintained a safe distance. Though I could seem contrite for letting years pass without contact, the truth was that I had been content with sitting on the periphery. Until this trip south, I had asked for nothing and expected nothing from my siblings. Today had been an act of faith, one that I now regretted. I had been a fool to trust Charlie. I hated him for forcing me to process the hurt he was causing me before my loved ones. Out here, there was nowhere to hide. I felt like an exposed nerve ending. I knew what Maggie had said, that more than anything, our father wanted the children united, but I could never forgive Charlie for this.

Other than the hush of bristling leaves and buzz of wings overhead, the back of the villa was silent. The door nearest to me was smaller than the others and equally inaccessible, but enough of the glass was gone that I could see a hallway and stairs to the second floor. I tried to imagine what our father had envisioned: a mob of grandchildren someday filling this very staircase with laughter, his children braving the road to Ayéné to seek solace from the capital and the harshness of Western life, to replenish themselves with the fruits he had planted, his children learning, in time, to love this place, even if their mother never could, this village he had left with nothing and returned to suffuse with abundance and, before it had begun to fall apart, beauty. I hoped that he would have been proud that I had sought him here.

Even through the grief of this moment, I could see that the colossal letdown of my visit south mattered less than I was ready to admit. No amount of house and goods, of photos and documents, of time spent at his tomb would ever fully explain he who did not want to be found. My father was, by nature and choice, an enigma. A man I could seek to unravel for the rest of my days. But Ayéné was as far as I was willing to go. I had new life to grow, to dedicate my heart to, and build a loving home for.

Resolute acceptance had a way of simplifying things. I had convinced myself that this place held the closure I needed to let go of any remaining traces of resentment toward him, as if its walls contained the missing pieces of a puzzle whose final form was amorphous at best. Perhaps it was the overwhelming dejection I felt, but I suspected, deep down, that in the end, no key would have unlocked the answer to the question of how the layers that formed my father's own life had weaved and tangled together to create his person.

I made my way to the front of the villa, and there, told my mom that I was ready, that we could go home now—a mere twenty-six minutes after first setting foot in Ayéné.

I had left DC with a distant portrait of my father and arrived here to find the same. But perhaps what I knew was enough to make sense of his effect on my life, and to decide whether to accept him as he was.

Perhaps this explains why, years after that appointment at the French consulate, his last name remains appended to mine. Assae Billé on my law school diploma. Assae Billé on my job offers. Assae Billé on the deed to my condo in DC. Only another set of letters has joined them. A. Bee on essays and stories, and A. Bee on this book. Another day, another christening.

Maybe new homes have remolded too much of my person for me to feel like a Jucquois anytime other than while I visit with my daddy. Or maybe begging one father for his acknowledgment has soured me to the endeavor. Some might speculate I wanted the credit to myself all along, worked backward from there. Perhaps they are right. All I know is that I stopped short of erasing the ghost, that she and I are still bound.

Whatever the case may be, it isn't out of a particular fondness for him. Hearing the name Ésaïe evokes a faceless composite of fading memories and a quilt of facts gathered from others. Someone who gave me a name, but nothing else, and therefore took none of me to his grave. Time has turned me into a distant observer of our relationship. I remember the disappointment and the anger, though both have dissolved. I remember the curiosity, though it's no longer piqued. There was never a person there for me to miss.

Still, I feel drawn to the map home, to this land I'd not set foot on until the summer of 2021, yet recognize as engrained in me. My name is a people and a place. And if I am to never feel completely at home in it, then I must make a new home of it. Rewrite it with a pseudonym, but also in the way that I live my life, that I treat my people, that I honor our values. I hope this is still the beginning, that there is still time to become a better Assae Billé—the kind of daughter who'd never kill her *mbômbo*.

Even at war.

∮

AS WE DROVE back to the capital, I thought of the life burgeoning in me. A child whose arrival would extend the bridge between my mothers' and father's clans. His mind would not imprint these past weeks, the steps we had taken, the food we had eaten, the music we had shaken our shoulders to, the paths we had trod as one—weeks that I doubted I would forget, but that would be nothing but stories to him. I hoped to bring him back someday, more often than I had gone in childhood. Cameroon would be a part of his history and constitution. A place that would claim him, and that, in turn, would be his to claim, regardless of what any embassy had to say about it. I felt the urgency of time, of passing down everything I could while our story was still in its beginning.

And so, here is what else I hope to someday tell the child who accompanied me all this way, my beloved, my son:

That your uncle Charlie contacted me two mornings later with a text message vaguely alluding to our missed connection, as if I had not yet guessed that his mother convinced him to ghost me, and that he, a grown man of fifty-two, had yielded to her, without regard for my feelings or your grandfather's dying wish that our family come together. Perhaps someday you will hear that I forgave him in time, but as I write this, I cannot tell you that I have.

But know that I did forgive your grandfather that afternoon, for myself, yes, but also for you—so you would have a chance to learn about him without the encumberment of past bitterness.

I hope to tell you, too, that my last three days in Yaoundé before our safe return to DC, your birthplace, were blissful and surrounded by your aunts and uncles, great-aunts and great-uncles, a sprawling family—too numerous to count—that adored you before any of them ever set their eyes on you.

And that as bleak and miserable as the drive back from Ayéné was, and heavens knows it was, for I could not help the rush of spontaneous tears each time I reconsidered Charlie's betrayal, it was on this day, this of all days, that I first felt you flutter in my womb, as if to remind me that the life that began with that strange summer of 1989, and made me the mother that you will perhaps seek to understand yourself someday, had also converged into new beautiful layers.

ACKNOWLEDGMENTS

A sincere thanks to:

My parents, Suzanne and Dave, Florence, Ésaïe, Laurent and Lisette, and Janet and Don, for everything.

My enormous family here, there, and back home, for trusting me with our stories. You mean the world to me.

My editor, Alessandra, and the small but mighty team at Astra House, for understanding me and bringing this book to life.

My magazine editors, for publishing excerpts of this memoir in their pages before its release: Nathan of *Current Affairs*; Nausicaa, Mark, Elias, Rachel, Laura, and Nick of *n+1*; Spencer and Ed of *Guernica Magazine*. Your work made mine better.

My friends, for miscellaneous acts of kindness, including but not limited to believing in me, lending me their eyes on early drafts, and supplying pep talks, snacks, and distractions: Sparky, Oren, Lyta, Cate, Adrian, Eli, Pete, Anna and Arik, Elizabeth and Josh, Emily and Melanie, Jacy and Billy, Dan, Gabi, Taryn, Sana, Marissa, Maryum, Autumn, Ben D., David, Alec, Matt, Caitlin, Liv, Sanaë, Ethan, Jesse, Jacob, Ben K., and Meredith. I could not have done this without you.

Our dear Fiona, for leaving us with a template for leading a good and kind life. How we miss you.

And last but certainly not least:

My agent, Elias, for the hours and hours poured into making this book the best it could be. I am so lucky.

My all-around favorite Sam. Codependence has never been so blissful. I love you.

My little Sufjan, for being the most delightful womb-mate on the last leg of this journey. Maman adores you (and secretly hopes you never write a memoir about her).

ENDNOTES

8. THE SPECULATOR

1 George W. Bush, *Remarks at St. Paul AME Church* (speech, Atlanta, GA, June 17, 2002), The American Presidency Project, presidency.ucsb.edu /documents/remarks-st-paul-ame-church-atlanta-georgia.

2 Chris M. Asch and George D. Musgrove, *Chocolate City: A History of Race and Democracy in the Nation's Capital* (Chapel Hill: University of North Carolina Press, 2017), 14, 191, 294, 454, *passim.*

3 Christine Sadler, "Our Town: Petworth Really a Community Conscious Area," *Washington Post*, October 3, 1939.

4 Marion Barry et al., *DC City Council Hearing* (hearing, Washington, DC, June 17, 1975), DC City Council Legislative Services Archive, B1-57, Roll 37 and 38.

5 Katie J. Wells, "A Housing Crisis, a Failed Law, and a Property Conflict: The US Urban Speculation Tax," *Antipode*, 47(4), (2015): 1053.

9. DON'T KNOW WHAT YOU'VE GOT 'TIL IT'S . . .

6 Youssef M. Ibrahim, "France Bans Muslim Scarf in its Schools," *The New York Times*, September 11, 1994.

7   Linda Villarosa, "Myths About Physical Racial Differences Were Used to Justify Slavery—and Are Still Believed by Doctors Today," The 1619 Project, *The New York Times*, August 14, 2019.

8   Kelly M. Hoffman, Sophie Trawalter, Jordan R. Axt, and M. Norman Oliver, "Racial Bias in Pain Assessment and Treatment Recommendations, and False Beliefs About Biological Differences Between Blacks and Whites," *Proceedings of the National Academy of Sciences of the United States of America (PNAS)*, 113(16), (2016): 4296–4301.

9   Sophie Trawalter, Kelly M. Hoffman, and Adam Waytz, "Racial Bias in Perceptions of Others' Pain," PLOS ONE 7(11), e48546, (2012): 4.

10   Lauren A. Wise, Julie R. Palmer, David Reich, Yvette C. Cozier, and Lynn Rosenberg, "Hair Relaxer Use and Risk of Uterine Leiomyomata in African-American Women," *American Journal of Epidemiology*, 175(5), (2012):432–440.

11   Reprudencia "Dencia" Sonkey. Interview by Jackie Long. March 21, 2014. *Channel 4 News*.

10. TONIGHT, WE SCREAM

12   Dan Cassino and Yasemin Besen-Cassino, "Race, Threat and Workplace Sexual Harassment: The Dynamics of Harassment in the United States, 1997–2016," *Gender, Work and Organization*, 26(9), (2019): 1228, 1236.

11. OF IRON AND SOIL

13   Gustave Flaubert, *Madame Bovary*, trans. Lydia Davis (New York: Penguin Books, 2010), 53.

14   Le Figaro and AFP, "Suicide des agriculteurs: une mission confiée à un député LREM," *Le Figaro*, February 23, 2020.

ABOUT THE AUTHOR

Vanessa A. Bee is a consumer protection lawyer and essayist. Born in Cameroon, she grew up in France, England, and the United States. Vanessa holds an undergraduate degree from the University of Nevada and a law degree from Harvard. She lives in Washington, DC. Follow @Vanessa_ABee on Twitter and @TheHomeBoundBook on Instagram.